CHURCH GROWTH BY DESIGN

A Complete Guide for Planning and Building Churches to God's Glory

ROE MESSNER
With Ruth Ann Messner

CHURCH GROWTH BY DESIGN

All scriptures quoted are from the Holy Bible,
King James Version and The Living Bible.

ISBN: 0-9745015-0-6

Published by
EMPIRE GROUP
P.O. Box 1281
Matthews, NC 28105

Printed in the United States of America

IF YOU ARE CONSIDERING
BUILDING A CHURCH FACILITY, CONTACT

ROE MESSNER
COMMERCIAL BUILDERS AND ARCHITECTS, INC.
P.O. BOX 1281
MATTHEWS, NC 28105
PHONE: 704-841-8994
FAX: 704-841-8910

DEDICATION

*This book is dedicated to my sons,
Richard and Ron Messner, for their love,
support and inspiration. I am proud that they have
followed my footsteps and are designing and building
churches across the nation. Their commitment,
dedication and accomplishments in God's
Kingdom fill my heart with gratitude.*

FOREWARD

As a pastor who recently completed an enormous enlargement to my present church building in Seoul, I understand very well the many factors involved in erecting a beautiful House of God.

In our day, a ministry that is needed more than any other time in history is building a House of God which is just the right type of building for the many, varied groups of believers, or congregations expanding their present facilities. What type is best, how to have it financed within the ability of the people and other insights into church financing are all a ministry.

I highly recommend that every pastor and church administrator have a copy of this book in his personal or church library.

In this book, *Church Growth by Design*, it will be obvious to the reader that Roe Messner is one of the most knowledgeable persons in this field. With him, church construction is a ministry. He and his excellent staff have spent many hours prayfully studying entire projects, architectural designing, interior designing and quality planning for every edifice with which they were involved. This has made him a trusted friend of pastors as well as a highly qualified person who can create a beautiful sanctuary within the cost range of each budget.

As he shares in this book, you will find that he has built more churches than any other person in the world, and each one was constructed specifically to meet the exact needs of the congregation. He often solved problems before they surfaced. And everyone was – and is – satisfied with the new building.

I highly recommend that every pastor and church administrator have a copy of this book in his personal or church library, before a building program is needed or additions are imperative, to assure a total view of services available and within reach of each individual congregation.

God bless you,

Paul Yonggi Cho
Pastor, Yoido Full Gospel Church
Seoul, Korea

Table of Contents

ACKNOWLEDGMENTS

The colleagues, consultants, and clients who contributed to the development of this manuscript have our sincere thanks. Without the individual knowledge of each professional, as well as the repeated requests for written information on church building programs, we wouldn't have been challenged to compile our years of experience into the pages of this book.

We wish to express special gratitude to the staff of Roe Messner, whose dedicated teamwork has produced church designs and buildings for congregations all across the United States. The registered architects, designers and professional engineers spent long hours in researching and defining information they felt would be helpful to pastors and building committees. We especially acknowledge the efforts of certain architects within the firm.

Registered architect Don Kimble, head of the R. Messner Construction Company design department, made invaluable contributions with information, editing and coordination. Also special thanks to my friend, architect Alvah Breitweiser. We have worked together for over 40 years.

Jerry Martin, president and chief executive officer of MMR Investment Bankers, a firm specializing in corporate and church financing, provided the important information to assist you and your church in meeting financial goals and objectives. Jim Young, president of American Audio, Inc., gave some "sound" information for acoustical design.

A very special acknowledgment and thanks goes to Ruth Ann Messner, whose editorial expertise and contributions to this book have been invaluable.

I am grateful to Jim Denk for the book cover design.

We especially wish to recognize – with love and appreciation – the many pastors, building committees and individual members of the churches whom we've worked with in the past, are working with now, and hope to continue to serve in the future. Several of these fine people made valuable contributions within the pages of this work. Their personal and professional support of our efforts through the years has made our business – and this book – possible.

We especially wish to recognize the many pastors, building committees and individual members of the churches whom we've worked with in the past, are working with now, and hope to continue to serve in the future.

PREFACE

"Our church is growing. Now, how do we go about a building program?"

What an exciting challenge!

During the past 50 years, I personally have talked to many pastors, church building committees and congregations about the total process of church growth - church building. I have participated in seminars that include leaders of progressive, visionary and vital churches across the United States. The bottom line is always: "We're growing...what about building?" This indicates the powerful move of God among His Church and in His churches all over this country and in the world.

Church Growth by Design is my written answer to all those pastors whose dynamic ministries are reaching out and touching lives. This book is a collection of church-building experiences, a useful guide to the practical steps of physical expansion and a suggested plan for harmonious growth. It contains handy resource and reference information on all aspects of planning, designing, financing and building a church – taking the reader from the basics of assessing needs, setting up committees, site selection, choosing an architect and builder, construction and after-construction details including maintenance of the building and grounds. A comprehensive "how-to" guide, *Church Growth by Design* is written to meet the needs of any church, whether the plans stipulate seating for 100 or 10,000 people.

And just why would I attempt such a project? Well, for one thing, I'm in the business of designing, building and financing churches. I have designed and/or built 1,710 churches in 47 states, with many more plans on the drawing board and in the discussion stage. However, I know – and you know – that no one has all the answers. There are exceptions to any rule when it comes to dispensing advice; and, there is only one Authority.

After more than five decades in the business, I've encountered almost every situation that possibly could be faced by a pastor, a congregation – and a design/build company! My recommendations, along with practical and spiritual suggestions from pastors for whom we've worked, will offer a lively and pragmatic guide to any

To me, building churches is a ministry, just as a pastor's ministry is to build and feed His Church.

church. But there's more to this venture – much more.

To me, building churches is a ministry, just as a pastor's ministry is to build and feed His Church. I started my career in 1949 at the age of 14, working for a general contractor. By 1953 I was in business for myself, building houses. Three years later I had the opportunity to build my first church – Douglas Avenue Assembly of God in Wichita, Kansas. Because of my church upbringing and involvement with all the programs throughout my life, I am well acquainted with the workings of a church – from the inside out. I know the decisions building committees face. I'm aware of how important it is for the church to function properly, and how each department must work separately, yet as a total unit.

As a personal testimony, I learned early in life to keep my priorities straight, through my favorite scripture: "Seek ye first the kingdom of God and his righteousness; and all these things shall be added unto you" (Matthew. 6:33, KJV}. This important passage in the Bible has helped me keep the Lord first in my life, personally and professionally. I truly believe that the Lord has given me the ability to design and build churches in His special way. There is no question in my mind that this promising Biblical scripture can be – and should be – the credo of every pastor and church congregation as God demonstrates His pattern for growth.

I will be the first to say that my company's accomplishments in His service are made possible by the blessings of the Lord, a lot of hard work and the phenomenal team effort of our professionals working together with churches across the country. This special responsibility we share has led to deep and lasting relationships. It's resulted in a continued association with many pastors as they move to different cities and find a need for a building program, or as growing churches for whom we've worked need to expand their facilities. I sincerely credit and compliment those individuals and institutions – many are mentioned in this book – who have encouraged and supported our business, our ministry. Their goal, synonymous with His, is the ultimate directive. After all, "Unless the Lord builds a house, the builders' work is useless" (Psalm 127:1 TLB).

As a result, and in return, I have written this book, *Church Growth by Design.* It is my prayer that leaders of churches, both small and large, will find expert guidance and His blessing as they begin the exciting challenge of building for the kingdom of God.

In His Service,

Roe Messner

Roe Messner

"Unless the Lord builds a house, the builders' work is useless."

Psalm 127:1 TLB

INTRODUCTION

What Is This Book About?

Church growth is the plan and objective of the Lord. It always was and always will be. Growing and building are companion commandments, twin tenets if you will, for God's Church. Not a new concept, you say? Hardly! It's as old as, well, considering the time we measure, some five centuries before the birth of Christ.

Let's take a look. 1 Chronicles 22:7-13 and 28:2-10 tell of David's desire to build a temple for the Lord, a plan that didn't happen to match God's timing. God did, however, promise David that his son, Solomon, would get the job done. In 2 Chronicles 2:4-6, Solomon enthusiastically shares with his friend Hiram the plan to accomplish God's promise. "I am about to build a temple for the Lord my God...It is going to be a wonderful temple because he is a great God, greater than any other."

No wonder he was excited! After all, the building of a house of worship is no ordinary task, and this definitely would be no ordinary temple. It was to be "greatly respected" as the physical symbol of man's recognition of God's glory, and built to that end. God's servant recognized that it would be a structure in which He was to dwell among His people and a sign that He was with them in this place.

Well, Solomon had the green light, and off he went! With confidence in his directive – and counsel from Hiram – he designed his master plan, selected a site, secured financing, chose his craftsmen and started construction. From all accounts, the project took plenty of vision, fearless dedication, unity and plain old hard work. Most important, it had the direction of God, the Master Designer. When construction finally was completed, Solomon dedicated the building with this prayer: "...Lord God, even the heaven and heaven of heavens cannot contain you – how much less this Temple which I have built. Look down in favor day and night upon this Temple – upon this place where you have said that you would put your name" (2 Chronicles 6:20, 21, TLB).

With the passage of time and another of God's great gifts to humanity – His Son Jesus Christ, and subsequently the Holy Spirit – the biblical references to "buildings" and "temples" took on new meaning.

In the New Testament of the Bible, we see another kind of temple in which God is to dwell. It is the Church – a body of believers – and it is the heart of the individual Christian who is now possessed

Solomon... designed his master plan, selected a site, secured financing, chose his craftsmen and started construction.

by the Holy Spirit. Jesus told Peter: "You are...a stone; and upon this rock I will build my church; and all the powers of hell shall not prevail against it" (Matthew 16:17, TLB). Some 20 years later Paul reinforces this message when he reminds the folks in Corinth that they are God's building...God's garden, God's co-workers. To all the new believers in Asia Minor, Paul elaborates on this concept, referring to them as "parts of a beautiful, constantly growing temple for God," the foundation of which are the "apostles and the prophets; and the cornerstone of the building is Jesus Christ himself" (Ephesians 2:20-22, TLB).

So there you have it, in a nutshell. What you've just read is hardly an in-depth, much less stirring, sermonic discourse. It was, rather, a humble but sincere attempt to discuss scriptural progression, taking the Old Testament concept of God dwelling in a special place, a special building, to His dwelling in a special people – His Church – those who accept the Lordship of Christ and His saving blood. And if you will allow, please, just one more homiletic outburst, we have come full circle. Paul, ever the great visionary, repeatedly reminded the new Christians in Colossians 2 that "...the body is of Christ...and knit together, increaseth with the increase of God." (Along with that promise, of course, he issued the warning to be aware of those who might stifle growth. A fact of life, in this one, anyway! I can tell you from experience - and you can ask any pastor of a church on the move – a handful of people with illegitimate complaints and criticisms will knock you out of the race before you even get to the starting line.) And, in Jesus' own words: "Look around you! Vast fields of human souls are ripening all around us, and are ready now for reaping" (John 4:35, TLB). It is God's plan, His commission and commandment for the body of His Church to grow and build.

And now we are to build people. We are to build each other as one might build a temple – for we are, in fact, the temple of the Holy Spirit. And in the process of "building people," churches in and outside of the United States have experienced phenomenal growth - especially in the last 20 years, a mere speck of time. Several books have been written about this recent surge of church attendance and growth patterns, about which denominations are growing, and speculating "why?" I have read with great interest, *The Large Church*, by John N. Vaughan; *The Complete Book of Church Growth*, by Elmer L. Towns, John N. Vaughan and David J. Seifert; *Understanding Church Growth*, by Donald A. McGavran, and *Design For Church Growth*, by Charles L. Chaney and Ron S. Lewis. Perhaps a dear friend, the Reverend E. M. Clark, had the best answer when he said: "Today is the day of the great harvest!"

Whatever the reasons, church attendance and church growth are at an all-time high, and appears to have no denominational boundaries. Pastors and congregations are accommodating this growth with new buildings. Many are huge structures with auditoriums that seat not hundreds, but thousands. And yes, those seats

We are to build each other as one might build a temple – for we are, in fact, the temple of the Holy Spirit.

are filled! First Assembly of God Church in Phoenix, Arizona, pastored by Rev. Tommy Barnett, completed a building project with an auditorium that seats 6,500. The complex is on a 60-acre site and has parking for approximately 1,500 vehicles, including the many buses used for the church's transportation ministry.

Reverend Ron Carpenter and the congregation of Redemption World Outreach Center in Greenville, South Carolina will dedicate a new sanctuary in 2004 that seats over 4,000. They have three Sunday morning services, plus a Saturday evening service to accommodate the growing attendance.

The super-church, of course, is the Yoido Full Gospel Church in Seoul, Korea. Pastored by Dr. Paul Cho, this church has a phenomenal membership of more than 800,000 people. These are just a few examples. The point is, we are in a time of "megachurches" like no other period in the history of our country. This trend is continuing and getting stronger every year. It most certainly appears that what we're experiencing is the prophecy of Joel: "And it shall come to pass afterward, that I will pour out my spirit upon all flesh..." (Joel 2:28, KJV).

Whatever the reasons, church attendance and church growth are at an all-time high, and appears to have no denominational boundaries

Who Is This Book For?

Pastors and church leaders, this one's for you!

Growing churches are following the scriptural pattern of the Old and New Testaments of the Bible – the building of His church and His Church of believers. It was God's promise to David, carried forth by Solomon, and a pure and simple directive through Paul to the Church of Jesus Christ.

No where in the Bible, however, does it say that a building project is easy. Quite the opposite. Church leaders face an awesome responsibility when they realize their present facilities are not adequate to meet the needs. Even with all the ingredients, it's no piece of cake.

On the other hand, there are ways to make it work, and make it work well. Since we know that growth and building is an Old and New Testament "given" and both are logical progressions of God's will, we also know that with the same logic, a building program can be an exciting challenge, a blessing to the entire church, and yes, even fun! After all, as Rev. Strader says from experience: "It is God who wants you to grow, and it is God who will direct you in that growth."

But we all are human. We all have questions. And if your church is considering a building program, you'll need some answers. There's no sense in re-inventing the wheel, so listen to those who have paved the way! The guidelines and experiences provided by many others who have undertaken and completed building projects hopefully will be an encouragement. From Solomon's A-B-C's of building to our contemporaries' plans of action, you can get the job done! Remember, please: God's directive, timing, master planning, financing, counsel, site selection, unity and enthusiasm. Building a church is not only an act of God, it is a series of actions by His servants.

To help you in your planning, we'll "walk" you through what we believe are the logical steps in church building, no matter what is the size of your project. We've included comments from pastors and churches for whom we've worked as architect and/or builder, with first-hand, "I've been there" advice. Illustrations and pictures from an extensive portfolio hopefully will give you ideas, and as a quick reference, an index and glossary is at your service. Please forgive us if the terminology used throughout the book is not in sync with that of your particular church. Thank goodness God's grace crosses denominational lines and language! We hope you'll discover easy reading, interesting and informative material, and most of all — the encouragement you need to achieve your objective in His will.

God bless you as you build for the kingdom.

Building a church is not only an act of God, it is a series of actions by His servants.

Central Community Church
Wichita, Kansas

SIX ESSENTIAL PRINCIPLES OF CHURCH GROWTH

Recently, a pastor asked, "Roe, I know you have built more than 1,700 church buildings, but have you come to any conclusions regarding what is needed for growth?"

I have given considerable thought to that question and have concluded there are six essential principles involved. Let me share them with you:

Principle Number One:
The Pastor Must Want to Grow.

Here's a mind-boggling statistic: Ninety percent of all churches run less than 200 in attendance. That includes the children in the nursery and those attending children's church or who are in other classes of some sort while the main service is in progress.

The number one reason for this is that *the pastor is content.* He is comfortable with a small congregation. As long as the church remains small he can golf more, travel more, or spend additional time doing the things he desires to do.

If a church is alive and growing it is because the pastor is *working* towards church growth. If it isn't expanding, it is because the pastor (or the deacons, elders or board members) don't desire growth. They have decided they like things "just the way they are."

I once attended a church like that. It was in the middle of a growing city. It would have been so easy to add a visitation program, so easy to publish the church schedule in the local paper with the rest of the churches. It would have been so easy for the Pastor to inspire his small congregation to invite and bring their friends to church. But nothing was ever done of this nature and I realized as I wrote out my last check to that church that, unless God intervened, nothing ever was going to change.

> *If a church is alive and growing it is because the pastor is working towards church growth.*

The pastor was complacent, he was satisfied with just over a 100 people. He didn't *want* the church to grow. He was making a comfortable salary, playing golf and enjoying life. He just was *not interested* in growth. My family and I eventually decided to leave the church. We ended up in a lively, exciting growing congregation.

I taught a Sunday School class that kept growing and growing.

Yes, the pastor and his wife were busy, active people. It was a miracle if he even took Monday off. But I've never seen a happier pastor or a more excited congregation.

The former church kept losing the few people they had.

I believe every pastor needs to focus on what I call the "Three P's."

1. *Promotion.* He must constantly keep the ministry of the church before both the congregation and the community.
2. *Personnel.* He must surround himself with the most gifted, dedicated staff available.
3. *Plain hard work* – or "Perspiration." There is no substitute for daily diligence in the pursuit of excellence and growth for God's Kingdom.

Principle Number Two:
The people must want to grow.

No matter how hard a pastor may work, unless the people catch the vision and also want the church to grow, it won't.

Far too many churches form "little cliques" of people within the congregation. This is dangerous to any body of believers. When new people visit, they do not feel they belong. There are members who have their favorite place to sit – and heaven help anyone if they should mistakenly sit down in one of those sacred pews.

Then there are individuals who place coats, purses, books or whatever along a group of seats – saving them for friends who are arriving late. To a newcomer it looks like it is a vacant seat until they walk up the aisle to sit down and are embarrassed to hear, "Oh, these are reserved."

In my opinion, the pastor should gently discourage this practice if he or she wants their church to grow. My wife and I have visited churches like this, where some people were just plain rude. We didn't go back!

During the process of building hundreds of sanctuaries, I have had a first hand view of church growth. In the construction process, you get to know the pastor and his congregation and understand the problems they face. I have been to churches that are run by

> *No matter how hard a pastor may work, unless the people catch the vision and also want the church to grow, it won't.*

"cliques." They are satisfied with things just the way they have always been. They don't want their little apple cart upset by new people coming into the church. They have done things the same way for years and they are determined that nothing is going to change if they have anything to do about it. Often, these people have been the financial backbone of the church, so the pastor is reluctant to even try to alter their way of thinking. After all, they usually vote the pastor out every two years – and his two years is almost up!

When this happens the church stagnates. A new pastor arrives, enthused about church growth and the programs he is going to insitiute to make it happen. Unfortunately, he is promptly notified, "We like things the way they are."

Confrontation is not a comfortable path for a new pastor to take, but if the church is going to grow, there may have to be one. What if some people leave the church? Perhaps a transfusion of new blood is God's way of rejuvenating the congregation.

For a church to flourish, there must be enough space and sufficient parking.

Principle Number Three:
Always provide extra space.

A church near where my wife and I live seemed like the ideal church – at least that is what we thought until we attended for the first time. It has a great preacher, the sound system in the sanctuary is extraordinary. Because of a hearing problem the sound is important to me. The choir is the best, and they have wonderful programs for all ages. They have three services on Sunday. The reason we decided *not* to regularly attend that church is because it became so frustrating to desperately look for a place to sit. Unless you arrive an hour before the service begins, you might as well go home.

Who wants to wait outside in inclement weather only to rush in with hundreds of other people to find a place to sit? *Not me!*

Then there is the parking problem. If you do not arrive early you have to park down the road and be bussed to the church. That is very difficult for older people and families with children. Then after the service you must line up and wait your turn for the next bus to come along to transport you back to your car. Consequently, you leave frustrated and in a bad mood – which is *not* what worship is all about.

The pastor of this particular church does not seem concerned about the problem. In fact, I think it is a bit of a boost to his ego that people are outside by the hundreds waiting to get in.

Many have left as a result of the overcrowded conditions. It's *not* a matter of finances for this pastor. The church can afford to expand and provide additional parking. But as long as they ignore the issue, there are going to be many more stories like ours. For a church to flourish there must be *enough space* and *sufficient parking*.

Whether your facility is large, like this one, or small, the problems of overcrowding and parking have the same effect on people. Pastor, your members will not invite visitors if they cannot easily find seating for them. They will be less inclined to attend church if it's freezing cold outside, or sweltering hot, and they have to walk a half block just to get inside the sanctuary.

If you have a desire for your church to grow you must provide ready access and make it easy on the people. That takes away two excuses! (1) "I don't want to go today because I can never find a place to park!" and (2) "I don't want to go today because I can never find a place to sit!"

If you desire growth, you must continue to build and add more space – and provide additional parking.

Principle Number Four:
Provide programs for all ages.

Your church is growing in leaps and bounds. The service is filled with crying babies and restless teenagers. It's a wonderful sign! Everyone is excited! Then you begin to notice that some of the older people are not attending as often as usual. You faithfully do your pastor follow-up and discover that the crying babies make it impossible for them to hear – or they are just plain agitated by the extra noise.

Your new teenagers are missing Sunday after Sunday. They seemed to enjoy attending church. What has happened? Again you do your pastor follow-up. "Well," says one teen, "There is nothing planned especially for us. We need something to do."

This is a very common problem in a fast growing church. The answer is simple. Pastor, you need to implement some good programs.

First, you need a nursery! It's one of the most important facilities in your church if you want new blood. Mom's *must* have a place they can leave their children, or *take* them when they are fussy. A good speaker system should be installed in the nursery so the people working there will not feel they have missed the service. In my opinion a large, well equipped nursery is vital to church growth.

You *must* institute programs for all ages! Kids, high school age, college age, young adults and senior adults. Everyone needs to feel like the church "cares about them."

Young people love to be part of a church band. They love sports, they thrive on just getting together and having discussions, and they

> *Everyone needs to feel like the church "cares about them."*

love to eat! My wife and I attended a church in Palm Springs, California, and Tammy's son called it the "donut church." His favorite part of attending was that after the service, outside under the canopy, they served donuts to everyone. You could also purchase a cup of coffee. People stood around, ate their donuts, drank their coffee and had fellowship.

Don't ever underestimate the power of food! It costs the church so little, yet makes people so happy! The adults, the kids, all eating donuts together – laughing and talking. What price can you put on fellowship?

Also, make sure you have a solid counseling program. Perhaps you can offer drug or alcohol recovery classes, divorce recovery, cancer survivors groups, etc. People need to talk to someone and "where two or three are gathered together" there are always problems that surface, A church that prays and works together stays together.

Get your people involved in all aspects of the church. You will find that those who were saying "I'm going to church," will begin to say, "I'm going to *our* church." That's what you want to hear. They must feel as if they truly belong.

Our true goal should be to grow more "spiritually significant" people.

> *Our true goal should be to grow more "spiritually significant" people.*

Principle Number Five:
Every church needs a good visitation program.

When we first moved back to Charlotte, NC, my wife and I needed to find a good place of worship. So we decided that we would go to the church Tammy's daughter was attending. We really liked it. Great music, good preacher, programs for every age. But we left after nearly one year of attending, paying tithes and offerings. Now we are *not* individuals who need to be "cow towed" to. In other words we don't need special attention. *But* we attended that church for almost a year, no one ever said hello to us, we never received a "welcome to the church" note, and we felt totally invisible! As a result, we felt unwanted and unaccepted by that congregation. And no one wants to attend a church where they feel isolated.

A visitation program is of the utmost importance to church growth. A kind word of acknowledgment means so much to a newcomer. It makes them feel comfortable and gives them a sense of being wanted and accepted by not only the people, but the minister. Pastor, it reflects on you, not the people, if you don't have a good follow-up, visitation program. It's been said," The buck always stops here." In a church, the buck stops with the pastor, not the people! I have always observed that a church is only as good as it's pastor.

- Caring church = caring pastor.
- Friendly church = friendly pastor,
- Giving church = giving pastor.
- Lively Church = lively pastor.
- Sedate church = sedate pastor.

Pastor, *you,* set the direction your church will take.

Lately, my wife and I have been attending a wonderful little church called "Hope Baptist." Pastor Don is a model minister. I wish everyone could attend this church just once. Pastor Don has been successful in actually making every one of the church growth suggestions work for the glory of God, and, consequently, the church is growing fast. He is one of those rare pastors that does visitation himself, along with his people.

I recently went to visit someone in the hospital and there was Pastor Don, weeping right along with the family. He not only has all the church growth programs in place, he drops in on them all. He's liable to turn up when least expected – to enjoy fellowship with the kids, the young adults or the seniors. He is faithful to his calling and loves being a pastor – and it shows in ever area of the church!

Principle Number Six:
A church must be friendly.

When I married my wife she was not attending church. When I asked her why she said, "Roe, the church people have hurt me so much, I just don't want to keep being wounded. My heart can't take any more hurt."

I felt so sorry for her, yet I knew what she said was all too true. I wasn't going to force her – and for several months after we married we did not attend church. That was very difficult for me as I am a church man.

One day we were standing in front of a restaurant waiting for our car to be brought up when a man approached us. "Hello Tammy and Roe. My name is Pastor Jeff Walker and I pastor Victory Christian Church just a few blocks away. We sure would like you to come visit our church next Sunday." Tammy immediately spoke up, Pastor Jeff, you wouldn't want us" – and she went on to give him all the reasons why.

Pastor Jeff just smiled and said, "Tammy, life goes on! We do want you. Please come next Sunday." With that he said goodbye, waved and walked away. Our car arrived and we got in and drove off. For a while Tammy was quiet and I could not tell *what* she was

> *Pastor, you set the direction your church will take.*

thinking. Then all of a sudden she said, "Honey, let's go to Jeff's church next Sunday."

I was dumbfounded at her sudden change of attitude. But I calmly agreed that's what we should do — wondering if she would really follow through when Sunday arrived.

But come Sunday morning she jumped out of bed and said, "Honey, let's go to church today." We got ready and Tammy went to the house of the Lord for the first time since she had been so hurt. My wife was trembling as we walked in the door. I could see her fear of rejection on her face. I thought she was going to bolt and run. Instead, something wonderful happened. There was a gentleman at the front door welcoming everyone. He was a huge man with a great big smile on his face. He grabbed my wife and gave her a big old bear hug. I will *never* forget his words to her, Welcome home Tammy Faye, we want you here!"

My wife's life was forever changed from that moment on. With tears streaming down her face she led me to a seat in the back of the sanctuary. That morning Pastor Jeff Walker welcomed Tammy Faye and Roe Messner to the church from the pulpit. He said he had watched her for years on television and was so happy to have us there. We began attending Sunday after Sunday. My wife's hurts were healed because a pastor dared to care – because an usher faithfully stood at the entrance to the church, greeting people and giving them a hug.

A church must be *friendly* in order to grow. You never know whose life you may eternally affect by showing you care – and just being friendly. Why is it that so many Christians look like they have been weaned on dill pickles? Remember, it takes fewer facial muscles to smile than it does to frown!

Pastor, please teach your people the value of being warm and welcoming. It will transform your church...and, it could forever change a life!

Why is it that so many Christians look they have been weaned on dill pickles?

1

YOUR CHURCH IS GROWING ... NOW WHAT?

Defining priorities with the help of a survey committee

Congratulations! You must be doing something right in your community. Your worship services, Sunday School and outreach programs are bringing in the people – a sure sign that yours is a church that provides the love to others as He loves us. And what's more, Jesus' commission to believers in Matthew 28:19 obviously is in action where you live.

So what's happening? Are the Sunday morning crowds forcing you to hold two – or even three – services? Are the Sunday School classes making the walls bulge? Is your parking lot attendant complaining that he can't find room for all the cars? Are there just too many people, and not enough room in your church facility? Ah, what a blessed dilemma! Well, you can't just sit there and stew, and here's why: that wonderful spurt of growth will soon become a drizzle if there is inadequate space for your dynamic programs. The hassle of parking, bad acoustics in the auditorium, kids complaining of hot and overcrowded Sunday School rooms or any other problems you're experiencing is the quickest way to put a cap on the well. It's time for a new plan of action!

Are there just too many people and not enough room in your church facility? Ah, what a blessed dilemma!

This particular scenario indicates a church building program whose time has come. Not too late, mind you, but certainly ready – if not past due – for consideration. And remember, don't sell your parishioners short. Congregations of growing and vital churches can become effectively involved in an exciting and upcoming expansion project – if, indeed, they know it's forthcoming! Ideally, regardless of how or why your church growth is happening, if you are 80 to 85 percent filled to capacity, you need more room. Now is the perfect time to start planning to build. If your church is in a growth pattern – and your goals, your vision and your ministry stay intact – there is a guarantee, in God's plan, that with expanded space you'll have expanded programs to reach even more people.

Now comes a logical course of action. With no plan and no definition of priorities, your flight pattern could, well, fall flat. And that, my friends, is not His plan – nor is it necessary. So, with logic in mind and God looking over our shoulders, let's examine a tried and true checklist for folks in your position.

We'll go into more detail in the following chapters. But as preliminary and pertinent information, these abbreviated steps for a building program are our recommendations to pastors. Assuming that you have a clear understanding of why your church is successful and growing, here's what's next:

Once you and your church leaders have established the building and property inadequacies, share them with the members.

- Meet with the leaders of your church to list and review what you all believe are inadequacies in your present facility.
- Get outside help. It's okay! Don't be afraid to request advice from a church building consultant (present company definitely *not* excluded!). It can save you money and grief in the long run. And go visit other pastors who have gone through building programs. They'll have some valuable words of wisdom at this point.
- Talk to your congregation. Once you and your church leaders have established the building and property inadequacies, share them with the members. This is important. At this time, also, request approval to structure a survey, or long-range planning, committee. This group's function will serve to study the needs and determine appropriate action. Everyone must feel as if they're involved.
- Put the committee to work! This job could take some time, as it involves taking a survey of the community and determining its needs. It's an important study that should piggy-back a definition of the church's program goals, the number of people who could be reached in those programs and an over-all statement of mission.
- Alright, the study is in. Now, do you do nothing? Do you stay at the same location and remodel? Or, do you relocate? If it's option two or three, a recommendation of the amount of property needed and/or the site location should be made. Keep in touch with the church members!
- Prepare a financial plan. Oh, yes. it always comes back to this, doesn't it? First, you need to take a look at your church's financial performance – past and present – and study the

trends. It's a good idea to make an initial contact now with a professional source for church fund-raising campaigns. After you've determined how much money you can raise within your church, investigate other sources for borrowing money, find out just how you can borrow, and get some tentative loan commitments. If you've done all your homework, you'll have a realistic picture of the maximum funds available for a building project.

- You're still not sure whether to stay at the same location and remodel or to relocate your facility? Why not get out the floor plans of your existing building and identify the uses of your present space, plus any temporary space you're utilizing. In this process, you can examine the structural condition of your building to see what needs replacing.

  While you're at it, get an accurate plot plan of the church's property or any other property you're considering acquiring. Now it's time to make a serious decision on the amount and type of new space needed.

- Go back to your church members. You've gathered some valuable statistics and information and your committee is ready to make a recommendation. You need the church's decision for action on: remodeling or relocation; acquiring properties; selection and employment of an architect with a go-ahead to prepare a master plan, design development plans, preliminary plot and floor plans, and cost estimate; and a plan for the project financing. If you haven't already selected a building committee, do it now. This trusted and active group of people will help preside over the entire building process, and probably should have, for advisory input, sub-committees on financing, music, kitchen, education, and all the other important working functions of the church. The building committee also will take part in selecting the architect and builder.

- Keeping an eye on your budget and considering your borrowing capabilities, buy your property – whether it is land surrounding your present facility, or a new site location. From the earlier studies, you'll know how much acreage you need.

- Choose your architect or architect/builder. Interview several you've had recommended to your church, and be sensitive to how well each of the candidate's philosophies and experiences "match" with your project. Once you've made this important decision, send your architect to the drawing board to prepare preliminary drawings in line with the church-approved development program. Be sure the architect understands he must keep the cost of the building within the budget!

- When your architect has completed this part of his job, and the plans have been approved by the building committee, go back to

Be sure the architect understands he must keep the cost of the building within budget!

the church for a progress report. This can be an exciting time for your members, actually seeing a plan – and possibly a color rendering – of their new church home. Please note: this process also can be time-consuming if the committee or the church is not satisfied with the architect's work, and the process needs to be repeated. Good communication is the key to saving time – and money.

- Start your fund-raising campaign! Actually, this process should be started immediately after you've secured the church's positive decision to proceed with the building project.

- Master site planning is a vital concept but not necessarily in this order of sequence. However, we feel it is important enough, as a separate point of reference, to highlight. After your long-range planning committee has made its recommendations, and along with your church's short and long-term goals for growth and ministry, you'll have a grand scope of your ongoing project. This total program needs to be discussed thoroughly and lucidly with your architect. An experienced firm can take your written program, then make valuable and money-saving recommendations to benefit you and your ministry.

- When the building committee and the church have made final approval of the architectural plans, choose your builder. You have several choices at this stage of the game, all of which we'll discuss later, and in depth. Whatever plan you select, let's assume your decision is made, and at last, you're ready to start construction! Now, don't forget to order your furnishings (your architect and builder can help you here), inspect the project periodically (although it's doubtful if you could be held back with horses from the site), and authorize payments to the contractor at appropriate times. Good stewardship will set a positive example in your community.

- Begin organizational enlargement, leadership training and promotional activities just as soon as that first shovel has broken ground – if not before! Just because the building is going up, there's no time to sit on your hands and expect the rest of the world to fall into place. There'll be a lot of natural enthusiasm in the community as the dirt is moved, but don't plan on too much unsolicited rallying. Every day of every week there needs to be a conscious and executed promotional plan for your continued growth – both in the church and in the community.

- Project completion – a great day! After a final inspection – you've approved and accepted the work when your contractor has completed everything according to the contract agreements, and the final payment is in the pockets of the architect and builder – you will have jumped one big hurdle.

Good communication is the key to saving time – and money.

- It's time now to complete financing for the building project, making final arrangements with the loan company (if you've gone that route) for permanent financing; set up in your budget the amount needed to make payments on the loan; and, secure the appropriate insurance for the new building.
- Your furniture should be delivered by now, so inspect it well, and if everything looks good – and the building's heating and/or air conditioning is in working order – the church is ready for occupancy.
- If the engine of your promotional and organizational activities are well oiled and on track, you can count on entering the new building with high attendance, and your operational plan is working at top efficiency. At your dedication service, you joyfully can say – as did Solomon – "O Lord my God! Look down with favor upon this Temple...arise and enter this resting place of yours..."; and as did Paul: "...all of you together are the house of God...the Spirit of God lives among you in his house..."

You've come full circle!

Starting Out ... The First Committee Study

With this encapsulated overview of the total building process in hand, you still honestly can say: "Yes! This is where we're going" – then go back to a logical jumping-off point.

With all due respect, pastors, your vision is not enough. You really must involve the church leaders in your aspirations for the ministry. Who they are depends on your denominational church structure. But whatever the pecking order, give them a chance to be a part of your plans. You need their support, and unity is crucial. Without a concerted effort of the leadership, any dreams for growth could become a nightmare from never-never land of the Twilight Zone in short order. We just happen to know of some examples. (All names and places will be omitted to protect the innocent!)

Once upon a time a pastor and his church board – somewhere between the Adirondacks and the Rockies – had grandiose ideas about building a large, new church that would include a 3,500-seat auditorium. Nice goals; but there was a major glitch here. After they commissioned – and received – a $200,000 set of complete architectural plans and specifications, then they went to the church for approval to sign a contract with the builder. You guessed it! In a landslide, no-questions-about-it, thumbs down vote, the church politely said "No." Who knows for sure how this chapter would have ended if things had progressed in a logical order. But one thing is certain: that church wouldn't have a $200,000 set of plans (albeit paid-for promptly) turning yellow in the drawer.

You must really involve the church leaders in your aspirations for the ministry.

On another occasion, deep in the heart of Dixie, an ambitious pastor spent several thousand dollars to have preliminary plans drawn for a 3,000-seat auditorium and church facility. This poor fellow struck out before he got past his church board, much less the congregation.

And then there was the unfortunate case of a church that went through three, yes three, pastors before a church was finally built.

These are good/bad examples of well-meaning leadership that sadly lacked one of the most important plays of the game – unity with the board, and in the Body. There is no intention here of exploiting someone else's mistake. Quite the contrary. Our hope is that an unpleasant situation can be avoided by the example of a hard-learned lesson.

So, assuming you're postured in a positive liaison with your church leaders, we advise the immediate organization of a committee. Whatever name you give this group can never be matched by its mission. Call it a long-range planning committee; call it a survey committee; call it a steering committee. Whatever you call it, the important thing is: call it into action! These people are going to do all the groundwork, so make your selections wisely and include church members who are active, involved, knowledgeable and dedicated to God's work and the church's ministry.

Their assignment should include the following jobs:

- A careful examination of the total church program, including past years – as far back as there are records – to the present. The immediate and future goals of the church need to be taken into account also, since those ministries are on what growth patterns are based.

- Your community should be analyzed in terms of population increase or decrease trends, educational opportunities, sociological needs, projected changes, industry, economics and transportation. After all, you must be sensitive to the city or town you're serving. All this information is available through your telephone company, the Chamber of Commerce, social service agencies including the American Red Cross, and the public school system, just to mention a few resources. It is possible, once this particular study is completed, that you'll see a definite pattern that will spell out certain needs in your ministry such as a day care center for children and/or senior citizens, a school, a gymnasium, nutrition programs, facilities for the physically challenged, a busing program or a special – and exciting – integrated ministry for the ethnic groups in your town.

- Your present facility should be very carefully examined for its adequacies and inadequacies. If parking is not, and can never be

Your community should be analyzed in terms of population increase or decrease trends, educational opportunities, sociological needs, projected changes, industry, economics and transportation.

available for the growing membership, it's a sure sign that a new location is on the agenda. If parking is no problem, however, if your present building is reasonably sound and can be remodeled, and if surrounding property can be purchased, perhaps the best choice is to stay put and remodel.

- Sunday School enrollment, church attendance and through-the-week activities should be considered. Not just the present programs, please, but your projected goals. Look at other ministries in your church, such as the choir and music program. Can you accommodate the growth, and is there room for an orchestra, dramatic presentations and special events? How many people should you plan for?

- Finally, what can you afford? Every church has its needs, its wants, but eventually its budget. What is the borrowing power of your church based on past and present income and can your members contribute substantially to a building program?

When you and your committee come up with the answers to these questions, you'll have a real and viable set of recommendations to present to your church. And as you know, combining God's work, groundwork and teamwork is the only successful way to proceed. "The person who does the planting or watering isn't very important, but God is important because he is the one who makes things grow" [1 Corinthians 3:7, TLB]. That passage of scripture gets one's priorities lined up in a flash.

The next decision belongs to the church membership. With a thorough study from you and your committee to consider, your congregation will make the next call. Will you make no changes? Will you stay at your present location and remodel? Or will you relocate and launch a major building program?

The jury is out.

Combining God's work, groundwork and teamwork is the only successful way to proceed.

2

BUILDING DECISIONS FOR YOUR CHURCH

The verdict is in on remodeling or relocating

T*alk about responsibility! We mentioned earlier the heavy obligation of the pastor, the board and the long-range planning committee during the process of evaluating your church's needs. Imagine, then, what your church membership felt when you laid it all out and said: "You decide; the buck stops here!" At least we hope that's what you said. Because yes, the congregation must decide and yes, it's their pockets. Paying for a project like you've just recommended calls for digging deep, whether your congregation comes up with the cash, the church instigates a major bond program, secures a bank loan, or all of the above. You're in this together as a team – and the congregation knows it. If you've done your job right, the membership will give you an educated answer which either will put up a road block – bringing your aspirations to a screeching halt – or pave the way to a successful building program!*

> *Your in this together as a team, and the congregation knows it.*

Bumping Heads

Let's just suppose your church membership switches on the red light. A no go. There could be a couple of reasons. We hope, for your sake, a negative vote means "We understand and like what you want to do, but the timing isn't right." This action could be positive in the long run and ultimately end up in a highly successful building program sometime in the future. (Remember David and Solomon!) Perhaps the timing *isn't* right, considering the reconnaissance of your long-range planning committee. On the other hand, if your church says "No, we like it the way it is; don't change a thing," you may have a situation in which you can't maneuver. If a church has no legitimate reason for not wanting to grow, it will wither away like a thirsty wildflower and eventually perish. Do you really want to be a part of the demise?

In too many cases, churches give God a poverty complex. They sell Him short and call His account overdrawn. From what we read, His line of credit is unlimited. "O my people, listen! For I am your God...all the animals of field and forest are mine! The cattle on a thousand hills! And all the birds upon the mountains! If I were hungry, I would not mention it to you – for the world is mine, and everything in it" (Psalm 50:7-12, TLB). Church growth is tied to this scripture. Limit God and your church will be limited. But, as with everything in this life, the choice is yours.

Making Amends

Ah, good! The church membership sees a good thing happening and catches the vision! But from all reports – parking capabilities, location, finances, purchasing and other existing possibilities – the rational decision is to hold on to what you've got and make it better. It's a vote. Stay where you are and remodel.

We must mention, at this point, that the choice to renovate could mean that your facility simply is outdated and in desperate disrepair, a real eyesore in the community. Your facilities may be perfectly adequate for the church's functions, but need a serious face-lift – a good and legitimate reason for reconstruction! If, however, you do need more room and want to stay where you are, you should know the pro's and con's.

Morale is an important factor in a building program.

On the Positive Side

- You don't have the worry of selling your present church building. Listen up! This can be a big item. Why? It's elementary. You have X amount of square feet in your facility; it is going to cost you X amount of money to reproduce that space somewhere else. The cold (cold as in cash) hard facts are: when you sell a building, no matter how much you'd like to receive remuneration that equals the real value of your property, you seldom do. The time element is another consideration. It may take eons to unload that building. Unfortunately, you can't assume people are standing in line to buy property that can or cannot be zoned according to their needs. We're acquainted with churches that have waited for years to sell existing buildings, or even ended up giving them away. It's a serious consideration that probably depends on just how long you can wait. How patient is your membership? How deep are your pockets? Morale is an important factor in a building program.
- The church that stays, stays together. Real-life experience tells us that relocating can have a devastating effect on a church if the

process is not approached with wisdom, sensitivity and pragmatism. Even with an enthusiastic, high-sell vote to move and rebuild, there's always the outside chance – if you're not careful or totally communicative – that a latent element in your leadership and congregation doesn't really want to, deep down, move from the east, the west, the north, the south or the midtown location. What can happen next is a church split.

We can give you one (or more if you'd like) example. A thriving church in a midwest state – and in a midtown location – was led by a powerful minister and board to relocate on the edge of town. Everyone was caught up in the exultation, for a while. When too many commitments were made, when it was too late to back out, a church was under construction. Before anyone really knew what was happening, the leadership became flaccid because of too much pressure; the congregation was confused and disoriented; and the ministry, diminished. The pastor resigned and an overwhelming number of disgruntled members split to other churches. This particular church – with some wonderful and dedicated hangers-on – is still reeling from the financial and emotional debts to which it committed itself. Too much, too fast.

The message here is: be aware – spiritually and cerebrally – of all the implications of moving. An effective inner-city ministry may become no ministry at all in another location. The key is unity laced with wisdom – and no strong-arming allowed!

■ Continuity in the community is a plus. Depending on the size of your town and the impact of your present ministry, where you are says a lot. If you've got the right amount of everything you need – and can acquire – for your present ministry and your projected growth, stay put! And let's face it – nine times out of ten, the tab for remodeling your existing facility will be much less than the cost of relocating and rebuilding.

The key is unity laced with wisdom – and no strong-arming allowed!

On the Negative Side

■ The energy efficiency of your present building probably is not up to snuff. Today, all new buildings must meet the current minimum energy code requirements, which are mighty stringent compared to the way they were twenty years ago. New buildings are significantly more energy efficient. Insulation is very good, and those monthly utility bills won't hit as hard.

■ Although we talked about the probable lower cost of remodeling, we don't want any surprises. Depending on the size of your project and how much land you need on which to expand, you could drop a sizeable amount of money buying up property. One church needed to buy the entire block around the existing facility. In the process of purchasing 15 houses, they were looking at a cool $1 million-plus price tag, still not a bad deal considering the location and property evaluation. And don't forget to add in costs for additional landscaping and parking facilities.

- If you can't provide enough parking space, you may as well start packing your bags right now! Most cities require a minimum parking ratio of four to one, so if you compute that into vehicles, an acre of ground will accommodate 140 cars – at the maximum. And, if you happen to live in a town that requires more greenbelt, you'll have to reduce that number of cars to 125 per acre. In the process of enlarging your sanctuary, you may not be able to get the off-street parking you need.

  Most of us are two-car families, and a three to one ratio is more realistic than four to one; however, most cities will let you figure the four to one ratio in your planning. But remember, you read it here: the parking situation usually is the deterrent of a well-meaning plan to stay at the present location. On the plus side, and if you're in an area where there are adjacent commercial buildings, you may be able to utilize that space – indoor and outdoor.

- Be aware of zoning restrictions! You might run into some attitudinal and actual resistance to an expansion program in your church's neighborhood. A rapidly growing church in the South had enough property to stay at its present location, remodel and expand. Obviously, the area had proper zoning for a church, adequate parking and all the other requirements to influence the congregation's decision. The city had other ideas. So did the neighbors. An existing ordinance allowed for a 500-member church within the city limits, but certainly not one for 7,000 as the plans projected. When the building committee appealed for an exception to the rule, the neighbors – who didn't want a megachurch in the area - howled in protest, and the church was forced to relocate in the county. It can happen!

- And finally – the design. Adding on to a facility that was built several years ago can be a real challenge. From an aesthetic standpoint – piecemeal is out! Merging the old building into the new is no effortless task for the architect or builder. It can be done skillfully. As in one movement of music easing into the next until the crescendo is reached – almost unnoticed except for the thrill of the finale. Or, like too many instruments out of tune, it can jar the senses with patterns of dissonance. Opt for accord, not discord, please,when your architect makes recommendations for a matching design. Don't underplay the trickiness of making it cause a standing ovation.

If you can't provide enough parking space, you may has well start packing your bags right now!

Moving On

And what if the congregation turns in a majority vote that shouts: "Put up the For Sale sign and let's go!" Well, there you have it. It's time to move along. Don't forget that you do have an alternative to building. There could be an ideal existing church building somewhere in your city just waiting to be bought. With only a few remodeling alterations – or maybe none at all – you could take a load off some other congregation and fill your needs at the same time. For obvious reasons, however, let's assume the church membership has given you the big O.K. to sell your property, buy some new land, and build the facility you need to accomplish the goals of the ministry. Heads up! You are ready to play out a major building program, and there's no reason why you can't be a winner with some time-tested game plans and recommendations. Keep your eyes open, however for some possible pitfalls:

Dollars

Don't do anything until you've got the money. As we mentioned before, you've got your needs, your wants and your budget. Pay attention to stewardship; it's important in the community. Since you have an idea what kind of program for master planning your survey committee created (see Chapter 8), you also have a hint about what kind of money you need if it's not there, don't do it – not now, anyway.

We know of one church that "stepped out in faith" several years ago to build a church that would seat 6,000 people. The money they had in their pockets covered the pouring of the foundation – and just enough walls to cause a snicker in the town. A decade later, those half-built walls were still there, and probably eliciting some major guffaws simply because there was no reasonable evaluation of the costs involved or, more importantly, the ways to cover the costs.

Situations like this can be devastatingly less than a good witness in your town, so be careful that you connect your building with your billfold. Timing is everything.

Design/Build

A building project requires the help of an expert – an outside consultant. This is not to imply that the pastor and/or church board does not have the built-in capabilities of carrying this program off. Maybe they do. But in most cases the pastor is doing just that – pastoring. Members of the church board have their hands full - making wise recommendations while they live out their own career obligations.

Out there in the big wide world there are qualified church-building consultants. Any one of them can give you solid and experienced advice on your master plan, your site selection, and

A building project requires the help of an expert – an outside consultant.

even provide a set of preliminary plans without a serious financial obligation. But just so you won't infer a commercial message from this dissertation, we want to stress that whomever you call on for expert advice – the important thing is that you hire someone who is accustomed to working with churches and their growth.

Dedication

Unless you see no other way out, pastors, don't try to run the project yourself. As we've said before, there are exceptions to every rule. A good and longtime friend of ours is one of those standouts. He got the job done, and he got the job done well. It seemed to be his only choice at the time. This pastor is an exceptional person with lots of energy, but even he will tell you that it can be a trying experience. Your personal and professional life can be pulled in far too many directions; the workload is heavy and suddenly, dedication can feel more like drudgery.

Several years ago, many churches in smaller communities sprang up entirely through the efforts of the leadership and congregation, and some still do. But today, and in most cases, our fast-moving and demanding lifestyles leave little time to undertake a building project on our own. It's dangerous ground to be treading.

Unless you see no other way out, pastors, don't try to run the project yourself.

Decorum

Be cautious of over-building. We are the first to admit that we are conservative in our recommendations. What God wills from there on out is between the pastor and Him! And, as we're ever-ready to admit, there are outstanding cases – such as Karl Strader's church in Lakeland, Florida, which frankly blew away, by a tremendous move of God, all serious and practical theories. But as a pragmatic rule of thumb, don't build a church for more than twice the number of people you are accommodating at the present. Leaders of one church entertained visions of grandeur and had a strange but not uncommon practice of counting ears instead of noses. They planned a building for four times what they were running in their Sunday morning services! That facility now is up for sale. The church is planning a new but logical building program that will comfortably adapt to future growth.

Determination

Don't ever think that a building program means guaranteed growth, or that you can for one minute abandon the effort to grow. In fact, this is the most crucial time in your growing period. If you can't fill that new space you're providing, your mission race has hit the skids.

Write Your Program!

When all information is accumulated by the survey committee, you're ready to pencil in your plans for the future! A written program is essential whether you're remodeling or relocating, and here's why: it will give an architect the pertinent information needed to draw the master plan. It will also determine a realistic time period for completion of the entire project, and each phase of the project, if you decide to go that route. A sample program, along with the resulting master plan of a recently constructed church, is included in Chapter 8.

To give you an idea about what you must have at your fingertips, please refer to the following sample Preliminary Planning Survey form. With all the information gathered and down in writing, you'll have a valuable resource tool while you're in the beginning stages of your program development. Ideally, you already will have hired a consultant and/or architect, and know where your money is coming from.

Now, get with the program!

A written program is essential whether you're remodeling or relocating.

First Assembly of God
Phoenix, Arizona

Preliminary Planning Survey

DATE _____

CHURCH NAME _____

Address _____

City _____ State _____ Zip _____

Pastor's Name _____

Telephone No.: Office _____ Residence _____

Building Committee Chairman _____

The Church plans to build in _____ months

Existing Facilities: Average attendance _____

Seating capacity _____

The Church plans to: (CHECK ONE)

Relocate _____ Build on present location _____

Offstreet parking requirement _____

Building code _____

FINANCIAL SURVEY:

Design according to: (CHECK ONE) _____ Budget, _____ Wants

Is this the first preliminary? _____ Yes, _____ No

Annual Income _____

Assets _____

Indebtedness _____

Building Fund on hand _____

Budget: Building _____ Approx. Sq. Ft. _____

Site & parking _____

Total _____

(CHECK ONE)

YES   NO

Has financing been secured?

Master Plan

	PHASE (1,2,3, or 4)	A floor plan is to be done on this Preliminary (YES or NO)
Sanctuary	_____	_____
Family Life Center (1st phase worship facilities)	_____	_____

Gym/Multipurpose (not used for worship service) . . . . _____ _____
Education . . . . _____ _____
Administration . . . . _____ _____
Retirement Facilities . . . . _____ _____
Athletic Facilities . . . . _____ _____
Other: _____ _____ _____

Proposed Facilities

SANCTUARY

Comments: _____

Seating capacity _____ Expandable to _____

Layout: ____ Fan, ____ Octagonal, ____ Rectangle, ____ Square, ____ Other _____

(CHECK ONE)

YES   **NO**

Balcony . . . . ____ ____
Baptistry . . . . ____ ____
Choir . . . . ____ ____   Capacity _____
Piano/Organ . . . . ____ ____   Location _____
Other Musicians . . . . ____ ____   How many _____
Choir Room. . . . . ____ ____
Robing Room . . . . ____ ____
Sound Booth . . . . ____ ____   Location _____
Storage . . . . ____ ____
Other: _____

FAMILY LIFE CENTER: (phase 1 worship facilities)

Comments: _____

Seating capacity _____

(CHECK ONE)

YES   **NO**

To be used as gym also . . . . ____ ____
Adjacent to Kitchen. . . . . ____ ____
Locker Room . . . . ____ ____   To accommodate _____ people
Baptistry . . . . ____ ____
Choir . . . . ____ ____   Capacity _____
Piano/Organ . . . . ____ ____   Location _____
Other Musicians . . . . ____ ____   How many _____
Choir Room. . . . . ____ ____
Robing Room . . . . ____ ____
Sound Booth . . . . ____ ____   Location _____
Storage . . . . ____ ____
Other: _____

FAMILY LIFE CENTER: (phase 1 worship facilities)

Comments: _____

Size of gym: ____ Jr. High, ____ HS, ____ College, ____ Other _____

(CHECK ONE)

	YES	NO	SIZE/COMMENTS
Pastor's Office	____	____	_____
Pastor's Study	____	____	_____
Conference Room	____	____	_____
Staff Offices	____	____	_____ How many _____
Secretary	____	____	_____ How many _____
Miscellaneous:			
Print Room	____	____	_____
Computer Room	____	____	_____
Bookstore................	____	____	_____
Library	____	____	_____
TV Production Room	____	____	_____
Radio Studio	____	____	_____
Fellowship Hall	____	____	_____
Fireside Room	____	____	_____
Chapel	____	____	_____
Kitchen..................	____	____	_____
Bride's Room	____	____	_____
Lunchroom	____	____	_____
Storage	____	____	_____
Other:			

FAMILY LIFE CENTER: (phase 1 worship facilities)

Comments: _____

	NO. OF STUDENTS	NO. OF CLASSROOMS		NO. OF STUDENTS	NO. OF CLASSROOMS
Nursery	____	____	Grade 8	____	____
Preschool	____	____	Grade 9	____	____
Grade 1	____	____	Grade 10	____	____
Grade 2	____	____	Grade 11	____	____
Grade 3	____	____	Grade 12	____	____
Grade 4	____	____	College	____	____
Grade 5	____	____	Adults	____	____
Grade 6	____	____	Other_____	____	____
Grade 7	____	____	_____	____	____

_____ Large classrooms   OR   _____ Classroom and Assembly layout

ARCHITECTURAL STYLE:

Comments: _____

(CHECK ONE)

	YES	NO
Contemporary	____	____
Colonial	____	____
Southwestern	____	____

Other: _____

Material:

	YES	NO
Brick	____	____
Stucco	____	____
Stone	____	____
Glass	____	____

Other: _____

Comments: _____
_____
_____
_____
_____
_____
_____

THIS FORM MUST BE ACCOMPANIED BY A SITE PLAN.

If a church is building on its present location, please include existing plans.

LIST ALL ITEMS SENT WITH THIS FORM

1. _____ 7. _____
2. _____ 8. _____
3. _____ 9. _____
4. _____ 10. _____
5. _____ 11. _____
6. _____ 12. _____

3

WALK A MILE IN MY MOCCASINS

*A useful map of the Building way
from those who have traveled the path*

W*e are architects, builders, consultants and financiers.
We do not pretend to be spiritual leaders. However, from
experience and inference over the years, we firmly believe that –
since you and your church have made the important decision to
build – you can get the job done with a maximum of blessings and
a minimum of anxieties.*

*Our step-by-step suggestions within these pages deal with
practicalities to safeguard your journey as you proceed. But along
with the necessarily mundane matters of a building project must
go some valuable advice from church leaders who have been
down the 'pike. The astute and spiritual observations are theirs
only to share, and we gratefully acknowledge the willingness of
four friends and clergymen to shed additional light on the road to
a successful building program!*

*Reverend Glenn D. Cole is the District Superintendent of the
Assemblies of God for Northern California and Nevada, and an
Executive Presbyter of the denomination. He is also the former
senior pastor of Capital Christian Center in Sacramento, California.
Under his ministry a sanctuary was completed that seats 3,000,
plus a chapel, gymnasium/fellowship center and a complete
educational facility were built for the needs of the school and
church. The total facility has 165,000 square feet of floor space
and is located on 63 acres. Rev. Cole is a graduate of Central Bible
College in Springfield, Missouri, where he was named Alumnus of*

Rev. Glen D. Cole

the Year, and was awarded a Doctor of Divinity degree from Pacific Coast Bible College in Sacramento. He and his wife, Mary Ann, have shared pastorates in Ohio, Washington and California. Their two sons are ordained ministers.

A popular conference speaker, the Reverend Cole has ministered in many nations of the world including Korea, Japan, New Zealand, the Philippines, Indonesia, East Africa, India, Germany and the Holy Land.

The following comments by Rev. Cole are from a seminar for pastors and building committee members, and were delivered while his church's building project was underway.

On Praying, Planning and Processing
By Rev. Glen D. Cole

> *Pastors, we must be convinced that we are doing what God wants us to do, and not because someone else is doing it!*

I have never seen a church with a greater spirit of revival, with more excitement and more unity – along with a sense of' destiny. There is no hassle! Our altars are full. Money is coming in; we're experiencing miracle after miracle. Some churches at this point are so discouraged...and even breaking up because of the pressure of a building program.

I am here to testify about a church that is enthusiastic and excited about what God has given us to do, and about the future that He is opening to us in our city.

Pastors, we must be convinced that we are doing what God wants us to do, and not because someone else is doing it! We need to keep our balance in the work of God. Building programs are far from a panacea; they can be the most horrible thing you go through if God isn't in it. If He's in it, it can be the most exciting thing you've ever experienced. But sometimes we get disoriented by seeing another church's building and think, "Oh, what I could do if I just had a building like that!" Then we tend to move ahead of God, and end up saying, "How in the world did I get into this?"

Disorientation is the pits, folks. I am heartsick to see disorientation in God's church, with people asking, "What in the world am I doing here; just how did I get into this?" Let's be sure God spoke to us in our building programs. Let's be able to say, "God told me!" Then, in my opinion, you can be successful, along with three important keys.

Plan well. Are you going somewhere significant? Have you established yourself as a leader in the eyes of your congregation? Do you have goals? Believe me, you'll also need a miracle – a series of miracles – so keep in touch with God. People must see that God is doing something unique and unusual. They must hear you, the leader, say, "Folks, we have a miracle. Things are really happening in the name of God, not in the name of man." Don't let vanity enter in.

Pastors, get ahold of your time. No. you are not a builder.You are a pastor! I'm not being arrogant, but my people and I have a love affair going; they're excited about me! This only means that I am not trying to be the builder. I am their pastor and their leader. I have given leadership, in the spiritual sense, to my staff and to my board during the building program. That's why I can truthfully say that the spiritual level of my church is higher now than I've ever seen it. I've got ahold of my time. Just because we're in the busy season of the building program, I don't overlook any elements of my pastorship.

I fill the pulpit; I don't bring in someone to fill it for me just because we're in a building program. I'm the pastor! And I must hear from God on every facet of church life – the preaching, the finances, the programs and how to raise the money for those programs...a mighty mountain of provision! You take a huge step of faith when you move from the pulpit down in front of the people and ask them to give you money to start and finish a building project. But when it happens – and it will happen – you must be ready and willing to shake their hands and say, "Thanks for being part of a miracle." In 1 Corinthians 16, "they brought their offerings weekly," and Moses encouraged the people to bring their gifts to Him – so it is scriptural. God said to do it. I am the pastor-shepherd, and the people are following.

Determine to be happy during your building program. Disgruntled leaders can be no inspiration or example for the people. Zepheniah said: "He will rejoice over you with joy." Excellence usually comes from the hardships, the difficult. And building churches will never be easy, in the sense that we understand it. They're exciting – but not easy! In fact, I'll be glad when ours is over. But if God gave the plan, He can help you through the plan. The pastor's role is to show the excitement to the people – not the difficulty. We keep the difficulties behind the scenes. And keep the perspective during criticism. You always get a certain amount of criticism during building programs, but you have to work through that if the enthusiasm is to be maintained. If you can answer an honest "no" when you question yourself if the criticism is true, then don't bother with it. Maintain a happy posture. The church needs a happy pastor and a spirit of joy permeating the place. I just wouldn't have it any other way. We plan it that way.

Pray well. It's important. Keep the building program in front of the people weekly in terms of prayer. Every Sunday morning, pray for the building program, the superintendent of the project and all the workers. In everything that is happening at our church, we pray that the Holy Spirit will cover the property and protect it from

Keep the building program in front of the people weekly in terms of prayer.

accident, the program and everything that surrounds it. Every workday morning, some of us are at the building site by seven-thirty. Whoever can stop on their way to work prays with us. Prayer helps your perspective.

When the spies went to Canaan to spy out the land, and then returned, ten of them lost their perspective. That's what can happen in building programs. You get the same report: "We can't. The land will devour us. The cities are fortified; the enemy is like grasshoppers in number." But there were two that had their perspective – and what a beautiful contrast! They said: "We can!...We will swallow them up; their protection is gone...and the Lord is with us." That's the perspective that comes with prayer. Some building programs, I suspect, don't have enough prayer. There needs to be a constant flow of prayer that God will make the building program a living witness in your community to what only God can do. Then, that prayer perspective can and will go on to bless the ministry. We must remember to keep before the people the message: things happen because of prayer, not just because of our expertise.

Process well. Selecting an architect is important. I went into a church once – the congregation had just moved in the new church. I saw some rooms in back of the platform and asked what they were for. They said, "Oh, we don't know yet; we're having a meeting tonight to decide." We don't process well if we, as church leaders, try to do something we're not capable of doing. Then there's the other side of the coin where we get licensed architects who don't even know the word "baptistry," or how it functions. Yet people sometimes hire these professionals to draw their plans, and it becomes a fiasco. Thousands of dollars can be wasted, and you still don't have anything. But there are those who do know what we're about, and can build in a profitable way to the local church. That is wisdom.

It's important to process well with the builders. There are exceptions to this next statement, but I believe you should go beyond your own congregation in the selection of your builder to avoid potential hard and bitter feelings. Besides, you can usually save money in the long run.

It's important to process well with your church leaders. Don't pull any surprises on them. Lay it out on the table. Be open and above-board on all areas of the building program.

Get everything approved through the church leaders, then bring them to the church and say: "Your leaders have agreed unanimously on this aspect of the building program..." How can they deny a 100 percent vote of their leaders? It makes things so simple when you process well through the church leadership. We keep them informed. We talk together, pray together and analyze together. I look at their giving record – the only records I look at – to make sure

> *I believe you should go beyond your own congregation in the selection of your builder.*

they are giving to the project, because I don't think I should ask the congregation to do something the leadership isn't willing to do.

We process well through the congregation. We keep them informed through mailings, announcements and taking small tour groups to and through the project. We keep them evaluated and informed of the daily miracles that are taking place.

A building program can be exciting, even fun, if you process well. Otherwise, it can be unpleasant, unenthusiastic, a drag and a drain. I read about a young man who called the newspaper to report that his wife had just given birth to triplets. The reporter said: "Would you repeat that?" The young man answered: "Not if I can help it!" Building programs can make you feel that way!

Plan well, pray well and process well – and God can give you a revival during your building program. He did that for us. Soon we will have a multi-million dollar asset. But the building is only a means to an end, reaching more people and being able to support more mission programs.

The anointing of the Holy Spirit is the "extra" in our building program!

Reverend Rang Morgan is a Southern Baptist minister who retired from the active pastorate in 1985, after serving Southern Baptist churches for approximately 40 years. Born in central Texas, Rev. Morgan was reared in Hillsboro, Texas, where he graduated from high school. He is a graduate of Baylor University and Southwestern Baptist Seminary in Fort Worth, Texas.

Rev. Morgan has pastored four churches in Texas and one in Kansas. His 16-year pastorate in Kansas was at the Sharon Baptist Church in Wichita. He led this church from 29 members to 1,700. During Rev. Morgan's years in the pastorate, he led his church in 10 building programs. Roe Messner was the general contractor in six of these programs.

The Reverend Morgan served as president of the Kansas Convention of Southern Baptists for two terms. He was the elected Kansas representative on the Executive Committee of the Southern Baptist Convention for seven years. The following are his comments:

Rev. Rang Morgan

On the Role of the Pastor in a Building Program
By Rev. Rang Morgan

A church building program is one of the most exciting activities that can ever take place within a local congregation – if it is done in a way that is pleasing to the Lord, and acceptable to the church members.

In any building program, large or small, the pastor must realize that his responsibility to the project is no small matter. His role is to lead, guide and direct. And, since there is no "good" time to build, the pastor needs to be a spiritual motivator to encourage church members. On his knees before God, he can find direction for the church. Then he must – with courage and boldness – say to his people, "This we can do!" And then, lead them to do it!

The pastor knows that progress results when planning is thorough. Too often, a church fails to plan well. When this happens, many problems arise that could have been avoided if enough time and energy had been spent in preparatory planning.

Wise is the pastor who uses many of his people in the planning and the subsequent follow-through of the building program. As more and more of the folks become involved, the building will become special to them.

In building programs of churches where I served as pastor, I used numerous committees to ensure participation of a large sector of the church. Some of these were long range planning, new building planning, building, building decorating, building finance, building memorials, parking lot, public relations. The list can go on and on.

The selection of the general contractor who will build the church is extremely important. Not only should he know church needs and limitations, but he should be able to relate to pastors as well. Also, unless the contractor can communicate with the laity at their level, his other talents will go unnoticed.

Those who labor on the project at all times should remember that they are working on a church building, and should be cautioned to conduct themselves accordingly. The general contractor will have great influence in this area.

A good beginning is a must. Spiritual momentum is like the starting gun of an exciting race. If the folks trust God, believe in their leaders and are excited about their future, this initiative will mean a great deal. Drawing from many passages of scripture, the pastor can plan his preaching to get the folks "ready" to build.

Unless the contractor can communicate with the laity at their level, his other talents will go unnoticed.

Reverend Hugh Rosenberg is the founder and served as the senior pastor of Tri-County Assembly of God Church in Fairfield, Ohio.

A graduate of Central Bible Institute in Springfield, Missouri, Rev. Rosenberg met and married Joan Schindell, a former pianist, soloist and trio member of the "Revivaltime" radio program. After graduation from Central Bible College, the Rosenbergs worked in the evangelistic field before serving as pastors of churches in Kansas, California, then Ohio.

The idea of a new work in the Greater Cincinnati area was born while Rev. Rosenberg was working as youth pastor and Christian education director at First Christian Assembly. The board and congregation unanimously agreed that First Christian Assembly would gift the evangelical effort. Land was purchased in Fairfield because of the growth potential and development of land in the surrounding area. A building was erected, and on the first Sunday of occupancy, March 4, 1962, 97 people attended the first service. Since that time, the attendance has grown, as well as building programs. Today, Tri-County Assembly of God Church is located on a 52-acre site with over 185,000 square feet of facilities and an auditorium to seat 3,700 worshipers. Ancillary programs at Tri-County Assembly include a singles and senior citizens ministry, a day care center for pre-school children, an elementary and high school, a summer camping program for all ages and a ministry and leadership training program.

Rev. Hugh Rosenberg

The Reverend Rosenberg has served as president of the board of Tri-County Christian Schools, chairman of the board of Cincinnati Teen Challenge, board member for Calcutta Mission of Mercy, a member of Evangelicals Together for Christ, a presbyter of the Greater Cincinnati Section for Ohio District Council of the Assemblies of God and Foreign Missions Secretary for the Ohio District Council of the Assemblies of God. Under Rev. Rosenberg's leadership, more than 100 young people from the congregation have gone into full-time ministry as pastors, evangelists and missionaries. He tells us what it's like to undertake a project like this as your own contractor.

On the Pluses and Minuses of Being Your Own Contractor
By Rev. Hugh Rosenberg

In the first 20 years as founder of Tri-County Assembly, 18 of these were spent in some form of building program. In all of these projects, we – the church – were our own building contractor, using, for the most part, volunteer labor. We built three sanctuaries, three school buildings, a gymnasium, apartments and several additions. We had help getting started with a master site plan and the first set of architectural plans for a 32-feet by 65-feet building, plus a 40-feet by 76-feet wing.

If you're considering this option for your church, here's some advice:

- To begin with, you must have good insight and a knowledge of building. You'll need expertise in codes, restrictions and technology, which today is very difficult.
- You should have a flair for dealing and buying. Unless you have excellent favor with all building trades, you end up paying more and getting less than would a professional contractor.
- You must know financing through and through for your projections and borrowing – a speciality in itself!
- You've got to have the tenacity of a bulldog, the patience of Job, a strong will, untold energy and great faith!

Sure, there are some pluses in self-building, *if* all the above attributes – and then some – are in place! You just might save some money; there is a sense of fulfillment; you make lots of contacts and, hopefully, friends. Often, you can move faster in your dreams and visions, or you can move at your own pace. We chose to move quickly, since it costs more money if you're not "in and out" efficiently.

Let the contractor build the church for you, pastor. Make it your business to fill it!

But success hinges on being able to make it all work. If you can't, you're stuck with a life-time failure. We believe we accomplished our goals, with good results. And when all was said and done, I realized I couldn't have done differently, being the person I was. On the other hand it would have been impossible to do it at all without spending a career lifetime in one place, using the same contacts over and over again, and establishing a credibility with our congregation and community.

But the pitfalls are too many and too deep to travel that road again. Our last major building project lasted six years, which included beginning-to-the-end plans, purchase of property, financing and the actual building process – a total of 115,000 square feet. If I had not built the trust and relationships with our city building department over the previous 20 years, it would have been impossible. OSHA, new codes, liabilities – all of which are vital for success and protection – are difficult and demanding on everyone.

The personal stress and strain on the pastor is not worth the effort. The burden of responsibility weighs heavily on your shoulders, especially since the congregation has undying belief that you can carry it all. Believe me, you can't. Besides, it's lonely out there on that road by yourself. If you make a mistake – and you will – too often, it's the end of your ministry. Your deeds follow you, whether good or bad. The energy needed for your ministry is sapped, and consequently, somethings are left undone and people can be hurt. The money you do save gives your people the illusion that you can always "get it for less" and you end up constantly faced with performing the impossible when you try to sell the next big project to your congregation.

Let the contractor build the church for you, pastor. Make it your business to fill it! You will live a lot longer, and – I believe – have more rewards that day in His Kingdom!

Reverend Karl Strader is senior pastor of Carpenter's Home Church in Lakeland, Florida. He came to Lakeland from South Bend, Indiana in 1966 when the weekly attendance was approximately 325. The church now serves several thousand people each week.

Rev. Karl Strader

Reverend Strader was born and raised in Oklahoma, and has a Methodist background. He received his Bachelor of Arts and Bachelor of Divinity degrees from Bob Jones University in Greenville, South Carolina, in 1954. Strader was awarded an honorary doctorate from Oral Roberts University in 1985.

Prior to his arrival in Lakeland, Rev. Strader pastored churches in the cities of Farmersburg, Gary and South Bend, Indiana. He was dean of men at Southeastern College in Lakeland for three years, youth president for the Assemblies of God Peninsular Florida District for three years, and four-year assistant superintendent of the District. He served for several years as a member of the Civil Service Commission for the City of Lakeland, and Foreign Missions secretary for the Peninsular Florida District for 13 years. He is a 15-year member of the General Presbytery of the Assemblies of God.

Rev. Strader and his wife, Joyce Wead Strader, have four children. He is the author of eight books.

A 10,000-seat sanctuary was built in Lakeland and named the Carpenter's Home Church. In addition an expansive Life Care Retirement Center has been completed, of which the Reverend Strader is president.

The following text is from the same seminar for pastors and building committee members in which the Reverend Cole directed his statements.

On Building
Rev. Karl Strader

From what God showed me through dreams and visions, it must be – it's got to be – God all the way. Believe me, that has kept me on my knees. If your church is not in God's will or in revival, I would not encourage you to go into a building program. When you open any kind of door – if you're worth your salt – Satan will kick you all the way through it, and all hell is going to break loose. Satan will see to

CHURCH GROWTH BY DESIGN

it that your life is diverted and your intentions are sidetracked any way that he can; he'll attack you personally, and attack your family. He'll cause a disruption if you start to do something for God. You've got to expect that.

I would recommend that before you start a building program of your own, you are on staff with a senior minister during one and learn from experience. Even then, it's dangerous. In fact, I wouldn't recommend anyone to build, unless, of course, God really speaks to your heart. If God does speak to your heart (for a building program), He will help you raise the money to do what He has called you to do. It's an awesome task and a great responsibility to step out with a congregation in a building program. And if I got a 100-percent vote of confidence from the congregation when I presented the plans for building, I would really shrink back and wonder if it was the will of God. Why? Because not everyone in the congregation is in tune with His will.

But, if you're fortified – through prayer, scripture and fasting – you can conquer!

Sometimes we have the tendency to get the methods and techniques without the principles. But there is no way to grow and expand or to know what to do about church building if you don't stay with God's principles. "Because the foolishness of God is wiser than men; and the weakness of God is stronger than men" (1 Corinthians 1:25, KJV). Methods and techniques have very little, if anything, to do with church growth. (If your church is not growing, if it's the same size as it was 30 years ago, you're not putting these principles to use.) Without naming all the personalities in the ministry today who are growing and making an impact, we know they have had a solid move from God. If you have had a 300-percent growth in 10 years, that's outstanding; a 400-percent growth, excellent; a 500-percent growth in 10 years, that's incredible! This is happening in some parts of the United States and the world today, and we thank God for it.

But don't start a building program unless you're in revival. If you are in revival and God lays it on your heart to build, then build. There has never been a revival in the church where there was not a price to be paid. But any excuse is ridiculous. If you're in God's will, you're in the right place and at the right time.

Have a trans-denominational atmosphere. God wants us to flow with the Spirit and with all denominations. Be flavored with every segment of the body of Christ. We must have that if we're going to expect growth and expansion. And the supernatural must be there – with all the manifestations. That's the finest advertising you can have. People will go where they can find the supernatural.

God wants us to have a joyful spirit in and out of a building

> *God wants us to have a joyful spirit in and out of a building program.*

program. The climate must be in tune with the golden honey of God's word. God will bless those who praise Him. Praise is a reason for church building – to worship Him and bow down. We must duplicate Christ's ministry in our own.

He said: "Follow me, and I will make you fishers of men." We must teach our people how to give to foreign and home missions. In the next five to 10 years, we plan to give 50 percent of our income to missions. That should be the commission of the megachurch, or any church. I like to accentuate the positive:

"Honour the Lord with thy substance, and with the first-fruits of all thine increase: so shall thy barns be filled with plenty, and thy presses shall burst out with new wine" (Proverbs 3:9,10, KJV).

"He that hath pity upon the poor lendeth unto the Lord; and that which he hath given will he pay him again" (Proverbs 19:17. KJV).

You say you get a headache...get sick when you fast? Well, join the club! There's just no other way to put the cutting edge on your ministry and on revival. The kind of fast I want is that you stop oppressing those who work for you and treat them fairly and give them what they earn. I want you to share your food with the hungry and bring right into your own homes those who are helpless, poor and destitute. Clothe those who are cold and don't hide from relatives who need your help. If you do these things, God will shed His own glorious light upon you. He will heal you. Your godliness will lead you forward, and goodness will be a shield before you. and the glory of the Lord will protect you from behind. Then, when you call, the Lord will answer. "Yes, I am here." He will quickly reply...Feed the hungry! Help those in trouble! Then your light will shine out from the darkness, and the darkness around you shall be as bright as day. And the Lord will guide you continually, and satisfy you with all good things, and keep you healthy too; and you will be like a well-watered garden, like an ever-flowing spring. Your sons will rebuild the long-deserted ruins of your cities, and you will be known as "The People Who Rebuild Their Walls and Cities" (Isaiah 58:6-12, TLB).

But remember this – if you give little, you will get little. A farmer who plants just a few seeds will get only a small crop, but if he plants much, he will reap much. Every one must make up his own mind as to how much he should give. Don't force anyone to give more than he really wants to, for cheerful givers are the ones God prizes. God is able to make it up to you by giving you everything you need and more, so that there will not only be enough for your own needs, but plenty left over to give joyfully to others... (2 Corinthians 9:6-8, TLB).

And He says in Matthew 25:31-40, on top of all that, we'll have eternal life! You don't have to give if you don't want to, but look what happens if you do!

The number one deterrent to church growth and building is

Don't force anyone to give more than he really wants to, for cheerful givers are the ones God prizes.

pride; an over-consciousness of our importance; having all the answers; a proud look; a more-than-frequent use of "I" or "my"; an over-awareness of good looks; a delight in ordering people around; loving titles, positions, rewards and compensations; doing things without God's motivation; an over-exhilaration about being around "important" people; having little concern for others; boastful of our goals, being negative and always voting "no."

Jesus said, "Beware of the level of the Pharisees." That "level" will deter church growth and keep you where you were 30 years ago – a holier-than-thou-attitude; hearing the Word and not doing it; fruitlessness; laboring for hire; isolation; praying and giving for show; thinking that being a member is more important than being a Christian; denominationalism; traditionalism over scriptures.

Think through everything you have read or heard – then do what God leads you to do. Those who are led by the Spirit of God are the Sons of God.

We trust that the words of these four pastors will be a source of help and encouragement if you are planning a church building project. It is our conviction that their personal experiences, combined with professional recommendations, will greatly enhance the value of this book for the reader.

> *Think through everything you have read or heard – then do what God leads you to do.*

First Assembly of God
Rockford, Illinois

Capital Christian Center
Sacramento, California

Carpenter's Home Church
Lakeland, Florida

4

THE RICHES OF WISDOM IN FINANCIAL PLANNING

A guide for fiscal responsibility in a building program

The writer of Ecclesiastes made some pretty pithy comments on good old common sense when it comes to money matters!

How about this: "To be wise is as good as being rich; in fact, it is better. You can get anything by either wisdom or money, but being wise has many advantages. (See the way God does things, and fall into line. Don't fight the facts of nature.) Who can straighten what he has made crooked? Enjoy prosperity whenever you can, and when hard times strike, realize that God gives one as well as the other – so that everyone will realize that nothing is certain in this life" (Ecclesiastes . 7:11-14, TLB).

Or this: "Finishing is better than starting! Patience is better than pride!" (Ecclesiastes 7:8, TLB).

And top it off with this, from Proverbs: "Any enterprise is built by wise planning, becomes strong through common sense, and profits wonderfully by keeping abreast of the facts" (Proverbs 24: 3,4, TLB).

Well, Solomon, there you go again!

It appears that nothing has changed much, since the tenth century, B.C., to render these words obsolete. In fact, with the increased interaction of national and global economics, common sense and perspective play a vital role in the pecuniary process today.

The holy enterprise of church building needs every bit as much financial acumen as the capital ventures of General Dynamics! Small churches are in the business of becoming larger, and larger churches are in the business of becoming even

"Finishing is better than starting! Patience is better than pride!"

– Ecclesiastes 7:8 TLB

bigger. Church leaders, like managers of any corporate enterprise, need an entrepreneurial vision that looks for solid groundwork and acute awareness of the money market. They must calculate profit and loss even as they act on their call to reach people through the expansion of their ministry. We know that it is God's will for us to prosper. It is also His plan that we use good sound principles as we build for the future. Starting a project is one thing; finishing is quite another! With prayer, patience and planning, you can do both with aplomb and enjoy the "profits"!

Long Range Projections

Wisdom dictates that a governing body of the church makes long range projections for church growth. These projections should be periodically updated as to the outreach potential of the church, the church's membership and attendance, as well as the financial condition of the church.

Advance planning is important to avoid bad medicine that could stunt your growth, such as space saturation, over-building or premature building. We've talked about the important work of the long-range planning committee; most of your questions should have been answered in that initial investigation. We're including additional material that should assist you as you make financial projections. To complement your earlier research, please refer to the Situation Survey form. Additionally, the Census Access for Planning in the Church (CAPC) can, for a fee, furnish a computer-generated analysis of a particular ministry area. CAPC is located at Concordia College, River Forest, Illinois 60305.

Know what a building project will cost! The rule of thumb (along with several years of building experience!) says that a building project will cost you from 65 dollars to 120 dollars per square foot, depending on the design and materials selection. This includes architectural plans, the building itself and carpeting. What other costs are on the horizon? For starters: pews, other furnishings, parking lot, sound system or any other "extras" you have in your projections. Basically, you can feel safe if you count on:

Advance planning is important to avoid bad medicine that could stunt your growth.

- Construction cost – 70 to 80 percent of total project.
- Furnishings – 5 to 10 percent of construction cost.
- Landscaping – 3 to 5 percent of construction cost.
- Parking Lot – $550 per car, paved parking lot.
- Construction Loan Cost – 8 to 10 percent of construction cost.
- Financing closing costs – 2 percent of construction cost.
- Contingency – 5 percent of construction cost
- Architect, other fees – 5 to 8 percent of construction cost.

Financial Records, Planning and Analysis

One of the first things you should do after making a preliminary decision to explore possible expansion is to analyze the financial condition of the church. Conduct an accurate survey of the church's income and expense statements along with a comprehensive and realistic balance sheet. Many lending institutions require a church to obtain an audit of the previous three years financial statements, plus a stub for that portion of the current fiscal year. In some cases, compilation review is enough, along with current and projected budgets. When this review is completed, you can arrive at a Safe Debt Limit for the church.

Debt-to-income ratio

Typically, a church should not borrow more than three to four times the previous year's total income, excluding any borrowed monies. This also does not include any income from a school, daycare center, radio or television ministry – anything outside of the tithes and offerings, missions and building fund offerings.

Debt service-to-income ratio

A church's debt service should not exceed more than 35 to 40 percent of the previous year's income. When the amount of debt service exceeds this amount, ministry programs and opportunities will suffer. The Financial Analysis Information from MMR Investment Bankers, and Budget and Ministries Debt Ratio forms are tools that can be used in your evaluations. If at this point your proposed building project appears to fall safely within these guidelines, now is the time to bring on board the professionals who will draw up master site plans and master building plans. Be careful that you and those professionals pay attention to, and stay within, the debt to income ratio and debt service to income percentage. Several denominations offer this consulting service, and of course, there are some qualified independent companies who specialize in church planning, building and financing.

Debt-to-collateral ratio

There is one more thing you should keep in mind. Most investment bankers and lending institutions require that the aggregate amount of debt should not be in excess of 75 percent of the appraised value of the properties pledged as collateral (after completion of the building project). Here's the formula for arriving at this percentage.

> *Typically, a church should not borrow more than three to four times the previous year's total income, excluding any borrowed monies.*

<u>Total Amount of Financing Needed</u>
Final Value of the Project (Buildings and Land)

It's usually necessary to obtain an independent appraisal of the church's property to accurately determine the debt-to-collateral ratio.

Funds Available for Expansion

Building fund

The first step in raising money for expansion for many churches is to start a building fund. This can be accomplished by setting aside a portion of the weekly contributions, or people may choose to designate a portion of their offerings for the building project. There's nothing wrong with taking advantage of holidays and special events to fire up the fund drive and stimulate added excitement among the congregation. But gimmicks are gauche! You can spend too much time, money and energy on giving away trinkets (or even living creatures, as has been witnessed) in return for a special offering. Preaching the Word and bringing the people along with you in the building program works better than bribes!

Capital gifts campaign

Church leaders often choose to enter into a capital gifts campaign. Church members are asked to pledge a certain amount toward the building project on a regular basis and over a one, two or three year period of time. Some churches conduct their own campaign, but the wiser route is to employ an independent company to launch and carry out the effort. That company should supply brochures and other tools to conduct an effective, low-key campaign, carefully designed to be inoffensive to church members. A church can realistically expect to raise 1.5 to 2 times its last year's annual income over a three-year period (excluding borrowed monies and any large one-time gifts). There are several companies who specialize in this type of capital gift program.

Investment Bankers

Many churches are turning to investment bankers as a source of financing. An investment banker is a full-service lending institution that offers consulting services to a church in the planning stages of its building program, technical assistance in the capital gift campaign, and provides the long-term financing through the issuance and sale of real estate mortgage bonds.

The first step in raising money for expansion for many churches is to start a building fund.

Your church must vote in official action to issue and sell bonds. A bond is a certificate of indebtedness – a promise by the church to repay a specific amount at a specific date and at a specific interest rate.

The church will pledge its property as collateral for bonds; the bonds then are sold to church members and friends in the community, as well as to the customers of the investment banker all around the country. Building projects financed through real estate mortgage bonds frequently are less expensive than those financed through banks or other institutions. Why? There is no "middle man" and the interest rate can be set lower.

Reputable investment bankers are members of the National Association of Securities Dealers and the Securities Investment Protection Corporation.

Denominational sources

New churches and smaller mission churches may want to check with their denominational loan fund to see if there is money available for building projects. And, many times a larger church will sponsor a home mission or satellite church. The former might furnish cash and pledges, guarantee a loan or commit to making part – or all – of the loan payments.

Conventional mortgage loans

Bank loans usually are for a shorter period of time, or they may be amortized over a longer period of time – but with a two- or three-year balloon. The interest rate usually fluctuates and is tied to the prime rate (the interest rate banks generally charge their best commercial customers).

Mortgage bankers sometimes have access to insurance companies and other investors who may have money available to loan. The interest rate at most savings and loan associations usually will be slightly lower than those of banks.

Loan Portfolio

When a church is ready to apply for its long-term financing, the first thing the board should do is draft a comprehensive building budget. This budget should set forth – as accurately as possible – the entire costs of the building program. Then, the board should reexamine the projected church budgets to be sure they have included debt retirement and other costs associated with a larger facility, such as higher utilities and increased staff.

Next, the board should prepare an attractive loan portfolio to

Building projects financed through real estate mortgage bonds frequently are less expensive than those financed through banks or other institutions.

present to potential lenders. This portfolio should present a confident, yet conservative, picture of the church's financial status and potential for growth. These items should be included in the loan portfolio:

Loan request and description of project

Right up front, state your request and the nature of the project. Describe, accurately and concisely, what you need and for what you are asking.

Your current church status

Succinctly and accurately present the current statistical information about the church and community. (See how necessary that first research is to your project!) It is important that you describe the legal statistics of your church as defined in your articles of incorporation, constitution and by-laws, or your denominational manual.

Define your denominational affiliation and include the organizational structure, history and statistics. Will your denomination assume all – or any – of the responsibility in guaranteeing repayment of the loan? Say so, and describe to what extent.

History and projections of your church

It's always helpful to a lender to know the complete background of the borrower. Start with the church's organization and the growth pattern of the church. Finish your background report with future projections. A list of the pastoral leaders of the church and the tenure of each one is beneficial. In addition, a biographical sketch of the present pastor should be included, highlighting his experience in leading other church building programs, if any.

List your current church board, the officers of the church and the people serving on your finance and building committees. Name and occupation, please.

Financial statements and/or audit

The audit of a qualified certified public accountant is always beneficial and impressive to a lender. If you don't have one, give him at least three full years of financial statements, showing receipts and disbursements, plus a balance sheet for each year. For good measure, show him your current-year operating budget.

The board should prepare an attractive loan portfolio to present to potential lenders.

General statistics

Chart your membership growth over the past three to five years. Chart the increases in attendance. Both of these could be showcased in a graph.

Include in this area your per capita giving. You might want to compare this with your denomination's average along with that of other denominations. (The average should be 12 dollars per person per week, minimum!)

If you have completed a capital gift campaign, or are contemplating getting one started, you'll want to describe the results or projections in detail. This will enable the lender to better comprehend the commitment level of your constituents.

Description of property to be mortgaged

Give a legal description of the property along with the number of acres owned by the church. Divulge any and all information regarding loans against the property, and say whether the other lenders are willing to subordinate their position to the new mortgage.

Describe in detail any improvements on the property. If an appraisal is available, it would help in arriving at any equity you might have in the property. And finally, list all equipment, and its value, owned by the church.

Additional Information

The loan portfolio also should contain:

- Design and architectural drawings of the proposed new facility, including the name and profile of your architect.
- The general contractor should be named, along with the type of contract you have with him.
- A list of sub-contractors, if possible at this point.
- A construction cost estimate from your architect and/or builder and a time-table for completion of the project.
- Identification and information on the church's attorney and bank.

When the portfolio is completed, the church board should carefully consider the options in obtaining long-term financing. Whatever your choice, it is prudent to start applying for loans well in advance of construction start-up. Four to six months usually are needed to finalize loan negotiations.

When the board makes a decision on the method of financing, the church membership must vote to mortgage the property in accordance with its constitution and by-laws, and must execute a

Chart your membership growth over the past three to five years.

resolution. If the choice is to go with an investment banker and a bond program, the resolution will need to be examined by the church's attorney, who then will write a legal debt letter and assist the church in obtaining a title policy. The mortgage or deed of trust then should be recorded at the county seat. Remember, a qualified firm has the expertise to walk the church through each required – and important– step to make sure the bond offering will meet the state security commissioner's requirements, as well as those of the National Association of Securities Dealers (NASD).

You should have enough basic monetary information now to forge ahead! With wise stewardship of the resources at hand and those He has provided, everything – as He promised – will fall in line and you can finish what you've started.

And as one of our staff members said to a group of pastors who were anticipating building programs: "If God is my source, that's all I need because He will never go bankrupt."

There are two ways of giving. One is giving by reason, and that is to figure out what you can afford. The other is to pray about it and ask,"'What can God channel through my hands?" But you must know God. Let me tell you, it works. It can start a miracle!

With wise stewardship of the resources at hand and those He has provided, everything – as He promised – will fall in line and you can finish what you've started.

Evangelical United Brethren
Marion, Kansas

Situation Survey

	Current Year	Past History 5 Years	Future Projection 5 Years
Church Constituency			
Sunday a.m. Attendance			
Sunday School Attendance			
State Population			
County Population			
City Population			
% of Population to Members			
# Community Churches			
Total Constituency (All Churches)			
Total Unchurched (City)			
Projected Growth			
Annual Giving (All Purposes)			
Building Giving or Expenditure (Budget)			
Average Income of Individual City Family			
Average Tithe for Church Giving Units x Average Income x 7%			
Future Giving Based on Projected Growth x Average Income x 7%			

Financial Analysis Information

Church _____ Phone (____) _____

Address _____ City _____ ST _____ ZIP _____

Pastor _____ Phone (____) _____

Is Church Incorporated? _____

Financial and Statistical Information

Church's fiscal year _____ to _____

20 _____ 20 _____ 20 _____ 20 _____ 20 _____ (_____ Weeks)

(current year)

Income $ _____ $ _____ $ _____ $ _____ $ _____

(all sources except loans)

Attending Families _____ _____ _____ _____ _____

Amount in Building Fund $ _____

Building Fund Pledge Campaign

   Contemplated   Date _____ Goal $ _____ OVER _____ YEARS

   Completed   Date _____ Goal $ _____ OVER _____ YEARS

Property

Estimated value of present buildings and land .... $ _____
   (excluding parsonage)

Estimated equity in parsonage .... $ _____

Indebtedness Against Buildings and Land (excluding parsonages)
   for additional loans, photostat this page)

	Loan 1	Loan 2
Present indebtedness .... $	_____	$ _____
How paid? ___ weekly ___ monthly .... $	_____	$ _____
Original amount	_____	_____
Date incurred	_____	_____
Years yet to pay	_____	_____
Interest Rate	_____	_____

Project   **Estimated Cost**

_____ Build new sanctuary .... $ _____

_____ Build new educational facilities .... $ _____

_____ Remodel or Repair.. $ _____

_____ Refinancing.. $ _____

_____ Other (please explain) .... $ _____

Total Estimated Financing Needed .... $ _____

Is Retirement of Indebtedness Included in this Estimate   _____ Yes   _____ No

If so, list which loans _____

Information compiled by _____ Date _____

Budget and Ministries Debt Ratio

	Enter Amount Spent		Show % of Total Income		Possible % Range for Comparison
	1 Year	3 Years	1 Year	3 Years	
Building Maintenance and Operation					5% to 15%
Salaries*					30% to 45%
Other Local Expenses					12% to 20%
District and General Expenditure					5% to 10%
World Mission**					8% to 10%
Total Program					60% to 100%
Amount for Debt (service) Payment					35% to 0%
Total Income			100%	100%	100%

* The larger churches will usually experience a lower percent under salaries. Be sure to project any added staff due to expansion.

** Many churches experience increased mission giving when local building and growth take place.

Recommendation: Maximum debt payments are usually limited to 35% of current gross income (payment includes principal, interest, and other costs). To spend more than this on debt service will take from the ministry budget.

Note: If the local economy is strong, it can be assumed that inflation will be absorbed by increased giving due to increased income. The above study is not designed to include inflation.

Construction Cost Projection

1. Construction contract (or professional estimate of cost)
   Including completion bonds and insurance $ _____

2. Architect Fee $ _____
   Acoustical Cons. $ _____
   Attorney Fee $ _____
   Survey Engineer $ _____
   Soil Analysis $ _____ $ _____

3. Site Work
   Grading $ _____
   Drainage $ _____
   Utilities $ _____ $ _____

4. Landscape Planting $ _____

5. Parking and Drives $ _____

6. Contingency (5% or more of above) $ _____

7. Furniture, carpet, and drapes $ _____

8. Stained glass and art $ _____

9. Sound System, TV System, Production and recording,
   including sound engineer. $ _____

10. Special lighting $ _____

11. Kitchen equipment $ _____

12. Interest during construction $ _____

13. Allow 4% of above for miscellaneous expense $ _____

    Project Total $ _____

Add land cost if applicable.
Including real estate fees, appraisal fees, and other related expenses.

5

SELECTING THE SITE FOR YOUR PLANTING

Smart-shopping tips for property acquisition

So you're growing a church! Now, where is the best place in town to break ground?

The process of locating the perfect site for your new building is an important one that calls for an abundance of serious thought, calculations and practical considerations. We're not saying that in your search you won't find yourself standing barefoot by a burning bush. Oh, no! Maybe, just maybe, you'll hear an angel of the Lord proclaiming that you've found a patch of holy ground. It happened once; it surely could happen again!

But God works in many and mysterious ways. A lot of time has passed since Moses lived out his years on this earth; the population has lustily procreated and filled almost every gap. What used to be pedestrian separations of space are now golden-arched, high-rised, shopping-malled pockets of "progress" connected and fueled by a battery of freeways. The masses have multiplied, and the land is limited! Simple choices have succumbed to complex decisions that might dumbfound even Solomon, with all his wisdom.

It's not an easy road to hoe, nowadays. That's why it's even more imperative to read The Directions. Carefully and prayerfully, mix His will with your God-given common sense when you go about the task of choosing – and buying – the property for your expansion project. Be watchful, like Moses. Be wise, like Solomon. But like any contemporary consumer, be wary!

Since you've already done your program planning, with the help of the long-range planning committee, and figured out just how much money you can spend to accomplish at least phase one of your project, let's buy that land!

Carefully and prayerfully, mix His will with your God-given common sense when you go about the task of choosing – and buying – the property for your expansion project.

Here are some pretty important things to consider: God does love a cheerful giver, but it will cost you more in the long run to accept a free or next-to-free gift-wrapped parcel of ground that's in an undesirable area. From your studies on community growth and socio-economic patterns, you've got a good feel for which part of town your church would have the most impact. Consider whom you want to reach, and how available it is from a transportation standpoint.

Unless your church will be within a comfortable walking distance for most of your members, you really must cater to the drive-in traffic. Good access is a must, whether cars will be approaching from a major freeway or a main city street. Have you ever driven down a busy thoroughfare and seen a skimpy little sign with an arrow directing you to a church six blocks down a narrow road? Do it right the first time: build your church – not your sign – on that premium piece of property!

How Does the Land Look, and What Is Adjacent to the Property Lines?

Schools, apartment complexes, and yes, even shopping centers make good neighbors and good prospects (maybe Wal-Mart will even share their parking lot - think about it). Reeking sewage disposal plants, smoke-belching factories or clamoring industrial areas can be unfriendly and unsightly. One church curiously purchased a piece of property not long ago next to an electrical substation. Imagine how charged the members were to see their church going up next to high voltage electrical lines! Be careful not to increase the risks by offending your congregation's senses while you're trying to appeal to their souls. Environmental pollution of any kind is likely to send your members scampering – holding their ears, eyes or noses! Not only that, it can cost an arm and a leg to control the undesirable elements to which you've moved next door.

How Much Land Do You Really Need?

As a rule, buy a minimum of two acres to build a church accommodating 400 people. This assumes those 400 folks will be using all the educational, auditorium and parking space you'll provide. (A church of this size requires a parking lot for a minimum of 100 cars.) Now, take it on up the scale. If you're looking at serving 1,000 people, buy no less than five acres. Obviously, this acreage will not allow for a baseball diamond – which needs approximately two-and-a-half acres – or even a two-hole golf course – but it will provide the very least amount of space you can buy, considering setback and greenbelt requirements in your city. This translates into approximately 45 square feet per person for auditorium and

As a rule, buy a minimum of two acres to build a church accommodating 400 people.

educational space – plus 30,000 square feet parking space for every 100 cars, matched by 30,000 square feet for city requirements. Please notice that we've stressed the words "minimum" and "approximately" since each building project and each city has variables that resist stone tablet inscriptions.

Square Is Fair

For any church building project, and especially the architect and builder, please, we beg you, resist the temptation, just because you may be getting a "good buy," to settle for a piece of ground that measures anything like 100 feet wide and 900 feet long. Get the picture? Setting the building on an odd-shaped site could result in an odd-shaped church and make it difficult to get full use of the land.

Be a smart shopper! The best way to do this is to ask the current owner to provide you with an engineer's certified survey of the property. This can tell you everything you want to know (or don't want to hear later) about the site you're considering.

A topographical survey can give you information that might give you cause to pause.

What's the Lay of the Land?

A topographical survey can give you information that might give you cause to pause. One pastor friend, for whom we were commissioned to build, assured us that his property was "flat as a pancake." After a bona fide survey of the situation, we discovered a seven-foot slope that required a mighty load of fill dirt to even-up the grade. Funny pancake! But not so funny to the person writing the check. And do you know what they call land that is built up by stream deposit, and that could again be visited by unwanted waters? You guessed it! Floodplain. Be careful; you're building a church, not an ark.

Another church we built already had paid good money for a piece of land that was eight-feet lower than the street. Once we got rid of the water, and the ducks, we filled it up and built it up. Expensive business. A thorough study of the land's elevations should give you a clear picture of any drainage problems. Consider, too, the visual impact on your parishioners. It's much more appealing to look up than down.

Don't build your church in a hole. Just about the time you think everything is going uphill, you might discover from your survey that some things just won't! A church in Florida had to run a sewer line for half a mile. Find out exactly what is the state-of-the-utilities. How deep is the sewer? Is there a sewer? The sewer situation can be a high-dollar item and should be anticipated. A good utility map from your city will also tell you about the availability of water, electricity and gas.

Types of Sites

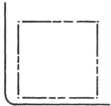

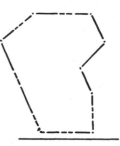

Corner
A site of this type offers good exposure to the community. A corner site also offers a variety of access and orientation.

Wide
This site type lends itself to a long and narrow development. Buildings and parking will be laid out in a linear arrangement.

Narrow
This type of site will have a minimum of exposure to the community. Access to the site will be restricted, with buildings and parking laid out deep into the site.

Irregular
This site type can be difficult to develop due to site restrictions. However, there is a potential for original and innovative site design development.

Conditions of a Site

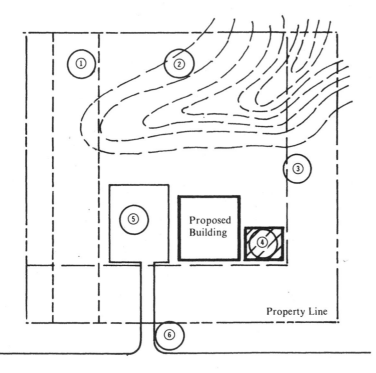

① Easements for utilities and other services

② Topography; contours, soil condition, water table level.

③ Building setbacks and code restrictions.

④ Special site consideration; existing buildings, trees, etc.

⑤ Off-street parking requirements.

⑥ Allowed access-egress from site.

FIG. 5-1

What's Yours Is Yours; What's Not, Is Not!

A land survey will (or should) make it perfectly clear where to draw the property lines. Stay in your own yard, please. One property owner in Chicago wasn't too happy when a congregation built a 50-foot church on what they thought was a 50-foot lot. (On some inner-city properties there are no municipal requirements for setbacks or greenbelt/which gives the owner full use of the land.) As it turned out, their lot actually had only 49 feet and nine inches. The next-door neighbors. who weren't very friendly in the first place, hung a hefty little price tag on those three inches, and probably never darkened the door of that church.

Did the church have a site plan? Oh yes, but it wasn't certified. The stamp of a professional can give you peace of mind. Even if you don't like what you find from a certified survey, at least you can be certain the legal description of everything in, on, under, around and about the property is accurate.

It's Dirty Work, But Someone Has To Do It.

A soil test can unearth a truckload of information. It can cause you to bury your head in the sand, butt your head against a rock, or smile and consider yourself well-grounded. However it affects you or your building project, you must obtain a soil test to dig up all the available information about the foundation on which you will build your church.

What do you need to know? Well, are you building on solid rock or the city dump? What does the soil contain that affects foundations, and what is the water availability and table depth? If you know everything there is to know about the soil, you and your architect will also know what modifications, and the costs of those modifications, will be. With up-front information, there are no midterm surprises.

We don't blame you for liking mountains – so do we. Just realize what you're getting into – what it's actually going to cost – if that's what you want. A church in Oregon had purchased property before they contacted our company. They were ready to build, and we were ready to go to work. When we asked the pastor to show us the site, he proudly pointed to a mountain! Our first job? We cut off the mountain – 30 feet to be exact – to find a place big enough on which to set the church.

Another church we completed takes your breath away when you see it sitting high on the hill at the edge of a Southwestern city. That particular city has what is called a "hillside" ordinance which means you can't build over 38 feet above the way the land lays. We petitioned for and acquired permission to go to 54 feet. In doing so, it meant that we had to dig into the mountain, down on the backside 19 feet. We blasted over 5,000 times during the excavation for a

A soil test can unearth a truckload of information.

total price tag of $360,000. Beautiful, but expensive. Just know what you're getting into and budget for it. God, money and modern technology specializes in things thought impossible!

Early in our construction career, before we learned the hard way that the absence of soil tests can cause fear and trepidation, we walked upon a lovely piece of property with the pastor who assured us that this was "virgin soil," perfect for the taking and what's more, at a real bargain price! We, innocently, took him at his word. But as we began excavating, we also began hitting heavy metal that looked suspiciously like parts of an automobile. When we uncovered the second car body, we knew we were in trouble. The pastor didn't realize it, but he and the church, also innocently, had paid good money - albeit not much – for the old city dump. Everything worked out, as it usually does. However, we had to dig 15 feet downward in some places before we were able to hit solid ground.

Herein are two lessons: "discount prices" don't always mean savings in the long run. And, never, never, buy land before a professional investigation of the soil is completed and studied for all the possible implications.

It's no secret to anyone, even a fledgling who had trouble passing Geology 101, that there are more than a dirty-dozen "soil variances in the U.S. of A. If you'd shovel your way cross-country, you would find about anything you can think of causes grief, and a big difference in building preparation.

Let's take Colorado's bentonite as an example. Because bentonite is a clay that causes expansion and contraction in the earth, which subsequently threatens to crack a foundation, builders need to sink a pier approximately 20 feet in the ground. On top of that goes a grade beam. Then there's the spongy, almost peatmoss-like soil-of-the South – "affectionately" dubbed bulltallow in those parts – that is filled with air and the aggravating tendency to compress to great depths. If enough layers of this porous terra *un*firma have oozed into the earth some 30 or 40 feet, the pier and grade beam plan goes into action. If it's a shallower pit of puree, it can be excavated and replaced with good fill dirt. It's an extra step that will cost more, but the precautions against cracking founda-tions are well worth the time and money in the long run.

Examine Your City's Zoning Ordinances Before You Cut the Check.

A church in the Northeast had great fortune in selling the existing building and impulsively bought another piece of property without doing the necessary homework. After architectural plans were prepared and submitted to the city for a building permit, the pastor and committee were graded down for lack of research and

As we began excavating, we also began hitting heavy metal that looked suspiciously like parts of an automobile.

told that the area was not zoned for a church. One would think an experience like this would teach them a lesson. But noooooo. They did the same thing three times before they graduated!

Another pastor bought 38 acres after he was told that zoning was acceptable for a church. What the city didn't tell him was about the "hillside" ordinance which said you couldn't build a building over 38 feet high. The proposed church structure required 58 feet. The church committee went before the city council for a variance, but was denied an appeal. They decided to sell their property and look elsewhere.

As we implied before, there's not a surplus of holy ground. It's not a simple matter to build churches anymore, and every inch of a city's zoning requirements must be memorized. You may even be required to convince a city council that your church will be an asset to the area. In that case, your previous studies – combined with some high-powered and heavy salesmanship – may be a required subject. Study for the tests!

Some cities won't issue a building permit with or without the proper zoning requirements. The lack of easements, streets, up-to-date platting or some other technicality within the city structure can stop your project – or at least slow it down. Put your heads together with the architect, an attorney, your real-estate broker and the local planning department to find out about the existing codes, setbacks, required greenbelt areas, parking, street rights-of-way, or even the possibility of existing liens or restrictions on the property. Keep in mind that building codes for your part of the country may be altered by the local rules and regulations. Your life will be easier if you hire a professional consultant to help you pull things together. You'll sleep better, we assure you!

You've been watchful, wary and wise. Now, one last thought from an in-house expert on good manners. Don't tarnish the Golden Rule by planting yourself too close to another church – especially of your denomination. Tending to the P's and Q's of turf etiquette can earn you stature and respect in the community. And even more important, where you chose the site for your "harvest" can make His commission to "go forth" easier to accomplish – and definitely within your reach!

Find out about the existing codes, setbacks, required greenbelt areas, parking, street rights-of-way, or even the possibility of existing liens or restrictions on the property.

Analysis Map for Choosing a New Church Site

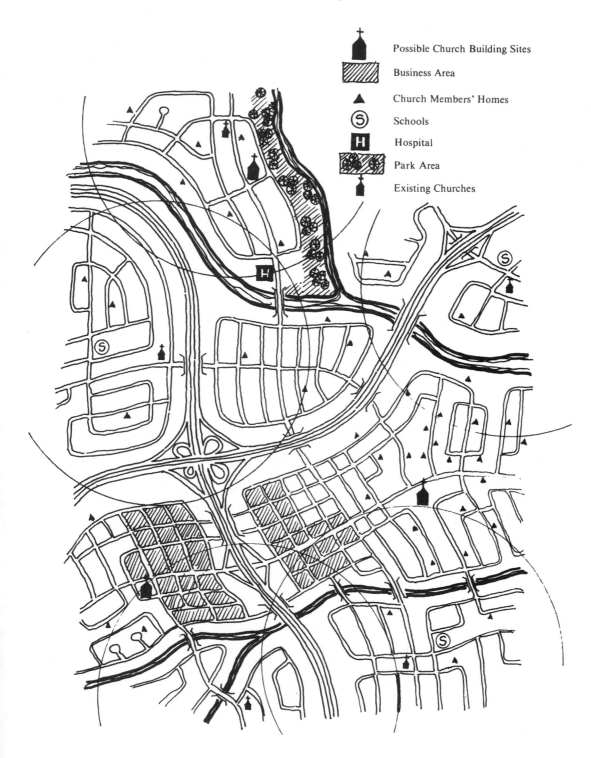

Possible Church Building Sites

Business Area

Church Members' Homes

Schools

Hospital

Park Area

Existing Churches

FIG. 5-2   71

6

BUILDING BY COMMITTEE – A WORKING PARTNERSHIP

Selecting a building committee and subcommittees

When you get down to the business of building, you have the luxury of rich resources at your fingertips.

The Body has brains, so use them!

When it comes to a building program, you're going to need all the collective grey matter with which your church is blessed.

But don't stop there. The very best conceptual, even common-sensical, brainwork could be left floating aimlessly in the clouds unless the rest of the "members" show some life. Hands, feet, eyes, ears and noses mobilize the mentality and activate the intellect, bringing down to earth the task at hand.

"Suppose the whole body were an eye – then how would you hear? Or if your whole body were just one big ear, how could you smell anything?...The eye can never say to the hand, 'I don't need you.' The head can't say to the feet, 'I don't need you.' Just as our bodies are composed of many parts and all the parts are needed to form a complete body, so it is with Christ's body, the church" (1Corinthians 12:12,17, 21, TLB).

Paul also heralds the good news that "God gives his people many kinds of special abilities...He "works through different people in different ways" and "manifests himself through each person for the good of the entire church" (1Corinthians12:6, 7, TLB).

When you get down to the business of building, you have the luxury of rich resources at your fingertips. Within your own congregation you have the leaders you need as representatives of the church. Each person you choose has individual talents and knowledge of the ministry into which you can tap. Some may even possess professional expertise worth its weight in gold! The eventual coalition is called the "building committee" – with possible spin-offs into "building sub-committees" – which will consider, investigate, take action on and report all aspects of the building program. The responsibility of this delegation is a heavy one, indeed, and plays a crucial role in the success of the project.

Pastors, you need these advocates. God chose you to "preach the Good News." Paul showed wisdom when he recommended appointing others to share in the business and to help carry the load. You, too – with a prudential selection of those who will be entrusted with the crux of your church growth – can establish manageable goals and accomplish His directive!

It's *old* news, of course, that each church – like each individual – possesses qualities of uniqueness. What one church needs in the way of committee representation can be significantly different for another. The Goose and Gander juxtaposition depends on the size, service and supervision of your ministry – or denomination, in some cases.

From experience, observation, words of personal testimony from pastors and building committee chairmen, we advise you to lock in this thought: keep your delegation small and workable. We suggest three, four, or at the most. five people. Rev. Harry Beall of the Bethseda Missionary Temple in Detroit, Michigan, has been through several building programs, including a 3,000-seat church. He knows what he's talking about when he says, "too many people on the building committee can mess up the machinery!"

There's no question about it. Building committees can slow down the building progress and speed up the blood pressure. But small, carefully-selected committees can be valuable in getting from point A to point B.

Small, carefully-selected committees can be valuable in getting from point A to point B.

Why a Building Committee?
Two reasons:

Help for the pastor

No pastor in his right mind would, or should, take on the awesome responsibility of going into a building program without support. Although the role of the clergy varies in each project, depending on the respective energies, strengths and ministerial goals, there's just too much going on for one person to oversee. Generally speaking, the building committee's job is to relieve the pastor of unending details, assist in making important decisions along the way, and oversee the actual construction of the church.

Representation

From a public relations standpoint, the building committee serves as a mouthpiece for the whole church. As representatives of the membership, this "working" party should make each person in the congregation feel comfortable in the fact he has a qualified advocate on the decision-making team. It all boils down to "taking the load off" – for the pastor and the people of the church. And after all, how many people really want to assume – and actually carry out – the burden of building? It takes dedication, hard work, long hours and wise consideration. Nobody said that God's assignments were easy. Be thankful there are people in your church ready, willing and singularly able to serve with you as you build!

> *From a public relations standpoint, the building committee serves as a mouthpiece for the whole church.*

Who Is the Building Committee and How Are They Appointed?

There are as many answers to this question as there are hairs on a camel. By the way, who ever said the dromedary was a horse designed by a church building committee? For shame! We do know it was Lucretius, in *On the Nature of Things*, who said: "What is food to one is to others bitter poison." Animals and analogies aside, the point is: pick yours! For informational purposes, however, there are several ways the process can be handled.

In some cases the building committee is elected by the membership. To make this congregational investiture complete, a chairman, vice-chairman, secretary and treasurer might be installed. Or, the newly-elected executive committee often will select officers among themselves.

Another approach is to have the official church board – or the pastor – select the committee, then present the list of candidates to the church for approval. If your church has a trace of totalitarian blood in its veins, with members who are happily content as subjects to authority, forget the election. Appoint your committee and proceed!

One church with whom we've worked simply appointed two "coordinators" – both with construction experience – to ramrod the entire project.

Then again, there are other cases when a church has a business administrator to whom the pastor assigns the job of running the building program. He, alone, may have the heady role of gathering about him the people he feels can best help him and the pastor through a successful building program.

So, to reiterate: whatever is best for you, your church and your ministry is workable. Only you have your finger on the pulse of the people. But you will best be served if those on the building committee are familiar with the workings of the church's ministry, have a good business sense, possess some organizational skills and enjoy at least a decent amount of confidence from the people. The chairman, whether he is a staff member or volunteer, should have a double dose of these admirable qualities since he will be charged with the task of guiding the committee, organizing and scheduling the meetings, making reports and recommendations, and generally stepping out as the diplomatic liaison.

One building committee chairman we know stresses the importance of the Lord's leading, but has this advice: "If you're on your deathbed, you want only certain people to come see you – to minister and to comfort...not everyone. The same is true when you choose your building committee...you want just the right ones for the task at hand. Then, because they each have a special expertise, let them do their job!"

Ah, yes. And back to the Bible: "We should make plans – counting on God to direct us" (Proverbs 16:9,TLB).

What *is* the Job of the Building Committee?

We talked earlier in this book about the long-range planning, or survey committee. In some cases, the same group of people, plus or minus a few, takes on the role of the building committee. In still other instances, the two are separate groups entirely. Whatever situation your church has chosen in this regard, the results of the previous groundwork is in your hands and by now you should know what you need. Look at every detail of the report. Make sure you understand it all. Mistakes and oversights are costly. Don't get caught with egg on your face by forgetting details.

Now communicate! Once your building committee and officers are in place, make it perfectly clear what their parameters of power include. Can they negotiate contracts? Deal with legal problems? Have access to the checkbook? Or not? If everyone knows, going in, what's expected and when, there should be good working rapport. This is not to say your committee members won't disagree now and then. As a matter of fact, some differing opinions can be healthy and productive. Overstepping boundaries and swimming against the tide of authority, however, can put unnecessary strain on relationships and progress.

"It was understood right from the beginning that we would have the authority to make recommendations to the pastor and board," says Dave Anderson, one of the two building coordinators for the completed Capital Christian Center in Sacramento, California. "But

Mistakes and oversights are costly. Don't get caught with egg on your face by forgetting details.

it's important to find out from the leadership what they want and how much they can spend. It's just like a business...pleasing your customers. If a building committee approaches the job like this, things should go smoothly."

We couldn't have said it better ourselves!

Other jobs for the building committee can include:

- Appointing subcommittees.
- Interviewing and selecting the architect and builder.
- Assisting in the choosing and purchasing of a site.
- Helping to secure financing.
- Handling contracts throughout the building program.
- Working directly with the architect and builder, meeting regularly during planning and construction.
- Authorizing payments.
- Staying abreast of the progress and reporting to the pastor, church board and membership.

"It's just like a business... pleasing your customers."

– Dave Anderson

The pastor and the membership: two other good subjects worthy of discussion.

Let's start with the pastor. Just how involved should he be in the building program? Read on, then decide for yourself.

Dave Anderson: "The main purpose of a building committee is to relieve the pastor of pressure and responsibility. It's a good plan if the right people are chosen."

"The pastor needs to be protected, since he has the job of preaching, teaching and visitation," says Barry Hummel, who was business administrator and committee chairman for the first-phase construction of Evangel Assembly of God Church in Camp Springs, Maryland. "It was my job to do the legwork, then report back to him for a final decision. This was easy, since I'm on staff and have his heartbeat."

Bob Morgan was the church business administrator and served as chairman during construction of Cathedral in the Pines in Beaumont, Texas.

"I am a partner with the pastor," says Morgan. "We tried to keep him as uninvolved as possible in order to let him handle what he's best at – spiritual matters. Our goal was to build a church without losing our pastor and creating dissension. Building the church was secondary. We tailor-made the project around the pastor. Then, he was wise enough to let people in the church do what they're best at...do what they know."

"Our pastor (Rev. Richard Exley) was very active in the planning and building...he knew just what he wanted, in every phase of the project," says Don Steele, who was chairman for the Christian

Chapel building project in Tulsa, Oklahoma. "I believe the pastor should stay in control...it worked for us. Because of his knowing what he wanted and because of good pre-planning, we had very few change orders."

The Reverend Harry Beall: "We as pastors (remember that his brother, Rev. James Beall, was senior pastor of Bethseda Missionary Temple) are very involved in the building program. We and the committee took a leadership role, and the church members have confidence in that leadership. My advice? Maintain the K.I.S.S. policy – Keep It Simple, Stupid! The simpler the program is run, the better. You know, the church is not really a democracy. You can't get bogged down with informing and getting input on every little detail from all the church members. The devil doesn't give us as many problems as that could!"

So there you have it! It appears that you can be as involved as you'd care to be, pastor. Just make that decision before you launch your building program, and let your committee know where you stand.

And now for the membership at large. Is your church run like a democracy – or with a hint of hierarchy? Whatever your answer, please, let's be fair! The members deserve to know something about what's going on with the plans and the progress. Besides, how can you maintain that explosive enthusiasm (which translates into double-barreled support) if you handcuff them outside with their noses pressed against the stained-glass windows!

Since we've already established the fact that too many bodies on the building committee can wreak havoc, there should be no argument with the Beall theory. Approaching the membership with every detail, every decision, could put your project completion date into the far distant future. But there are a couple of ways to make your people feel a part of the new building program.

Christian Chapel in Tulsa provided a suggestion box in the foyer of the sanctuary as plans for building unfolded. They were pleasantly surprised with some of the good ideas!

Another method we have used is to plan an all-day meeting at the church – perhaps on a Saturday – with the members, the building committee, the architect and builder. Invite everyone to come, give input to the plans and have a chance to speak. Who knows? Some good, workable ideas might well be incorporated while others wouldn't stand a chance. But at least you've listened. And besides, it's less painful to hear from an architect and/or builder why something wouldn't work – logically – than to be told by a pastor or building committee: "Thanks, but no thanks!" If, after this one and only all-inclusive church meeting, you feel compelled to involve certain other people, consider organizing ancillary

The members deserve to know something about what's going on with the plans and progress.

committees to assist with details.

Subcommittees – Who and What?

Same song, fifth verse.

There are no hard and fast rules in this department, either. The usefulness or practicality of subcommittees hinges on your need and your operation. One building committee chairman even waived the idea of a long-range planning committee: "Why have one? The people were coming in by droves. We knew our needs. It would have been like redesigning an intersection after 15 accidents had already occurred!"

You see? Records exist, however, which prove that subcommittee contributions can speed things along and create an opportunity for more individual involvement in your building project. But don't let them get unwieldy. You know what they say about too many cooks! Besides, it's more difficult to guide large numbers of people with effectiveness.

Here are some of the ways to go about the business of subcommittee appointments:

Design your operation to fit your function

- The church membership can elect the subcommittee chairman who, in turn, appoint the members. The chairmen may become part of the building committee, or just may be available at appropriate times to report to the main committee.
- The pastor or building committee members may appoint the subcommittee chairmen and members according to qualifications and building requirements.
- Each building committee member may assume the role of a subcommittee chairman, naming and organizing the group from which he needs input.

The point here is: design your operation to fit your function. Please refer to the "needs" list following this chapter. If you appoint subcommittees, though, here are some areas of representation you might want to consider:

1. Construction
2. Finance
3. Site selection
4. Publicity/promotion
5. Sanctuary
6. Education space
7. Recreation/fellowship space
8. Administration space
9. Kitchen
10. Interior decoration
11. Landscaping
12. Parking
13. Sound/lighting
14. Music/instruments
15. Furniture
16. Maintenance
17. Transition or church growth

Obviously, some of these subcommittees can be combined under a single heading, depending on the number of folks you have, or want to have, involved.

Another thing to remember. Not all subcommittees will be working throughout the entire building project. For instance, once a study and/or decision has been made on the amount of educational space needed, that job could be completed. Carrying out the dictates of the subcommittee should be taken over by the building committee for execution. Speaking of spoiled stew: you really don't need the day-to-day supervision of everyone on your subcommittees. And maybe your church won't be able to afford what everyone determines are absolute necessities in each department.

Choose people, if you will, who have a commitment and a vision, but who are able to adjust to the budget. The idea of having any committee, after all, is to help solve problems – not create them!

"There are always enough pitfalls during a building project," says one weathered committee chairman. "The committees should make it their business to miss them!"

> *Choose people ...who have a commitment and a vision, but who are able to adjust to the budget.*

World Harvest Church
Columbus, Ohio

Initial Research Questionnaire

Base Information:
- Age/Sex Distribution of Community Population
- Income Breakdown of Community
- Church's Annual Income, Assets, Indebtedness
- Survey of Religious Groups Serving the Community
- Projected Property Needs (offstreet parking requirements, access to Site)
- Building Code Requirements
- Existing Facilities Seating Capacity (Average Attendance)

Project Goals:
- Will this project be a new building or an addition to an existing structure?
- Should the design be concerned with budget taking precedent or the needs of the church?
- The proposed master plan will consist of . . .

	(phase 1,2,3, or 4)	Floor Levels
Sanctuary	_____	_____
Family Life Center	_____	_____
Gym/Multipurpose	_____	_____
Education	_____	_____
Administration	_____	_____
Retirement Facilities	_____	_____
Athletic Facilities	_____	_____
Other: _____	_____	_____

- What style of design is desired (contemporary, colonial, southwestern, other).
- What elements are requested (glass curtain wall, columns, low hip roof).
- What materials will be used (brick, stucco, stone, glass, other).

Sanctuary:
- Layout desired (fan, octagonal, rectangle, square, other).
- Proposed seating requirements. (future requirements that need to be dealt with)
- Areas requested . . .

(CHECK ONE)

	YES	NO	
Foyer	____	____	
Chapel	____	____	
Prayer Room	____	____	
Balcony	____	____	
Baptistry	____	____	
Choir	____	____	Capacity _____
Piano/Organ	____	____	Location _____
Other Musicians	____	____	How many _____
Choir Room	____	____	
Robing Room	____	____	
Sound Booth	____	____	Location _____
Storage	____	____	
Media Center	____	____	
Other: _____	____	____	

Family Life Center:
- Seating Capacity Required
- Areas Required

	YES	NO
To be used as gym also	___	___
Adjacent to Kitchen	___	___
Locker Room	___	___
Baptistry	___	___
Choir	___	___
Piano/Organ	___	___
Other Musicians	___	___
Choir Room	___	___
Robing Room	___	___
Sound Booth	___	___
Storage	___	___
Other _____	___	___

Size and type of cooking required _____

How many _____

Capacity _____

Location _____

How many _____

Location _____

Gym/Multi-purpose: (Not for Worship Service)
- Size of Gym Desired   (Court Size)

Elementary 36' x 52'	varies
Junior High 65' x 86'	42' x 74'
High School 79' x 96'	50' x 84'
College 100' x 104'	50' x 94'

- Areas requested . . .

	YES	NO
Adjacent to kitchen	___	___
Locker Room	___	___
Basketball Carpet	___	___
Storage	___	___
Other _____	___	___

For _____ people

If no: _____

Administration/Miscellaneous:
Areas Requested . . .

	YES	NO	Size/Comments
Pastor's Office	___	___	_____
Pastor's Study	___	___	_____
Conference Room	___	___	_____
Staff Offices	___	___	How many _____
Secretary	___	___	How many _____
Print Room	___	___	
Computer Room	___	___	_____
Bookstore	___	___	_____

Library . . . . _____ _____   _____
TV Production Room . . . . _____ _____   _____
Radio Studio . . . . _____ _____   _____
Fellowship Hall . . . . _____ _____   _____
Fireside Room . . . . _____ _____   _____
Chapel . . . . _____ _____   _____
Kitchen. . . . . _____ _____   _____
Bride's Room . . . . _____ _____   _____
Lunchroom . . . . _____ _____   _____
Storage . . . . _____ _____   _____
Other: _____ _____ _____   _____

Education:
- Areas Requested

	NO. OF STUDENTS	NO. OF CLASSROOMS	Comments:
Nursery	_____	_____	_____
Preschool	_____	_____	_____
Grade 1	_____	_____	_____
Grade 2	_____	_____	_____
Grade 3	_____	_____	_____
Grade 4	_____	_____	_____
Grade 5	_____	_____	_____
Grade 6	_____	_____	_____
Grade 7	_____	_____	_____
Grade 8	_____	_____	_____
Grade 9	_____	_____	_____
Grade 10	_____	_____	_____
Grade 11	_____	_____	_____
Grade 12	_____	_____	_____
College	_____	_____	_____
Adults	_____	_____	_____
Other_____	_____	_____	_____

- Check Local Code Requirements
- Decide if Large Classrooms or Small Classrooms are Desired

Retirement Facilities:
- Areas Requested:

	YES	NO	Comments:
H.U.D. Housing	_____	_____	_____
Duplex Units	_____	_____	_____
Apartments/Condo's	_____	_____	_____
Skilled Nursing Home	_____	_____	_____
Intense Care Facilities	_____	_____	_____
Club House/Pool	_____	_____	_____
Park/Picnic Area.	_____	_____	_____
Maintenance Building	_____	_____	_____
Other _____			_____

Athletic Facilities:
- Areas Requested:

	YES	NO	Comments:
Baseball Field	_____	_____	_____
Running Track	_____	_____	_____
Swimming Pools	_____	_____	_____
Gymnasium	_____	_____	_____
Tennis Courts	_____	_____	_____
Marinas/Boat Dock	_____	_____	_____
Camp Facilities	_____	_____	_____
Basketball Court	_____	_____	_____
Playground	_____	_____	_____
Other _____	_____	_____	_____

Immanuel Baptist Church
Wichita, Kansas

7

PICKING THE PROFESSIONALS TO BUILD YOUR CHURCH

Working with an architect, builder. . . and contracts

Rare are the cases when a congregation can design, draw, and build their "temple of God" without paying a big price.

Gone are the days when a pastor blithesomely shouts, "Praise God, I'm going to build a church," then strikes out to do it on his own. Rare are the cases today when a congregation can design, draw, and build their 'temple of God" without paying a big price. The task of church design and construction is hardly like building a sundeck with a hot tub. It can't be assimilated through the pages of a "How-to" manual in 30 days or less!

Perhaps you'll forgive the recurring theme of "Power-to-the-Professionals" that keeps playing in the background of this book, when you realize that qualified architects, engineers and contractors have been associated with church building through the ages. You'll surely agree that, since the first century "cell group" meetings in homes, the development of architectural styles – from Basilican (325-525 AD.), Byzantine (525-1453), Romanesque (775-1200), Gothic (1160-1150), Renaissance (1420-1600), up to the Colonial era (1700-) and the contemporary designs of today – bore the touch of an artist, not an archbishop!

There are the exceptions, of course, as in the early days of our country, when mission churches were going up expeditiously and abundantly, and even today in underpopulated areas of the U.S. – and the world. But now, with local, regional and national regulations, building codes and prevalent structural concerns, "self-building" is seldom worth the risk.

It's the day of the specialist! And if your church will blend the individual talents of the clergy, the church leaders, the architect and builder and all the other human components needed to synthesize the project, you can create a master-piece-of-a-place to gather in His name.

The Assets Of An Architect

When do you hire an architect?

Starting the architectural service tab too soon will waste your money and his time. Until the day your initial survey is completed and the committee's recommendations are approved by the church board and congregation, your effort is better spent shopping, not buying. There's no sense running up an exorbitant bill for thumb-twiddling while you do your research. But once your projections are determined, you know what you want, need and can afford – and your subcommittees are hard at work – it's time to purchase a professional's services.

Why now? It takes time to get acquainted. An architect worth his salt will want to become involved with the church. He'll familiarize himself with the total program – including the financing and budget – and come to understand what you've done, are doing and about to do. With the accumulated information from your survey committee, an architect who is experienced in the field of church building can be a great help in writing your program.

Space allotment, site selection, structural recommendations and cost containment are just some of the areas in which an able architect can advise you. He can counsel you on obtaining soil tests, surveys and city codes which could prevent needless waste and frustration. It's almost too late when an architect is hired only to find out the church has purchased property in a floodplain, on a city dump, a rock pile or spongy soil! What fun is it for you or the architect if the city says you can't build that 50-foot steeple you had your heart set on, because of building height limits? You'll only fritter away more money selling that land and looking for something else, or end up implementing expensive modifications.

You can make good and productive use of your architect if your selection is careful and timely. Then, once the choice is made, consider him an active team member whose multifaceted job description is that of an advisor, artist-designer, visionary, pragmatist and economist!

How do you hire an architect?

An architect worth his salt will want to become involved with the church.

Don't be afraid to ask questions. Perhaps someone you know and respect – someone who has gone through a building program – can make a positive recommendation. You can see for yourself what work the architect has done, in how timely a fashion he did it, and how he related to the church and the builder. Hiring an architect is like any other job appointment. Say your prayers and check his references! Selecting whom you want by this direct approach can expedite your project. You will know beyond a shadow of a doubt that his credentials are backed up by jobs well done.

Another approach is to do some comparative shopping. Select several architects, then invite them for one-on-one personal interviews. ("One" is as in one building committee or individual appointed to choose the architect, and "one" as in candidate.) Give each architect ample time to "sell" you on his qualifications and his desire to fill the job. References are a criterion, of course, and as in either method of selection, must be combed with fine-toothed precision.

No matter how you choose the architect for your job, get all the information you need to determine the necessary qualifications that will stand up to the test.

Professionally, you should ask questions about:

> *Say your prayers and check his references!*

- Qualifications. Is he or principals in his firm properly educated and licensed?
- Experience. How many years has he been in the business, and in how many church projects has he participated?
- Engineering disciplines. Does his firm have in-house mechanical, structural, electrical and civil engineers, or whom will he use in this capacity if he doesn't?
- Design support. Can he supply experts for interior design and decorating? What about landscape design?
- References. Can he give you names of projects he has completed or has on the drawing board? You wouldn't be out of order to ask for any pictures, brochures, slides or color renderings he could supply.
- Insurance and financial status of his company.
- Insurance and financial status of your project in relation to his proposed structural design.
- Budget. What does he project, how does he plan to handle it and can he stay within its confines? Getting an architect to stay on budget can be your Number One problem. We recommend a contract which spells out very clearly that if the building comes in over what you've allotted, it is the architect's responsibility – at his expense – to re-draw the plans within the agreed budget.
- Scheduling. Can his work load allow him to adhere to your time frame?

- Acoustics and lighting. What are his qualifications and expertise in these areas, or whom would he recommend as consultants?
- Master site planning. Has he done it, and can he? It's important to you.
- Personnel. With whom from his firm could you expect to be working?
- Stability. There is a fair amount of turn-over in architectural firms; will they stay together to see your project through?
- Costs. What are his architectural fees as they relate to construction costs? There is a wide range of architectural fees - anywhere from four to 10 percent of the construction costs.

Personally, you should be satisfied about:

- Interest. Will your project be just another job in the hopper, or will your architect have the time and tenacity to make this one close to his heart? An architect's personal attention to the program, whether it's small, medium or extra-large, will make everyone happier. If the interest isn't there, neither will be the time – nor energy.
- Experience. Traditionally, architects are generalists with the ability and talent to organize space and volume. Your project can go faster and smoother if you employ an architectural firm that has extensive experience/or, preferably, specializes in church design. The firm that can whip out 18-story bank buildings may not be so deft among the unique trappings of a church building project.
- Communication. You need an architect who can "speak your language." If the ritual of baptism means one thing to you and quite another thing to the architect, you could end up with plans showing a baptistry in front of your pulpit, or a "sprinkling" system behind the choir! "Form follows function," we always say, and an architect must be cognizant of your church's programs and goals. On the other hand, you must let him know what you want and need. Give him input; but make sure he's listening. Don't let anyone design a "monument" and try to fit you in! An effective church building must be planned around what goes on inside.
- Personal traits. Ego, procrastination or problematic behavior doth not a happy marriage make. Be careful of an architect with his head in the clouds. He could be mindless of the fact, for instance, that an aesthetically-designed dome is an absolute disaster for an auditorium's acoustics. Drawing and finalizing the preliminary plans can take some time, we know from experience. But if your architect begs for six to eight months to

There is a wide range of architectural fees – anywhere from four to 10 percent of the construction costs.

complete the working drawings, you've got a foot-dragger on your hands. Working with a pastor, board, building committee and all the subcommittees requires finesse and patience. Your architect needs the personal relations skills for this tall order. Pouting, temper tantrums and a surly attitude are reactions you don't need in the already-stressful building program! On the other side of the coin, it is in your best interests to employ an architect who can say "no" sometimes. After all, you are paying for his expertise.

Once your church has made the all-important decision on the selection of the architect and he is officially employed, what's next? Schematic – or preliminary – drawings can be prepared when programs have been written, analyzed and approved. This can take some time, considering the amount of input your subcommittees must make. When the collective stamp of approval has found its mark on the preliminaries, the architect can begin working drawings – or plans. These eventually will be given to contractors for bidding. It should be mentioned here that since the architect will serve as the representative (agent) of the church (owner) he is responsible for helping get bids from prospective contractors and awarding the contract. Any additional services from an architectural firm should be clearly stated in a contractual agreement. Better to be safe than sorry – it's all part of communications and the business of building.

Any additional services from an architectural firm should be clearly stated in a contractual agreement.

Bonding With a Builder

Selecting a contractor is another area in your decision-making process that offers some options. Choose wisely, like Solomon, and while you may not get Huramabi himself, a master craftsman is not out of the question! Actually, you can go one of four ways:

Conventional: architect and builder

It's simple. The architect is employed by the church to prepare schematic and working drawings. The latter is given to contractors for bidding purposes, and the contract is awarded – usually to the lowest bidder. In this *modus operandi*, the architect (depending on his contract with the church) has the responsibility of overseeing the construction project by periodic reviews and supervision of change orders, which by the way, there always are. (Either because of changed minds or changed prices of materials, change orders are a fact of life in the building business. A church would be wise to allow a small but certain portion of the budget for these unforeseen and inevitable expenses.) Then, when the project is completed, the architect makes a final inspection of the building project. If or when any corrections need to be made – and they are, indeed, completed

– the architect is authorized to approve final payment to the contractor.

The architect and builder have no contractual agreement between them in this system; the contract is between the builder and the church, or owner. Although the architect visits the site and makes several inspections, he can only advise the owners if he finds something that is not up to snuff. The perfect situation, of course, is a happy relationship between the architect and builder. There is no reason why this can't be a reality if everyone is performing at his peak and paying attention to business. You should be aware, however, of the pluses and minuses to this method.

First, on the *plus* side, you do have competitive bids. This gives you an opportunity to realistically compare the costs of building. Secondly, there is the third-party influence. With the church, the architect and the builder all involved, each being accountable for schedules, costs and quality, you have a comfortable cross-check in action.

On the *minus* side, the first thing you need to know is that your project can cost more money. Architectural fees can be higher. Secondly, the architect can't guarantee the cost of construction. On numerous occasions we have seen churches give an architectural firm their program and their budget; the plans come in and are put out for bid. What happens? A couple of things: the plans weren't "formed for the function," and the bids submitted are thousands of dollars over the allotted budget. This situation doesn't have to happen, but the truth is, sometimes it does! Fouled-up communications, misunderstanding or mistakes in evaluating personality link-ups could result in problems. Another fact to be faced is that some architects simply don't have a handle on real construction costs.

Finally, a lack of experience in church design and construction doesn't mean that an architect is not a skillful craftsman. It does mean – in most cases – that unless you're careful, your project will be less easily understood; and the resulting design, less functional.

The architect can't guarantee the cost of construction.

Design/Build

The same person, or firm, wears two hats on this occasion! The design/build method of church building has become very popular among congregations in the past decade, but, like the conventional way, has its pros and cons.

■ You can look at less dollars in a design/build project; it's been proven over and over in the past 35 years. One firm becomes one profit center, not two. Plans will be included in the submitted price which means, in essence, you can save money on architectural fees.

■ There is consistent management control. With the same firm working with a church through planning and building, fewer communication problems exist.

■ The design/build firm will bring with it a reputable background of experience. There are only a few large companies in the U.S. that specialize in church building, but any one of them would be more than willing – if not eager – to be of service!

■ Having just one firm to deal with, change orders are more easily negotiated – in action and in price.

■ The buck stops here! There are no lengthy or costly arguments between an architect and builder about whose fault it is if something goes wrong. If a mistake is made, design/build firms have no place to hide. They must face the error of their ways – and correct it!

■ The only criticism with the design/build method is the lack of the third-party "inspector." This needn't be a major draw-back, however, since most churches have someone within the congregation who is qualified to make inspections. Or, the church could employ a third party for that purpose. Also, a certain amount of trust is called for among the "team." If your church is willing to place all its confidence in an architect, why not make that commitment to the same person as the builder?

You can look at less dollars in a design/build project.

Construction management

If your church decides to take on the role as general contractor, but would like some help in the process, construction management is an option. A construction firm serves as a "manager" – for a fee – to guide you through the building program, and supplies a superintendent to be on site from beginning to end. Although there is no guaranteed price for the cost of construction, a church can usually save money in the change orders, taxes, discounts on materials, and even donated labor and supplies. All things being equal, construction management is the least expensive way to build your church.

Construction management with a guaranteed price

This is like having your cake and eating it, too! The same principles apply here as in the straight construction management method. The difference is, the contractor gives the owner a maximum, or fixed, price to get the job done. Again, the church assumes the responsibilities of a general contractor, but as a bonus, receives all the built-in savings from donations, discounts and tax exemptions. Each construction company may approach this differently, but if the total cost of the building ends up to be less than the fixed fee agreed upon, some will split the profits with the church on a 50-50 basis. It's a win-win situation, and one that has our recommendation.

Shake On It - Then Sign Those Contracts

You've picked all your professional service firms. Congratulations and handshakes all around.

Goodwill is a great beginning, no question about it. But remember what our old friend Solomon says about finishing being even better than starting. If everyone (including the church) knows his responsibilities, sees them in writing and solidifies them with a signature, you're more likely to end up on a happy note – on time and within budget.

Alas, we all have feet of clay! And in this busy life, it's hard to remember what we said we'd do and when we'd do it. So let's get it in writing and give everyone the benefit of the doubt. Before you start work on any phase of your project that requires professional attention with an exchange of work, property or money, prepare and sign a written contract. It's a smart way to protect you, the church, and those from whom you are buying services, such as:

Let's get it in writing and give everyone the benefit of the doubt.

- Lawyers
- Real estate brokers
- Financial consultants
- Financial institutions
- Property owners
- City or county corporations
- Utility companies
- Architects
- Engineers
- Design firms
- General contractors
- Sub-contractors

You'll no doubt be dealing with most of these professionals during your building project. Any and all of them would welcome a contractual agreement.

Although the Standard American Institute of Architects (AIA) forms often are used in a owner-architect contract, it may be necessary to develop an additional letter-of-agreement depending on the arrangement decided upon by the principals. The Standard Form of Agreement Between Owner and Architect, officially labled AIA Document B131, is a fair guideline for the description of an architect's basic services and costs. According to the B131, "The architect's basic services consist of five phases and include normal structural, mechanical and electrical engineering services."

Here they are, albeit condensed for a modicum of length and lethargy, along with the accumulative fees:

15 percent

Schematic Design includes initial meetings with the owner to review the written program, which spells out space and site requirements/restrictions, and the prepared budget. The architect will then prepare drawings and other documents showing the site plan, the scale and relationship of the project components for owner approval. Accompanying this phase of work should be an estimated cost of construction.

35 percent

Design Development comes after the schematic design and studies have been approved. This phase includes the preparation and presentation of drawings and other documents to fix and describe size and character of the entire project as to such essential components as structural, mechanical and electrical systems, suggested materials and other related details. Again, the probable costs should be counted for the owner's enlightenment.

75 percent

Construction Documents is the next step. From the approved design development, the architect prepares working drawings and specifications detailing any requirements for construction of the entire project. The architect must provide all necessary bidding information and be ready to assist in preparing bidding forms and contracts between the owner and contractor. If the probable costs have been altered for any reason, the owner must be apprised.

80 percent

Bidding or Negotiation follows the owner's approval of the construction documents and the latest cost analysis. In this phase, the architect helps the owner obtain bids or proposals and takes part in awarding and preparing construction contracts.

The architect must provide all necessary bidding forms and contracts between the owner and contractor.

100 percent

The Construction Phase starts with the award of the construction contract and ends when the final certificate of payment is presented to the owner. The architect has the responsibility of ensuring the fulfillment of the construction contract as agreed upon between him and the owner. Further involvement with construction includes periodic site visits to follow the progress and the quality of work as it relates to the construction contract. Based on observations at the site, the architect can determine the amount owed to the contractor and issue certificates of payment. In addition to preparing change orders, the architect reviews and approves drawings, samples, and any other submissions from the contractor in order to maintain compliance with the design concept and construction contract.

Whatever form of contract is used with any company, it is essential that it is written in language everyone can understand. Architect-ese, legal-ese or any other-ese is not necessary and could confuse a Rhodes scholar. This is the Communication Age, remember? And don't mince words. Make sure everything is covered from A to Z, with a heavy emphasis on "C" for Cost and "I" for Insurance.

The message here is to proceed in a wise and orderly fashion. The enterprise upon which you are about to embark calls for careful consideration as you choose counsel from the experts. The architect and builder – with a perfect blending of the church's vision – can bring abundant life to the plans for your ministry!

> *Make sure everything is covered from A to Z, with a heavy emphasis on "C" for Cost and "I" for Insurance.*

Redemption
World Outreach Center
Greenville, South Carolina

8

MASTER SITE PLANNING FOR THE FUTURE

Mapping out for tomorrow your dreams of today

B y now, you should be jogging right along in your building program plans. Perhaps you're even humming a little Moses praise: "He did great and awesome miracles...and has brought us to this place and given us this land..." (Deuteronlmy. 26:8,9, TLB). So you've got the land – your site. What are you going to do with it? Don't trip up now by stumbling over the most important step in your path – the master site plan.

And just what is a master plan? Simply speaking, it is putting the pencil to your long range goals with a graphically formulated program of action on your land. You could refer to it as a master site development plan, or master plot plan, since it involves full and practical use of your property – for now, and for the years to come. "'Plot' implies," says one reference book, "laying out in...distinguished sections with attention to their relations and proportions." Who can argue with a genuine Merriam-Webster? Clearly, folks, your assignment has been defined!

Let's review. From your survey, or long-range planning research, you've determined your growth patterns and projections. You know the scope of your ministry, you've written your program and know what facilities you want to offer the community.

The master plan is the next step. It is the visual and orderly arrangement of building locations, parking lot, recreational areas and landscaping. Whether you take the big leap and go for

> *The master plan...is the visual and orderly arrangement of building locations, parking lot, recreational areas and landscaping.*

everything at once or walk through your construction in phases, a master site development plan is the most important regimen for Body-building!

Pay Now, Not Later

In Chapter 5, "Selecting the Site For Your Planting," we talked about building codes, zoning ordinances, height limitations, parking requirements, setbacks, greenbelts, surveys and soil tests. If you did all your groundwork, and were aware of the peaks or pitfalls common in your area before you bought the property, you're halfway there. If, for some unearthly reason, you were star-gazing and missed those critical details, for heaven's sake do it now! Pay what it takes for a professional's help on these agenda items; it's money well spent. (Remember the drainage debacle...the uphill battle...the steeple stymie?) With a clear head and cool hand, you can feel comfortable putting on paper your proposed program for current use of the property and projected growth patterns, knowing you've covered all the bases.

What Next?

While you're thanking Him for bringing you to this land "flowing with milk and honey," keep your feet on the ground when it comes to stewardship and building. Recognize and get a firm grasp of your needs and desires. Remember that they are two different things.

If you and your finance committee know you can't afford to build everything you want at one fell swoop, our advice is to start out with a multi-purpose building for use as an interim auditorium. Later, when money is available and the church is growing at a nice clip, you can add facilities to meet the demands – a family life center, more educational space, an auditorium – you name it, you can add it, if you can pay for it! Warning: in "phase" building, an oft-committed mistake is starting with an auditorium, or sanctuary. Too many times, churches limit their growth with this order of business. Or sometimes growth is miscalculated, and you end up needing more sanctuary seating after a few years. But, if your plan is to start with the sanctuary, don't build yourself into a box! Plan an expandable facility (there are several ways this can be done) to accommodate all those folks who will eventually be a part of your ministry.

Know Your Place

Let's assume that your first-phase, or first-unit, construction calls for a multi-purpose building. Now, put it where it belongs in the broad scheme of things! This is where the master plan comes in handy. Draw up your development program, showing exactly where

In "phase" building, an oft-committed mistake is starting with an auditorium or sanctuary.

Generalized Code Map

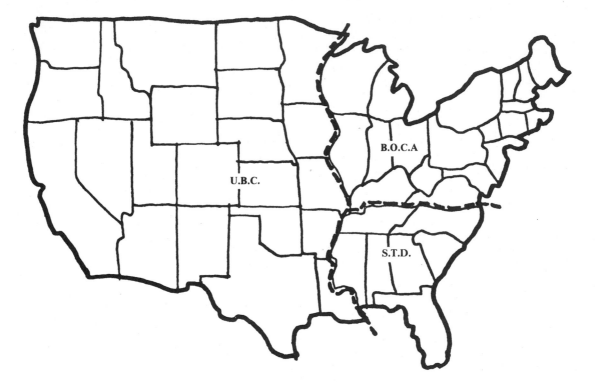

U.B.C. — Uniform Building Code

B.O.C.A. — Building Officials Conference of America
   Both of these codes require that pews shall not exceed 21'-0".

S.T.D. — Standard Building Code
   This code states that 30'-0" is the maximum pew length.

Note: This is a generalized code map. Some states and cities vary in their code usage. (St. Louis is BOCA, Illinois is UBC.) One should always check local requirements.

FIG. 8-1

each projected building will be located, and keep your first unit in its assigned position. Show at least a 10-year growth plan, including a time frame for every phase of construction. Ideally, you should start from the back of your property and work forward, with the sanctuary, magnificently viable and visible, as the grand denouement – the crowning touch! There's not only a time – there is a place for everything in God's work.

In Need?

Indeed!

Developing a master site development plan could be Greek to you unless, of course, your seminary courses included architectural training in that language! This is the time to employ the professionals. Architects and engineers are your best bet when it comes to transferring your program from a dream to the drawing board. Their expertise and that of city and county representatives, landscape architects – and yes, even vendors of products you'll need to purchase – is valuable input in these important areas of consideration:

- zoning, codes and ordinances
- setbacks, greenbelts and easement requirements
- parking requirements
- lighting, interior and exterior
- signage, or graphics
- provisions for the physically impaired
- recreational areas, interior and exterior
- energy sources and alternatives
- sound and lighting systems
- musical instrumentation and storage
- design and decoration
- interior space requirements for ministry functions
- accessibility, circulation and entrance

Show at least a 10-year growth plan, including a time frame for every phase of construction.

The list could go from here to eternity, depending on the scope of your program; but surely you catch the vision! (Detailed information on most of these subjects can be found in previous or forthcoming chapters.) The biggest job now is tying all the ends around a perfectly functional package.

We can't stress enough: professionals who have experience in church planning can give you great peace of mind in the areas of space requirements, design and money-saving techniques (you know your budget). The aesthetic appeal of your new facilities can make a powerful statement to the community. However, if all the well-designed components of your project aren't engineered for comfort and convenience, it just won't fly.

Design to get in easy.
Design to sit easy.
Design to see and listen easy.
Design to get out easy.
Easy does it. Make your plant work for you!

The Bane of Basements

Before we show you an example of a general written program and resulting master site development plan, we ask your indulgence for an editorial comment. Basement talk is included here because, whether you plan to remodel and expand at your present site or take off on a major new building project, you might be considering a facility with – yes – one of "those!"

A word to the wise: it's much better to go up than down! Don't build a basement unless you have to. You do have to, you say? Well, in our opinion, there should be only two reasons for that decision: land limitations and energy conservation. Why? We'll guarantee you, basements are not cheaper to build and there are several other negative considerations involved.

Don't build a basement unless you have to.

If you're building a house, you can put a basement under it and say: "Wow! I got a lot of space for just a little bit of money!" You've heard that, haven't you? Maybe even said it yourself? Well, consider this: in a home, you build a standard eight-foot basement wall and end up with a seven-foot, six-inch ceiling. Sorry, but you can't do that in a church. The average basement wall in a church building is 13 feet high – five feet higher than the wall of a house basement because of the depth of floor joists and duct work. When you go above an eight-foot form in commercial construction, the cost is automatically tripled. Then, of course, there is the cost of excavation, hauling off the dirt, installation of drain tile around the inside and outside, tar waterproofing and sump pumps you wouldn't have if the building was constructed on grade. And it should come as no surprise that carpenters, electricians, plumbers and heating and air-conditioning contractors charge just as much money to work downstairs as they do above ground level – or that the cost of concrete is not less in a basement. Hold on, there's more!

The minimum cost to put in a suspended floor structure above a basement to carry the floor upstairs is $12.50-plus, per square foot. This cost must be figured against the price of the basement since it wouldn't be required if you built on top of the ground. And if you have dreams of a sloping floor in the sanctuary, add some dollar signs for additional bar joists and beams. (With no basement, the

Wall Section

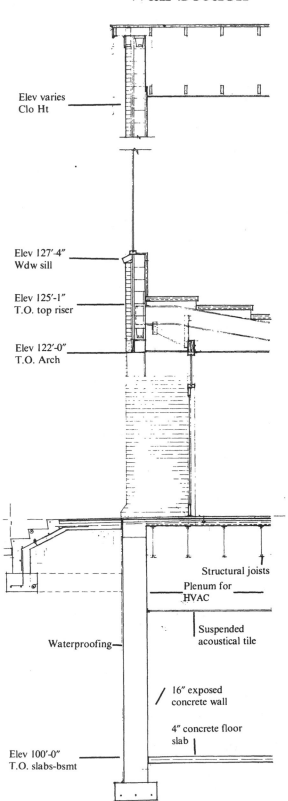

Elev varies
Clo Ht

Elev 127'-4"
Wdw sill

Elev 125'-1"
T.O. top riser

Elev 122'-0"
T.O. Arch

Structural joists

Plenum for
HVAC

Suspended
acoustical tile

Waterproofing

16" exposed
concrete wall

4" concrete floor
slab

Elev 100'-0"
T.O. slabs-bsmt

FIG. 8-2

ground is prepared for the slope before the concrete foundation is poured.) If plans call for a basement to be used as educational space, sharpen your pencil before you add in the price for partitions (you have live loads and dead loads – you'll need columnar support, which automatically disallows a large, unobstructed area), a sprinkler system and fire exits which are required by the Uniform, BOCA and Southern Building Codes. Basements are damp; basements have no natural lighting or ventilation; and basements often leak, no matter how well waterproofed they are. Gloom and doom, in our opinion.

One last point in our ban-the-basement campaign speech. Consider your new building as an advertisement to the community. The Lord Himself knows how churches compete against one another for bodies to fill the pews. So why hide half of your building 13 feet under ground? Wouldn't you rather have your brand new facility entirely visible for the whole town to see?

Think about it! What you build and where you build it will speak volumes to not only your church membership, but to your neighbors in the community and those you're trying to reach.

Why hide half of your building 13 feet under ground?

Getting from A to B to XYZ

Now, let's get back to the matter at hand: master site planning from general program requirements – to ensure a job well done.

It's been no secret throughout our career-experience – and this book – that there's more than one way to see the light. Program specifications and master site plan developments can be as unique as Saul and Paul. Different goals, same guts. Getting to the right place at the right time is what matters, in any case.

For your enlightenment, we are providing an example of a written program and the resulting master site development plan for Bethesda Missionary Temple in Sterling Heights, Michigan.

"BETHESDA"
New Building Project
Sterling Heights, Michigan

General Program Specifications

The information contained in this Appendix has been gathered to serve as a resource tool for use in the preliminary stages of program development. While not considered exhaustive on any one topic, this Appendix is the result of observation, evaluation and experience over many years of church planning.

Site

1. A 92-acre site has been purchased in Sterling Heights, Michigan. The site is rectangular in shape, approximately one-half mile by one-quarter mile in size. Its location is at the intersection of Metropolitan Parkway and Schoenher Road.

2. The site will provide land area for the physical plant, off-street automobile parking, landscaping, outdoor recreation and fellowship activities and any other church plans.

3. Approximately 75 percent of the site is usable land area.

4. An awareness of community planning, zoning restrictions and location of all easements to the site are essential.

5. It should be noted that the necessary footage will be donated to the county of Macomb to enable them to extend the proposed boulevard to the south point of the site along Schoenher Road.

6. Off-street parking will be provided on the site for approximately 1,000 automobiles. Using the ratio of three and one-half persons to one parking space, approximately six acres of land will be needed for this project. Pedestrian walkways must be included in master parking plan. Special care must be used in providing the best ingress and egress from parking area. This is especially important because all traffic must enter and exit from the same road (Schoenher). Adequate lighting is essential for safety and visibility. Parking area must be of hard surface material marked for efficient use of space.

7. Landscaping plan must be developed for entire site.

8. Outdoor recreation. It is desirable to provide space on the site for fellowship and recreational activities. Separate areas and play equipment for various age groups should be provided. Restrooms, first aid supplies and storage for equipment should be readily accessible from the recreational area. Outdoor activities will include baseball (hard and soft), soccer, track, basketball and tennis.

Using the ratio of three and one-half persons to one parking space, approximately six acres of land will be needed for this project.

Sanctuary

The worship of God is the heart of the church. The church must be used to lead individuals into a meaningful participation in worship. The atmosphere of dignity and reverence must be a dominating factor. It must provide for the participation of all. The worship service must stimulate the evaluation of ideals in Christian service on personal living. All care and planning must produce a marriage of sight and sound.

Size. The sanctuary must provide comfortable seating and worship space for 3,500. This will necessitate allowing approximately 35,000 square feet of space. The sanctuary will consist of three parts; main floor, balcony and chancel (platform).

A. Main floor
    1. Seating will accommodate approximately 2,500.
    2. Type of seating to be theatre seats with pew back on 36-inch centers.
    3. Sanctuary floor to be sloping from rear to front.
    4. Seating arrangement of sanctuary to be fan-shape.
    5. Lighting to be indirect plus down lighting with additional chandeliers for aesthetics.
    6. Consideration should be given to provide for all three areas to be under common ceiling.
    7. No natural light or ventilation should be considered for sanctuary.

B. Balcony
    1. Will accommodate approximately 1,000.
    2. Provision will be made to allow access to the main altar area from the balcony.
    3. Balcony seating will follow style of main floor.

Provision will be made to allow access to the main altar area from the balcony.

C. Chancel
    1. Will accommodate space for choir (150).
    2. Orchestra, (50).
    3. Organ, piano.
    4. Ministerial staff.
    5. Drama, concert area.
    6. Theatre-type lighting to be provided for concert and drama presentations.
    7. Lighting to be installed in chancel's ceiling and sanctuary ceiling (concealed if possible).

Foyer

1. The foyer is to be a large, pleasant area with natural lighting to accommodate approximately 200 people.
2. Approximately 7,500 square feet of space should be provided.
3. Ceiling height should be a minimum of two stories.
4. Space should be provided for conversational areas.
5. Foyer should be conveniently located to the main parking areas with convenient access to other building and activity areas.

Chapel

1. Ideally, the chapel will be in a location completely separated from the main sanctuary to provide simultaneous use.
2. The chapel is to accommodate approximately 500 with a square

footage space of approximately 6,000 square feet.

3. Seating is to be provided by padded pews on 36-inch centers.

4. A flat floor will probably be sufficient for this size room.

5. Ceiling height is to be a minimum of two stories (flat ceiling not to be considered).

6. Lighting will be indirect with additional chandelier lighting.

7. Natural light could be used in chapel area if appropriate (by design).

8. No overflow area to be provided.

9. The platform area of the chapel should be approximately 1,000 square feet.

10. Space for organ and piano should be provided either on platform or altar area.

Project Image

The central theme or image of the "proposed" project must be carried out in all phases and expressions of the physical plant and campus. It is our desire to convey to the area the image of a large, vital, progressive church community. Our facility will minister to the family and entire community.

To those driving along Metropolitan Parkway, the project should speak of size and balance, causing a desire to "come and investigate."

To those driving along Schoenher, it should provide a wide, sweeping view of the facility - being inviting and easily accessible. Approaching the facility by automobile should generate interest to the passengers. A tree-lined approach leading to the physical plant should be an inviting introduction to the "campus."

Approaching the facility on foot should bring the feeling of entering a planned, well cared for and quiet community.

The buildings and grounds should give an impression of importance in this order:

1. Sanctuary
2. Foyer
3. Office
4. Chapel
5. Landscaping
6. Parking Area
7. School
8. Social Facilities
9. Drive Areas
10. Playgrounds

Architectural features should include use of skylights, stained glass and other amenities.

The project should speak of size and balance, causing a desire to "come and investigate."

The grounds should be enhanced by the use of planting areas, tree groups, possible small lake to provide an "overlook" from the fellowship hall or other buildings.

Nurseries

The nursery departments play an important part in the ministry of the church – not only ministering to the children, but to the parents, other family members and congregation.

Much thought should be given to the development of these departments to create areas in which the children will feel at ease, be safe and enjoy a teachable atmosphere. Attention must be given to the teachers and supervisors of the nursery ministry, remembering that they are a volunteer group upon which the church is greatly indebted, and with the awareness of their personal needs and comfort. They are the "life-line" between the church and the "young marrieds."

At the present time, the nursery departments of Bethesda are divided into seven divisions, each serving a different age group:

The nursery departments play an important part in the ministry of the church.

1. *Tweety's Cage* *[0-6 months]* *[20 children]*
   Needs: play room
        sleeping room
        lavatory, closet, storage, coat racks
2. *Bugs Bunny* *[6-10 months]* *[20 children]*
   Needs: play room
        sleeping room
        lavatory, closet, storage, coat racks
3. *Roadrunner* *[10-13 months]* *[20 children]*
   Needs: play room
        sleeping room
        lavatory, closet, storage, coat racks
4. *Raggedy Ann* *[13-20 months]* *[30 children]*
   Needs: play room sleeping room
        lavatory, closet, storage, coat racks
5. *Sesame Street* *[20-30 months]* *[50 children]*
   Needs: play room
        sleeping room
        story, table room
        toilets (4), lavatories (2)
        closet, storage, coat racks
6. *Muppetville* *[30-42 months]* *[60 children]*
   Needs: play room
        story, art and music rooms
        closet, storage, coat racks
        lavatory, with toilet area close by

7. *Peanut Gallery* *[3 ½ – 4 years]* *[60 children]*
   Needs:　　　play room (shared with Muppetville)
   　　　　　　story room
   　　　　　　closet, storage, coat racks
   　　　　　　lavatory, with toilet area close by

General Nursery Needs:
- A common reception room in close relationship to each age group;
- A laundry room with washer and dryer;
- A storage room for laundry and supplies for all nurseries.
- The above nursery departments should provide proper care and space for a total of 260 children.

Bible Class Area
The importance of the study of God's Word should be shown by the thought and design of this most important part of the church. The location of the Bible classes should be in the administration/religious education building with additional classroom space in the parameter of the sanctuary (if provided in design).

1. *Beginner Department* *[4 ½ - 5 years]* *[Approx. 200]*
   The first floor would be best suited for this age group. Fifteen rooms of approximately 225 square feet should be adequate. A large assembly room for 200 should be located between Beginner and Primary Departments for sharing. An office for the department should be provided – approximately 400 square feet with space for a private office and teacher office. Storage must be available for supplies.
2. *Primary Department* *[5 ½ - 8 years]*
   A duplication of the Beginner Department should be sufficient.
3. *Elementary Department* *[8 - 9 years]* *[Approx. 250]*
   May be located on any level near a main corridor. Provision should be made for 250 students. Fifteen rooms of approximately 300 square feet department office space, storage and assembly area should be included in the planning.
4. *Junior Department* *[10 -11 years]* *[Approx. 200]*
   Should be adjacent to the Elementary Department so the assembly area can be shared. Fifteen rooms of approximately 300 square feet for 200 students should be provided. Space for office and storage should be included, sharing the storage with the Elementary Department.
5. *Youth Catechism* *[12 years]* *[Approx. 200]*
   The Catechism Department is a unique part of the training of young people in the fundamental doctrines of the church. The

The importance of the study of God's Word should be shown by the thought and design of this most important part of the church.

location can be anywhere, since these classes meet three times weekly. An assembly area should be provided to handle up to 200 students, with 15 rooms of approximately 300 square feet. Office space should include two private offices, one larger than the other. One large main office will have four desks, files and storage space.

6. *Intermediate Department   [15 years]   [Approx. 125]*
Can be located anywhere, with assembly area for 125 students, four classrooms with capacity to seat 35, and space for two offices.

7. *High School Department   [Grades 9 - 12]   [Approx. 250]*
This department should be in a separate area or confined to one floor, with an assembly area to accommodate at least 250 students, and having a stage area of approximately 500 square feet. A lounge or entrance area should be designed at the rear of the assembly room for "fellowship" with four departmental offices close to this area. Classrooms for grades 9 and 10 should be separated from grades 11 and 12. Classrooms will provide space for approximately 30 students. Additional room is required in girls' restrooms for this age.

8. *Special Education   [various ages]   [Approx. 20]*
Should be on the first floor with easy access to the outside, and with provision for 20 students of various ages. Two large rooms, with space for two offices, would be sufficient for the Special Education Department.

9. *Leadership Training Department   [Approx. 100]*
Can be located anywhere. This department requires an assembly-fellowship room for 100 students. Two rooms - one for 50 students and one for 60 students is needed, along with office space for two private offices and one general staff office.

10. *Adult Cathechism   [Approx. 200]*
Can be located near chapel area. An assembly room for 200 should be provided unless the chapel area can be used in proper relationship to overall function of the class. This department will need 10 counseling rooms that will hold approximately 20 students in each room; a square shape is desirable. Office space should include one room for the teacher and one for staff.

11. *Young Adult Catechism   [Approx. 50]*
This requires an assembly room for 50 students, four counseling rooms with capacity to hold 15 students per room.

12. *Music practice room*
This room should be located conveniently to chancel area of the sanctuary – ideally on same floor so instruments do not have to be brought up and down – with easy entrance from parking areas. The music room should accommodate 150 singers and

Special Education ...should be on the first floor with easy access to the outside.

chairs, risers, 30 instruments and a piano. Robe-changing and storage areas should be adjacent. Other requirements: music room office space, music storage space large enough for instruments and music, restrooms and large powder/dressing room for ladies.

13. Bookstore

Location of the bookstore would best suit its operation and purpose by being in the administration area of the church, accessible to those using the sanctuary as well as to people from the outside. Retail area of the bookstore would need approximately 1,000 square feet, which would include work area and storage connected for the office workers. A private office and private restroom would be necessary for the bookstore manager.

14. Communion Preparation Room

This should be provided in the administration building, and will need approximately 125 square feet with cupboard space for storage of communion supplies. This area possibly could be coordinated with the employee lounge, using the same lavatory and refrigeration facilities.

15. Adult Bible Classes

Provision should be made for 1,700 students, with room sizes to accommodate the following:

          1 room for 20 people
          8 rooms, each for 40 people
          3 rooms, each for 50 people
          6 rooms, each for 60 people
          2 rooms, each for 75 people
          2 rooms, each for 100 people
          2 rooms, each for 150 people
          1 room for 200 people

Location of the bookstore would best suit its operation and purpose by being in the administration area of the church.

Mechanical/Electrical

1. All utilities supplied to the project must be underground, and would include water, sewer, electrical, telephone and gas. All light poles on driveway will also be underground-fed. (A study should be made of the electrical service to see if it would be advisable to purchase primary or secondary current from Detroit Edison.)

2. Type of heat – hot water. Forced air handlers to be used to balance the air temperature as needed. All units shall be controlled by a computer. There shall be a boiler room provided which shall be located in the area where it will be most adequate to supply all areas.

3. The fuel to be used at boilers will be natural gas type.

4. Cooling – air handling units can be air-cooled or water-cooled

with a water tower depending on the location where the units can be installed.

5. Vehicle storage will include outside storage for four school buses and inside facilities for four vans, two tractors and a dump truck.

6. There will be a mechanical shop provided, 80-feet-by-80-feet or 6,400 square feet with a 12-by-12-feet electric operated door. The work shop will Include work benches, a drain in the center with floor pitched to the drain, and gas unit heaters.

> There will be a woodworking shop 1,000 square feet with work benches and a gas heater.

> There will be an electrical shop 600 square feet with work benches and a gas unit heater. There will be a paint storage room approximately 250 square feet with a gas unit heater.

> There will be a small office approximately 10-by-12-feet or 120 square feet.

> There will be a garden tool storage area of approximately 200 square feet.

7. Closet areas. There will be janitor closet storage in all areas as needed.

Your brainchild will have its own personality and patterns.

That's it: a written program for a building project! We give special kudos to Rev. James Beall and Rev. Harry Beall for giving us permission to incorporate this information, along with the following master site development plan for Bethesda Missionary Temple. You realize, of course, the program and master plan in this chapter is the embryo and development from just one church, one denomination and one set of circumstances. Your brainchild will have its own personality and patterns.

We trust, however, that by setting the example, we have provided helpful guidance as you plan for healthy growth in His domain!

Master Site Plan, Bethesda, Michigan

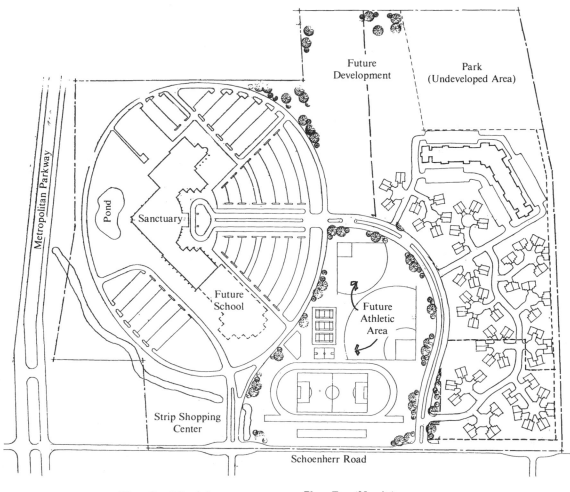

Phase One (17 units)

2 "A" Duplexes
  2 bedroom/ 1 bathroom

5 "B" Duplexes
  2 bedroom/ 1 bathroom

10 "C" Duplexes
  2 bedroom/ 1 bathroom

Phase Two (35 units)

3 "A" Duplexes
  2 bedroom/ 1 bathroom

9 "B" Duplexes
  2 bedroom/ 1 bathroom

23 "C" Duplexes
  2 bedroom/ 1 bathroom

Main Building (3 floors)
  96 units/ 1 bedroom/ 1 bathroom
  24 units/ 2 bedroom/ 1 bathroom
  120 units total

FIG 8-3

9

CREATING AND CONTROLLING A PROMOTIONAL PLAN

How to be your own best advertising agency

"You are the world's light – a city on a hill, glowing in the night for all to see..."

– Matthew 5:14, TLB

Publicity challenges our passivity every day of the week, every week of the year. We're constantly cajoled into consumerism, and - more often than not - buy into the ballyhoo.

With a thousand or so advertising messages invading our senses, some of us are destined to drive on Michelin, charge with Duracell, wash with Dove, gargle with Scope and subscribe to the Sweepstakes – at least once. And that's not counting 99 percent of the hype we tune out!

But do we really want to trade in our Corvette? Or have we simply been convinced that the savings of a Kia will make our lives richer? The strategy, you see, is to create an awareness of, then proffer ways to fill a basic need.

We all know that effective advertising pays, whether it's in the selling of a President, a product or an opinion. Lots of people in the business are earning big money by their powers of persuasion. Careers depend on campaigns to spread the news of a package that may or may not hold water.

Ah, wouldn't the ad agencies love to have His business – with Solomon and Matthew as the account executives! "Good news...is like cold water to the thirsty" (Proverbs 25:25, TLB). "The intelligent man is always open to new ideas. In fact, he looks for them" (Proverbs 18:15, TLB).

"You are the world's light – a city on a hill, glowing in the night for all to see...Let it shine for all; let your good deeds glow for all *to see, so that they will praise your heavenly Father (Matthew 5:14-16, TLB).*

It's a ready-made campaign:

- A Good News product.
- Smart buyers, with a need.
- Customer satisfaction eternally guaranteed.

Before you recoil at the crassness of church advertising, ponder this:

1. We're commanded to make His program palatable. "You are the world's seasoning...If you lose your flavor, what will happen to the world" (Matthew 5:13, TLB).

2. It's good business to promote your "city on the hill" which is growing and ready to expand. Go-and-tell is what evangelism is all about.

3. Your own parishioners deserve to be kept well-informed about the progress of the church. After all, it's their collective energies, plugged into high voltage leadership, that will produce the glow.

All things considered, there is nothing inappropriate about advertising/promoting His work. And a building program has a perfect "hook" for attracting attention. What's more, you can do it yourself without having to spend a fortune.

But the game of advertising is played in a competitive arena, so your church's campaign should go for the gold. It also must be consistent and on-going – before, during and after the church is completed.

Now, gather the prolific resources from your midst. With a few practical guidelines patterned from the greatest creation of all – and applying your own "earth-time" divisions – you can write a viable, ongoing marketing plan.

From the Beginning ... Create an Awareness

When a church acknowledges the fact that a union of dynamic forces has produced the need for a larger facility, a new promotion begins.

But even selling the brainchild in-house can be a multi-level endeavor.

Starting at the embryonic stage, "someone" must convince "someone else" that a building program is necessary. Perhaps a layman makes the first suggestion to the pastor. Or, it may be the pastor who initiates the action. Whoever provides the impetus to

Go-and-tell is what evangelism is all about.

link the chain of events, members of the church board must be sold on the idea. They, then, must get the attention and approval of the congregation.

Speak out

A lot can be accomplished during this time by open communication with leaders of various church programs. They know the space crunches caused by growing attendance. In fact, inadequacies that could restrict further expansion are probably a high priority concern in getting their jobs done. Acknowledging these needs is a sure-fire way to stir up conversation. And you needn't have been an Explorer Scout to know how important each leader is in helping blaze a trail! Gather their suggestions. Enlist their help. Ignite their enthusiasm. You'll need these people in your camp if you want your project to catch on. Talk to them.

Remember that somewhere in between the respective introductions, a survey must be started and completed in order to present a well-researched reason for building. As we mentioned in Chapter 1, the survey committee should be a cross-section of the membership. Their analysis of growth patterns, conditions of the present facility, and final recommendations will be valuable tools in structuring a building program. Think of Job as you go through this period; it takes time to accumulate thorough studies, which is the foundation to support what you hope to achieve. Then, use this information for in-house marketing.

In the meantime, put the power of positive politicking to work! Supportive conversation among leadership groups can, by osmosis, help develop the mind-set of the membership. Since you already have announced the study-in-progress to the parishioners, they'll be primed for a decision. Subliminal selling!

Use the pulpit

Communication behind-the-scenes is acceptable in the very beginning stages of planning, but as soon as possible you should be up front with the congregation - and vice versa.

The pulpit is the obvious place from which to inform the people before and during the building program. Without abusing or bullying, church leaders can help create interest and action in several different ways:

Announcements. Informational messages regarding the plans, progress, leadership and committee appointments, fund-raising and special events are appropriate. Take care not to over-kill. Move

> *You needn't have been an Explorer Scout to know how important each leader is in helping blaze a trail!*

methodically, with well-thought-out planning steps. Be careful not to press too quickly, unless the congregation shares your sense of urgency.

Sermons. An occasional didactic discourse from the minister, with the building program as the meat of the matter, is a good opportunity for challenging the congregation. The scriptures have plenty to say about growth, stewardship and outreach!

Guest speakers. With all due respect, pastors, hearing from another minister who has been through a building program and lived to tell about it can have great impact. From testimonials, your people can learn to expect blessings in a well-organized project. Other speakers might include members of the various committees for updates.

"Day" One: Enlighten the People

Promotion committee

Once the church leaders and members have joined forces and elected to forge ahead with the building, the next step is to appoint work groups. The promotion committee should be toward the top of your list. Your church may have enough qualified staff people to do this job. Otherwise, a few creative and energetic individuals from your membership may be recruited. They should be familiar with the functions of the church and the community. An established working relationship with the media would be helpful but not necessary; that will come!

The jobs of the promotion committee are:

The scriptures have plenty to say about growth, stewardship and outreach!

- Keeping abreast of all phases and facets of the building program, as well as the work of the other committees;
- Assisting in writing a campaign plan which will include identifying events and promotional opportunities, timely dissemination of information to church members and the community, preparing a budget and interacting with the media;
- Reporting regularly to the central, or building committee and leadership on activities planned or in progress. Granted, it's a tall order; but you can do it – together. With an in-house-agency concept, you'll save money and accomplish more. Your own people have a better understanding of the "product." There's bound to be a deeper dedication. Turn-around time is quicker, and you should expect a maximum of efficiency.

The names of the game

Advertising is the action of calling something to the attention of the public, especially by paid announcements for publication or broadcast.

Promotion is the act of furthering the growth development and acceptance of something through advertising and publicity.

Publicity is an act designed to attract public interest and attention.

Public relations is the business of inducing the public to have understanding for and goodwill toward a person firm or institution.

Or, look at it this way:

If you put up signs around town and say your church is presenting a Christmas music and drama extravaganza that's **advertising**.

If you take one of those signs, hang it on a camel and walk the camel through town, that's **promotion**.

If the camel walks through the mayors yard and his garden, and it gets in the newspapers, that's **publicity**.

Now, if you can keep the mayor and his wife smiling the entire time, that's **public relations**.

With Webster's words of wisdom in hand and Jim Lukaszewski's application from *The Executive Television Training Handbook* in mind, it should be clear that the promotion committee is charged with several correspondent assignments. If done properly, they will all work together for good!

"Day" Two: Separate the Systems

Special events for promotion

Pencil them in. You can count on several built-in promotional opportunities during the building process. They come with the territory and can be played to the hilt. Don't be bashful. These are legitimate events that, if publicized well, will communicate your intentions to the public.

Site selection

Once you've closed the deal on your property purchase, you can whip out a news release to the local media. Don't forget to include denominational newsletters or magazines on your mailing lists. For the membership, make a pulpit announcement and church bulletin advisory. Some churches build on this occasion with a special site dedication service. In this case, invite members of the media and

> *You can count on several built-in promotional opportunities during the building process.*

local dignitaries.

Architectural and Construction Contracts

Announcements all around. This time, however, you might include a black and white photograph with the news release regarding contractual awards. You might even consider a personal introduction of the firms' representatives to the congregation. This can amount to two separate occasions if you don't choose to go with one design/build firm to handle your entire project.

Selection and presentation of architectural plans

Again, you may want to capitalize on two occasions here: first, a presentation of the working, or schematic drawings, and second, when the architect is ready to show the final plans, design and color rendering. The latter event has more visual appeal and can stimulate a lot of interest in the community. Notify the media and send copies of the rendering. If your community has one special place where there is a high traffic pattern, ask permission to display an enlarged picture of the new church. The facility where you bank is one choice; you'll probably think of others.

Notify the media and send copies of the rendering.

Fundraising or capital campaign

The congregation and the general public should know about the kick-off of this important phase of the program. If you're selling church bonds, it's likely that many people outside the church will be given the opportunity to participate. To facilitate the stewardship drive, a four-color presentation brochure packed with information about the church, the goals and the benefits of the new facility is a great marketing tool. You should include a floor plan, a picture of the church, seating availability and any other facts and figures that will sell your project. Print enough brochures for each church family.

Groundbreaking

Here's your chance to invite political, community and denominational dignitaries who will bring out the news media. While this is a monumental step in the program which deserves a well-balanced bearing of solemnity, it's also an event that can stretch your imagination. There's nothing wrong with having a little fun at groundbreaking services, and it's a time where everyone can feel involved. Give everyone a shovel to make the first turn-of-the-earth. Make a chalk outline of the new building to surround the participants. Put a 50-foot rope on an old one-piece plow and let the people pull. Use a backhoe, a scraper, a bulldozer, a horse and a plow. Or be traditional and settle for a spade!

Cornerstone

To keep the community and congregational interest piqued, and to get some more good, free publicity, plan for a cornerstone laying when the building is nearly completed. Invite members of the news media. A container, placed behind the stone, can hold memorable information about the church and the building program. Plan ahead, and make sure you advise the contractor of the activities, so he can leave a niche in the building. And while you're at it, give him the exact dimensions of the box to be installed. At one cornerstone laying in which we participated, the church deacons brought a box that was too large to fit into the designated receptacle. The service went on, of course, and the cornerstone was laid – with no box. The deacons finally got it right, but the brick masons were a little testy the next day when they had to rework stone for the insertion.

Changing scenes

The completion of the new building and an imminent move is definitely a call for celebration. The last service in the old facility you're about to vacate is also a good time to commemorate the many good experiences you've shared. From a public relations standpoint, this service can be planned to ease the "transplant syndrome" and any sadness among the members on leaving an old, familiar church home. A thoughtfully-planned event can help transfer emotions from sentimentality to anticipation in one fell swoop!

Dedicating the new building

This event is the culmination of many months' hard work, expectation and participation. By contacting the news media, you can expect good coverage; but it's also a good idea on this occasion to buy advertising space. Dedication Day should be scheduled for a time when you're comfortably settled in the new church and everything's working smoothly – especially the air conditioning. This can be not only a big media attraction, but also an opportunity to invite special guests to help honor Him and others who have assisted with the building program. The Sunday morning service is an appropriate time for the event; or, a special Sunday afternoon dedication ceremony can be effective. A reception for church members, special guests and the media may be scheduled after the

The completion of the new building and an imminent move is definitely a call for celebration.

service in the fellowship room, or at a local hotel.

Perpetuating the promotion

Keep your creative juices flowing! There are many other events and efforts that can call attention to your church activities, even after the building program is completed. Special services, open house, mortgage burning, guest speakers and music/drama presentations can all be billed as media events. The goal of any promotion campaign is to create and sustain an awareness. This is even more applicable to His church, "...the world's light...for all to see..."

"Day" Three: Plant the Seeds

Overall church promotion includes advertising, publicity and public relations. But the total, perfect mix isn't complete without the basic grassroots ingredient in place. We're talking about one-on-one contact – better known in church circles as personal evangelism. This groundwork obviously is being done, since you're about to grow a new church! Now, in order to "burst forth" on a larger scale, you need the fertilizer. But it's not free.

Here are some of your options:

- Print advertising (newspapers, newsletters, magazines, brochures, flyers, telephone book yellow pages)
- Electronic advertising (radio, television, audio/visual presentations)
- Outdoor advertising (billboard, church signage, travel terminal posters, bus posters, bus-bench messages)
- Direct mail to a diligently-developed list of members and prospects
- Gimmicks (pencils, pens, cups, T-shirts, caps)

The bottom line is your budget.

Any or all of these avenues of promotion can be effective, but you should keep in mind some basic principles:

Target your market. Then, decide which methods best fit your needs.

Research the demographics and psychographics of the media you're considering. Radio station RONG might not reach your audience; station RITE may be the ticket.

Position yourself with a positive, consistent and identifiable image that will be carried throughout your promotional messages. You can combine sight and sound effectively.

In whatever media you choose to advertise, create an upbeat

Position yourself with a positive, consistent and identifiable image.

message. With print advertising, tell your message in the headline, then go on from there. Unfortunately, lazy readers are not the exception. With radio and television spots, you don't have much time, so keep it succinct and simple. Write copy that will make people act! Someone from your local stations may help you with suggestions or even writing. Media salespeople can be accommodating, especially once they know you're buying.

Freebies

You don't always have to spend money to get media exposure. News releases and personal contacts with the "right" people, especially in smaller communities, can result in nice coverage.

Keep in mind that reporters, editors and public affairs people are very busy people with daily deadlines. You'll get a star in your crown and story in the paper if you'll remember a few strategic pointers:

Compile a media list which includes each newspaper, radio and television station, major industry newsletter and advertising agency in your area. With each medium, list the address and telephone number, the manager, editors, and news and public affairs directors. Having this information at your fingertips will expedite the dissemination of information on any occasion.

> *Get to know the key people in each news organization.*

Get to know the key people in each news organization. They can be friends, not adversaries. A personal visit to their office or over lunch will familiarize them with you, also. Then, when a news release or phone call comes from your group, the bells will ring and you'll be more likely to get the coverage you need. How reporters feel about you and your church can influence the way your news – good or bad – is covered.

It's also a good idea to be aware of media deadlines or schedules and make a note of this on your media list. You can become a perennial nuisance by calling at inconvenient times. If you're in doubt on this subject, simply ask: "Is this is a good time to talk?" Don't take it personally if they tell you to call back later. News people have their job to do, also. If you're targeting a magazine, or needing special production for a print ad or radio/television spot, allow enough lead time.

News releases

You're competing with many other people for space when you submit a news release to the media. By preparing your message in an acceptable format and with good copy, you'll stand a better chance of response.

- Use letterhead that easily identifies the church or program you're promoting.
- Clearly state that your communique is a NEWS RELEASE.
- Include the name and telephone number of the contact person at the church in case an editor may want further information. If a reporter calls you after receiving your release, get back to him or her right away.
- Type the date of the news release. Depending on the event, you may want to state that the information is FOR IMMEDIATE RELEASE or FOR RELEASE AFTER SUCH-AND-SUCH A DATE. This will allow the editors to file the copy appropriately.
- Write a brief, but attention-grabbing headline. Editors and reporters get lots of releases each day, so make yours special. If a headline has no newsworthy appeal, they may have a tendency to ignore it.
- Double-space your text to leave room for editing. (Don't pout; most copy gets edited to fit the available space.)
- Start your release with a paragraph that says who, what, when, where, why and how – the major points of your story. The following paragraphs should be written in descending order of importance.
- Don't be flowery in your writing style, but do try to provide some special angle to attract readers or listeners. Never assume that just because you think your project or event is the greatest thing since Baskin-Robbins, everyone else will, too. Bring it home. Nothing interests people more than news that may arouse feelings of identification and anticipation. If you're able to make mouths water with your release, a reporter will add the rest.
- If your release is more than one page, let the editor know by using the word "more," centered at the bottom of the page. Also, indicate the end of the copy with a closing mark such as 30, "-end-" or ###.
- If you're including a photograph with the release, provide a black and white glossy, 4x5 inches or 8x10 inches. Clearly identify the subject(s) by typing the information on a label and attaching it to the back of the print. Don't write on the back of the photograph. For color, check with the paper or magazine as to their requirements.
- A fact sheet is helpful in delivering a concise message. Include information on the specifics of the event, the "where," "when," "What, who" and any additional information or contact names you want to mention.
- Once you've sent the release and allowed enough time for it to be delivered, you may want to make a follow-up phone call. Use good judgement on this point. You may have discovered this

Write a brief, but attention-grabbing headline.

additional contact is acceptable to some, but a pain-in-the-neck to others. When the media gives you good coverage, or is especially cooperative in any of your ventures, write a note of appreciation. Too many expectations – and no gratitude – won't endear you and your church to those who are in positions to help.

"Day" Four: Mark the Days

You have some good ideas now, but don't run amok. Before you set out to promote your church and building program, discipline yourself and your activities by developing a time-line. Then stick to it.

On a penciled diagram or computer spread sheet, map out promotional activities by the days, weeks, months and years. This methodical approach will keep you organized, on target, within budget and able to evaluate the respective responses. All church leaders should have a copy of the planned strategy along with their expected participation.

Constant exposure to the public is an ideal situation. Weekly advertisements, even on a small scale, should be a budget item. Scheduling additional, larger ads and promotional events that could activate media attention may be planned according to what you can afford. This is one strategy.

Another is to spend the bucks on limited "flights" of high-level advertising during times when people are more likely to attend church, such as Christmas and Easter, and pin your hopes on special event coverage from news releases.

The building program affords tremendous opportunity to (1) beef up the church's on-going promotion to the community and (2) keep the congregation informed and involved.

"Day" Five: Be Frugal, and Multiply

Church promotion is an important part of the church budget. And when you're planning, don't underestimate the power of advertising in bringing in the numbers. Too many times a company will stop spending money on advertising when business is slow. And what happens? Business gets even slower. The same thing can happen in a church.

The main considerations in arriving at a budget figure are to set forth your objectives; decide what needs to be done to accomplish these goals; then, determine the costs. It may take some time to get complete estimates from the media on advertising rates, but it's an absolute must for planning purposes. Once you've passed these three guideposts, then decide how much of the budget needs to be allocated for promotion.

In his Creative Leadership Series book, *Church Advertising, A Practical Guide,* Steve Dunkin suggests that a growing church

Map out promotional activities by the days, weeks, months and years.

should spend a minimum of five percent of its total budget on publicity. Declining churches should spend more.

You may think this is too much, or not enough, money for your particular program. It's your decision, of course. Just don't start up the creek without the strong arm of information. You could sink the ship you've built without a generating force.

"Day" Six: Create the Image

In a world of skepticism, competition and yes, even fear, representatives of His church need to be the most competent public relations practitioners of the age.

When God saw everything He had made. He determined that "it was excellent in every way" (Genesis 1:31, TLB).

Heaven only knows what He thinks now! But the believers on earth's present sojourn are definitely privy to the knowledge that many of our fellow humans have a nasty streak. As the old English rhyme says: "When I did well, I heard it never; when I did ill, I heard it ever." It is our job, therefore, to be image-builders and active contributors in winning over prospective "clients" to His church. This particular commission goes beyond the "let's-get-our-name-in-the-paper" mentality. What we're talking about here is an amicable bridge between you and those you want on board.

As your building project gets underway, the pastor, the leaders and every member of the church must be challenged to represent His church in a positive way. Everyone involved should anticipate resistance and be prepared to respond with confidence.

Alee Benn, in his book, *The 22 Most Common Mistakes in Public Relations,* makes some practical suggestions: "Do not confuse public relations with paid advertising. Remember that the press must be persuaded, cannot be forced, and should not be deceived... Mass communications differ from one-to-one communications. Prepare a carefully considered plan based on a knowledge of the realities of public relations and the nine determinants: purpose, audience, subject, source, media, authorities, professional, time available, and budget."

It is our job ... to be image-builders and active contributors in winning over prospective "clients" to His church.

"Day" Seven: Take a Break

You can relax now, if you've created a promotional plan and approved it as "excellent in every way." No one should be in the dark as the architect and builder turn your plans into reality.

10

THE SYNERGISTIC SANCTUARY

A place of worship and its surrounding blessings

"**G**etting together" is not only a sociological need, it's a Biblical theory.

For instance, when Paul wrote his letter to the Corinth church and queried, "Don't you realize that all of you together are the house of God?" (1 Corinthians 3:16, TLB), he was attempting to prove that symbiosis-by-solitude was not in the books. In fact, his assignment to "talk with each other much about the Lord, quoting psalms and hymns and singing spiritual songs, making music in your hearts to the Lord" (Ephesians 5:19, TLB) could not have been more in focus. "Getting together" is a tested dictum for spiritual good health.

David wasn't a loner, either! He and cantor Asaph even formed a choir of priests who had this didactic song for the congregation:

> "...give thanks...and pray to him
> ...tell the peoples of the world
> ...sing to him; yes, sing his praises
> ...glory in his holy name; let all rejoice
> ...seek the Lord; yes, seek his strength and...face
> ...remember his mighty...marvelous miracles and authority
> ...bring an offering
> ...worship the Lord
> ...give thanks to the Lord, for he is good
> ...forever and forevermore.
> And all the people shouted 'Amen!' and praised the Lord"
> (1 Chronicles 16:8-36, TLB).

All the people. Together. In one place.

As we know, most of these spontaneous expressions are

> *"Getting together" is a tested dictum for spiritual good health.*

translated personally within the Church – the body of believers – day in and day out. But for the practical purposes of shelter and fellowship, the church building represents symbolic, and sometimes literal, refuge. Thus, for thousands of years the "gathering place" or "house of worship" has been a religious signal to the world, with the liturgical center known as what it truly is – a sanctuary.

With today's competitive state-of-affairs and the trend toward super-technology, the Biblical directives offer a real challenge. Church leaders vie for not only spiritual, but visual, audible, educational, operational, mechanical, practical – and continual – excellence. Twenty-first century space created for a church congregation must include functional supplementary facilities surrounding the pivotal worship room – all with a total environment of propriety.

The "getting together" of His people, and all the workings of a church for worship and expression, is part of His Plan. With planning, wisdom and sensitivity, your new sanctuary – with all its vital tributaries – can draw the contemporary Corinthians together and make yours the church of their choice.

Going to church should be as pleasurable and hassle-free as possible.

Most people – coming off a week's worth of work, school and a frantic schedule – are ready for change. There's a greedy anticipation for a calming of the storms and stilling of the waves. "What a blessing is that stillness, as he brings them safely into harbor!" (Psalm 107:30, TLB). The best is The Rest.

Going to church should be as pleasurable and hassle-free as possible. It's crucial that the approach to your sanctuary is planned for the ultimate invitation. A well-placed and identified entrance location is as important to a church as it is to a retail business. Then, an accessible parking lot, easy entryways and the warm arms of the foyer and worship area can wrap your congregation in the unruffled peace that passeth all understanding!

Communications – Again

How can you create that perfect panacea? It's simple, if everyone does their job.

First of all, you should know by now – beyond a shadow of doubt – what your needs are: parking, access, education and administration space, worship center size and the functional relationships. You also know the habits of your growing group of worshippers from years of pastoring experience. You've obviously learned how to communicate with them, while allowing them to communicate with you. Hopefully you also are aware of the importance of communication among themselves.

Secondly, you're anticipating even more growth – new families, new faces – when your new building is completed. Unfamiliarity breeds contempt, said one sagacious gent, and those are two things you want to avoid. From review and consultation with the designer, you'll learn to know the architectural plans like the back of your hand. Just make sure the layout doesn't leave visitors groping in the dark.

As you turn over the awesome task of designing and building your house of worship, be aware of the fact that most architects aren't in the church communications business (unless they have lots of church plans under their belts). Knowing you and your require-ments, however, they can – effectively and aesthetically – design a facility to create the ambience for communication.

Signs

Good signage can communicate perfectly what your facility offers. Get your church name, the directions on how to get there, where to park and how to enter in plain sight! Good, simple and useful information should be clear as the morning air in Kansas. If there is more than one way to get to the foyer, and eventually the sanctuary, say so! It's inhumane to entice people into your building, then let them wander around in an ill-planned corridor/concourse searching for their destination.

C. M. Deasy. FAIA, in collaboration with Thomas E. Lasswell, Ph.D., sums it up in his book, *Designing Places for People.* He says, "If businesses can get a customer inside the store, they have a chance to demonstrate the superior nature of their service. If they cannot get the customer inside, the quality of their service is irrelevant."

From the viewpoint of a new viewer, there is a series of ques-tions that a building design should answer so that the viewer may determine whether the building satisfies any current needs or interests:

- What is it?
- What benefit does it offer me?
- How do I get in?
- What is inside?
- How will I be received?

The first impression made by most buildings, or the first information communicated by most buildings, occurs during the approach to the building when these basic questions are answered.

Your challenge? Keep the old business coming, and get the new

Good signage can communi-cate perfectly what your facility offers.

business in! A well-planned church and sanctuary of functional design will enhance the ministry.

The Foyer, or Narthex

The entry foyer – an anteroom or entrance to the sanctuary – is a transitional area, an along-shore relief from rough sailing to the smooth waters of the harbor. It is a place for spiritual preparation, whether in arrival or departure, and should set the mind and heart for expectations. As people move toward the church – to and from the parking lot – the flow should be natural and easy. A sheltered unloading area is a nice element. Well-planned landscaping, walkways and benches for seating will enhance the entry.

National and local building codes require a defined number of entry and exit doors, depending on the number of people you're accommodating. But even so, don't skimp. If you can afford it, plan for more than the minimum ways to get in and out. And be sure to meet everyone's needs by referring to the American National Standards Institute, Inc. (ANSI) regarding specifications for making buildings accessible to and usable by physically handicapped people and the elderly. (See Chapter 16, please.)

Clearly define the main entrance and foyer, then consider going one step further; define the sanctuary itself. A circular concourse around the sanctuary is an option. But watch your signals! If someone not familiar with the church marches through the foyer into the sanctuary with no direction, he could easily walk right onto the platform. Not good.

Establish easily identifiable entrances to the sanctuary seating and make everyone feel at home. The doors which open to the worship center should have the look and feel of "something special."

The size of the foyer has denominational variances, of course. But ample space allowed for the foyer can be designed for several functions.

For minimum use, it can serve merely as a vestibule from outside elements to the calm of the worship room. We have also designed foyers large enough to be used as dining halls, with adjacent kitchens.

The design of this important area depends on the occupancy of the sanctuary and the functions it needs to serve. Ideally, and if you can afford it, we recommend the foyer to handle 20 percent of the sanctuary space. If you're planning for 10,000 square feet in the sanctuary, allow 2,000 square feet in the foyer. This boils down to approximately two square feet per person.

If yours is a gregarious, friendly group, the anteroom can be an ideal place for greeting and fellowship before and after the church

The doors which open to the worship center should have the look and feel of "something special."

Entry Gate Elevation

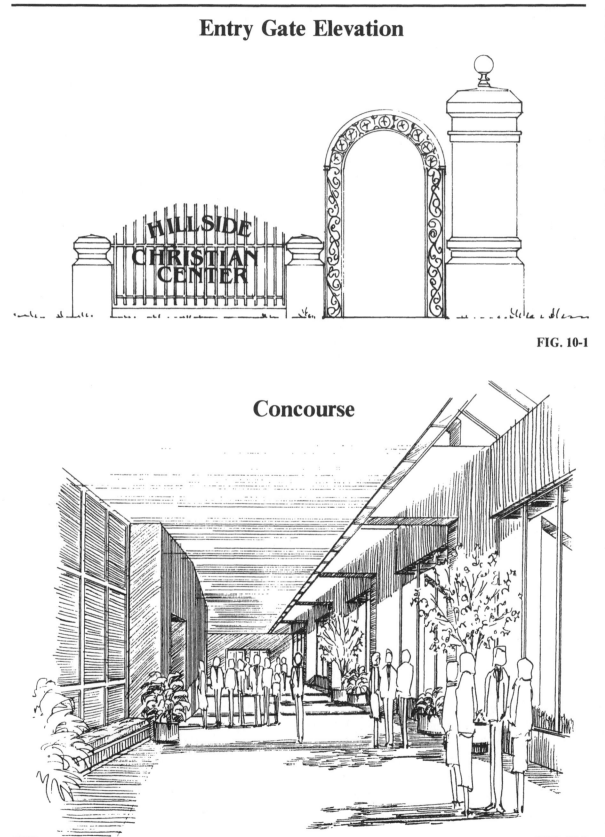

FIG. 10-1

Concourse

FIG. 10-2

service. For larger congregations, we recommend that you provide seating for those with small children and others who prefer to sit while socializing.

The question was: "How will I be received?" There is no better way to make folks feel welcome and comfortable than inviting them into an open, well-lighted and tastefully decorated foyer. If your church has plans for a balcony, the ceiling can be two-stories high with lots of natural lighting. Color, wall material selections and green plants are important, of course, but the keys to a well-planned foyer are Welcome, Warmth, Easy Movement and Accessibility.

The foyer is a perfect and natural sound-buffering area. Noise from the outside and inside – the nurseries, the educational areas and restrooms – can be held to a minimum from the sanctuary. Think wear-resistant and sound-absorbent when you choose the floor material in the foyer and sanctuary. Carpet is best, since hard-surfaced floors have a potential for noise when sanctuary doors are open. (One church we built, however, preferred parquet wood flooring in the foyer and sanctuary. They wanted the noise and the audio hub-bub during the congregating of the people. What's more, they're very happy with this choice!) Wall and ceiling treatments also must be designed and built with acoustical considerations in mind.

Support activities

Optional uses for the foyer should be considered when planning your new church. Additional educational space, reception areas and fellowship functions can be incorporated in this area with proper planning.

- Literature distribution and/or sales is handled very well in a designated, well-identified area of a large foyer. If this activity is a big part of your ministry, you may want to consider a separate sales room or book store which can be locked during off-hours.
- Open coat storage in the foyer area or concourse is one preferred method. The traditional, separate coat room is another. Coat hooks and shelves on specified wall alcoves can be integrated with the hallway design; this is economical and acceptable. A separate room is more expensive (and congested). But if wall racks, hooks or pegs offend you, and if your climate calls for heavy-duty wearing of coats, count on only 30 to 50 percent of the people who are willing to give up their coats. Most take them into the sanctuary and the pews. As a general rule, hang six coats per 12-inch lineal length whether you choose hallway space or a separate room. If you decide on the latter, the proximity of the room to the entry, exits and the

As a general rule, hang six coats per 12-inch lineal length.

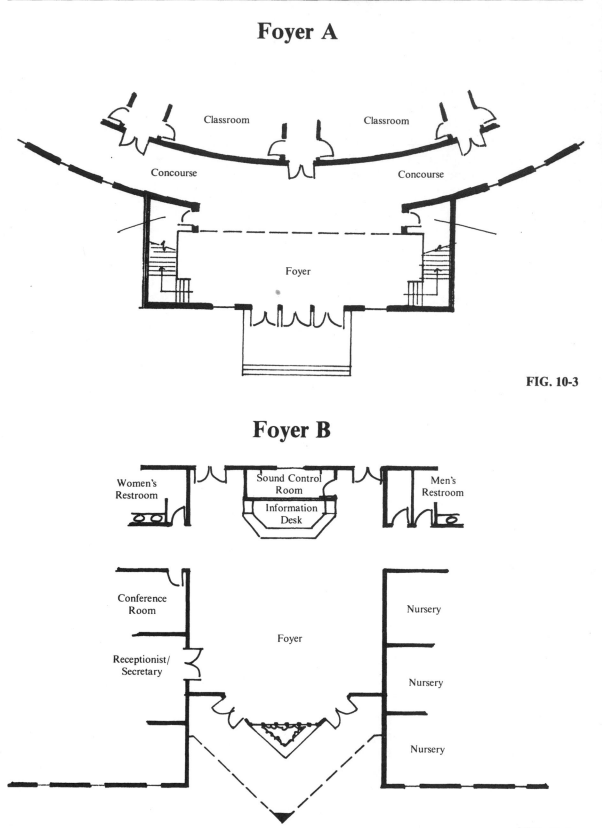

Foyer A

FIG. 10-3

Foyer B

FIG. 10-4

Foyer C

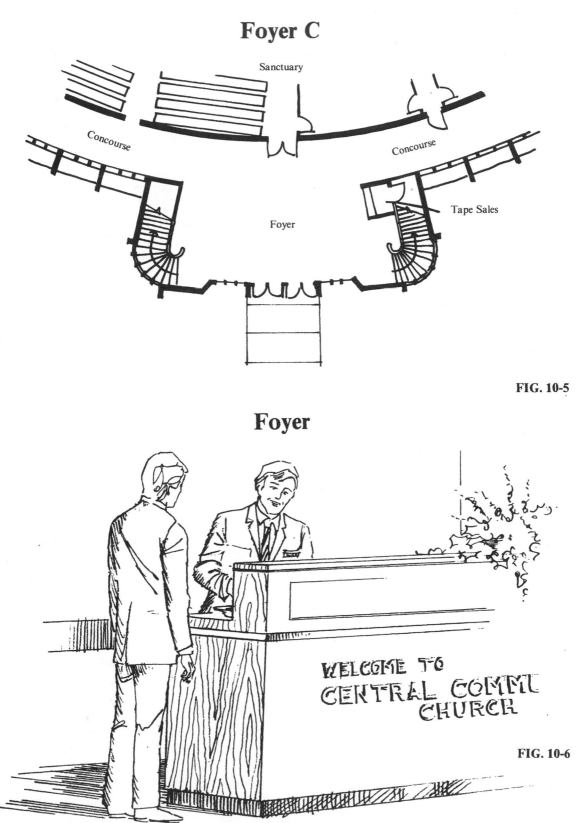

FIG. 10-5

Foyer

FIG. 10-6

concourse flow is important. Coat rooms that can be "walked through" facilitates circulation and helps avoid claustrophobic crowding.

■ Storage space for janitorial supplies, communion plates and any other items or equipment should be close to the foyer. Consider plumbing for a sink in this area.

■ Ushers need space for planning and preparation of their duties. A room for this purpose could also double as a station for security personnel and vault. This room, or a special place in the foyer, could have a telephone/audio equipment directly connecting to the platform or pulpit.

■ A parlor, or "fireside" room is an added feature you may want to consider. A small and cozy area close to the foyer can serve as a family room for funeral services, a bride's room, or even a small dining room if your plans have the kitchen facilities close by.

Ushers need space for planning and preparation of their duties.

■ Many churches have liturgical services which include a ceremonial procession through the congregation by the celebrant or minister. A sacristy for the storage of vestments and ceremonial utensils can be located near the vestibule and the sanctuary. A place for the clergy and any other participants to meet and robe, this location also makes it handy for ministers who greet and bid farewell to people in the foyer. If this is not the case, the vesting room could be located closer to the altar area. Assistants, or acolytes, also need vesting space which should be located near the sacristy.

■ The nurseries must be found easily and as near to the sanctuary as possible. It's a nuisance for young parents to search, then walk a mile to deposit their babies and belongings. Locate the nurseries close to an entry, if not the main entry. The problem with this is, of course, that visitors with children won't know which designated entry to approach. Again, well-placed and explanatory signage is a welcome help to new-comers. (See Chapter 13, please.)

■ Pastoral and administrative offices should be easy to locate from the foyer. Whether this space is close to the main entry depends on the size, work habits and inclinations of the staff. Its not likely that folks will be looking for this area on Sunday mornings; but after all, it's business-as-usual throughout the week. Since your church is thriving and growing, the office complex can be a real hub of activity and drop-in traffic. Make it perfectly clear where to find the people who make it all happen! (See Chapter 12, please.)

■ Restrooms need to be located near the main entry and close to the sanctuary. It's also a good idea to have a door connecting this area to the bride's room. Space for a lounging area could be included in the ladies' restroom and even be used as the bride's room. Be sure to make these areas large enough for the influx of people before and after services. Stay tuned to the building codes. Their minimum fixture specifications are adequate. Then, add what you can afford. Speaking of codes, check the ANSI book on restroom requirements for the physically handicapped. (Refer to Chapter 16.)

Sanctuary

Denominational variances come into play with every aspect of church building, particularly in the main church room. Nomenclatures may differ but the function is one in the same. Worship. To this add teaching, evangelism, celebration and yes, even entertainment, and you've got the sum total of sanctuary services from almost every church in the yellow pages! How this all translates into form for the function is up to you and your design architect. But there are certain practicalities and considerations that are applicable for any church getting ready to build.

We've brought you into the building and through the foyer. Now let's go find a seat.

Access

Getting into the sanctuary and seating area should be easy. Several entrances from the foyer/narthex can solve problems of congestion and allow free-flowing, non-distracting access. A concourse that wraps around the entire seating area is a good idea. This plan provides the opportunity to enter the sanctuary from any one of many locations at each aisle and eliminates the need to go to a "cross aisle."

Aisles

Strict building code requirements dictate the width in direct proportion to the length of the aisles, and the planned seating capacity. For example: the minimum code requirement is a three-and-a-half-feet aisle with a one-and-a-half inch increase for every five feet in length. In some areas of the country, however, a church sanctuary aisle must be six feet. Period. Your architect must know the codes. Remember, the aisle "leads" people to the platform. Strips of aisle carpet should be used to accent the path of travel.

Getting into the sanctuary and seating area should be easy.

Standard

Continental

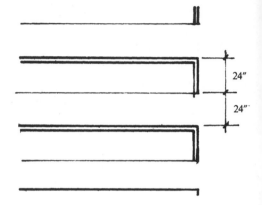

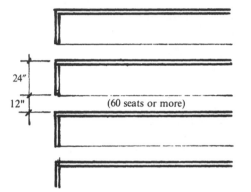

24"

12"

(60 seats or more)

24"

24"

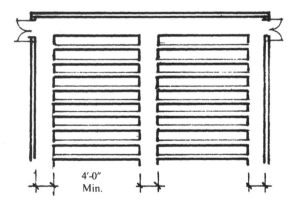

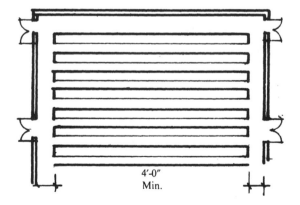

4'-0"
Min.

4'-0"
Min.

Standard seating requires that pews shall not exceed a maximum length established by local codes (UBC, BOCA — 21'-0"/STD — 30'-0"). At the end of these rows there shall be a minimum 4'-0" aisle. The depth of the pew spacing shall be a minimum of 36".

Continental seating requires that chairs can be continuous with no intermediate aisles. At the end of the rows there is a minimum 4'-0" aisle. One pair of doors will be available for every five rows. The depth of the chair spacing depends on the length in the row of seats.

FIG. 10-7

Seating

You're aiming for several things when you plan for seating in your auditorium. Accessibility, convenience, comfort and aesthetics are parts of the target. But again, the code books write the rules of the game when it comes to length, width and depth of pews. The requirements range from 21 to 30-feet pew lengths. There must be 12 inches from the front of a pew to the back of the one ahead; or, back to back, 34 to 36 inches. In churches where worshipers kneel for prayer, the spacing must be increased and kneelers should be planned as part of the pew. When you're selecting furniture, be sure to provide a storage space on the pew backs for hymnals, prayer books, pencils, envelopes and communion cup holders. A pew screen, sometimes called a pew front, is recommended for the front of the first row of pews with an approximate 36 inches between it and the first pew back, and a height equal to the pew backs.

An alternative to pews is theatre, or continental seating, which are individual seats with self-rising bottoms. The 12-inch requirement still applies, but fold-up seats can increase the length of the row. This option is favorable for easy access and exiting, and is certainly more comfortable. There are some considerations, however. Because of the width of the seat and added space between back-to-front rows when the seats are up, you can design very long rows. Theatre seats take up more space, per person and square feet. You can't seat as many people within a given space. The seat itself is more expensive than pews or portable folding chairs.

Whatever choice you make in seating, keep in mind that the pew design and fabric are important interior design decisions. We believe that what people can feel and touch will effect their perception of the total church experience.

There must be 12 inches from the front of a pew to the back of the one ahead.

$$$$

Since we've broached the subject, let's talk costs. Ten to 12 square feet per person is a reasonable allowance for the sanctuary. But don't under-estimate. When you start adding large platforms, baptistries, surrounding concourse, administrative and educational areas, the square footage per person could go even higher. Once more, it all depends on how the scope of your ministry ties into your budget.

Square Sanctuary (Small)

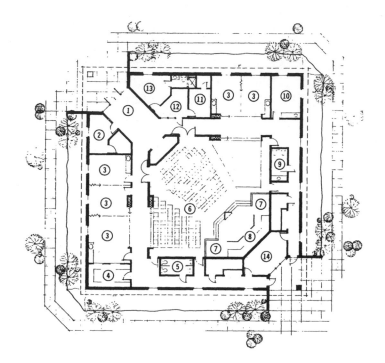

①	Foyer
②	Bookstore
③	Classroom (Sanctuary Overflow)
④	Kitchen
⑤	Men's Rest Room
⑥	Sanctuary
⑦	Orchestra
⑧	Choir
⑨	Women's Rest Room
⑩	Nursery
⑪	Office
⑫	Receptionist/Secretary
⑬	Pastor's Office
⑭	Choir/Prayer Room

Seating Schedule

Sanctuary	243
Choir	28
Overflow	120
Total	**391**

FIG. 10-8

Square Sanctuary (Medium)

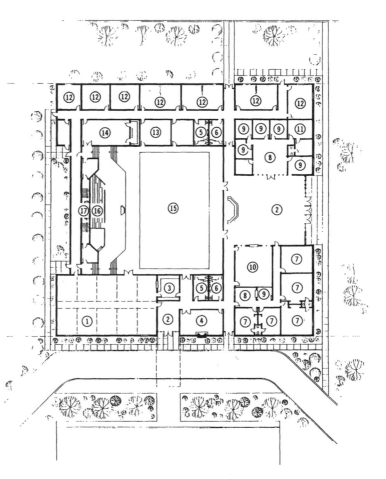

1. Fellowship Hall
2. Foyer
3. Kitchen
4. Fireside Room
5. Men's Rest Room
6. Women's Rest Room
7. Nursery
8. Receptionist/Secretary
9. Office
10. Library
11. Pastor's Office
12. Classroom
13. Prayer Room
14. Choir Practice Room
15. Sanctuary
16. Choir
17. Baptistry

Seating Schedule	
Sanctuary	1000
Choir	60
Total	**1060**

FIG. 10-9

Square Sanctuary (Large)
First Floor Plan

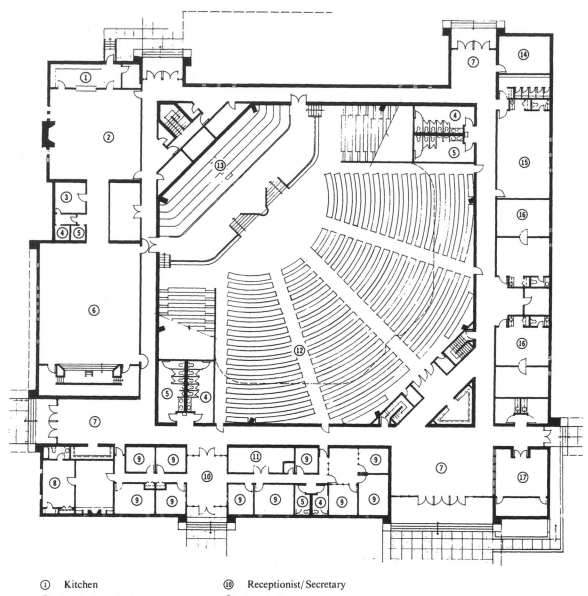

①	Kitchen	⑩	Receptionist/ Secretary
②	Parlor/ Board Room	⑪	Work Room
③	Bride's Room	⑫	Sanctuary
④	Women's Rest Room	⑬	Choir
⑤	Men's Rest Room	⑭	Dressing Room
⑥	Chapel	⑮	Children's Choir Room
⑦	Foyer	⑯	Nursery
⑧	Pastor's Office	⑰	Bookstore
⑨	Office		

Seating Schedule

Sanctuary	780
Choir	120
Balcony	780
Total	**1680**

FIG. 10-10

Balcony Floor Plan

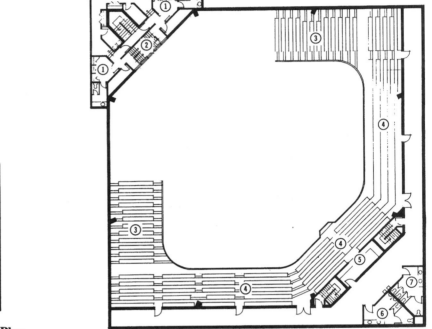

Partial Second Floor Plan

① Sound Control Room

① Dressing Room
② Baptistry
③ Gallery
④ Balcony Seating
⑤ Sound Control Room
⑥ Men's Rest Room
⑦ Women's Rest Room

Seating Schedule

Sanctuary	1000
Choir	60
Total	**1060**

FIG. 10-11

Octagon Sanctuary (Small)

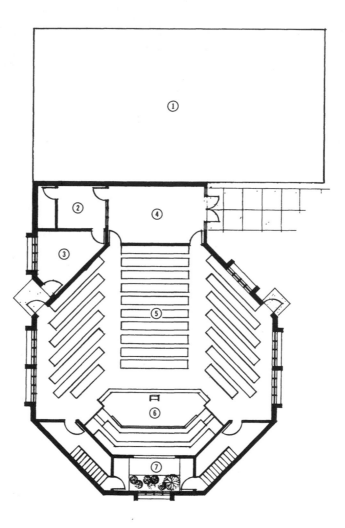

①	Existing Building
②	Receptionist/Secretary
③	Pastor's Office
④	Foyer
⑤	Sanctuary
⑥	Choir
⑦	Baptistry

Seating Schedule

Sanctuary	250
Choir	38
Total	**288**

FIG. 10-12

Octagon Sanctuary (Medium)

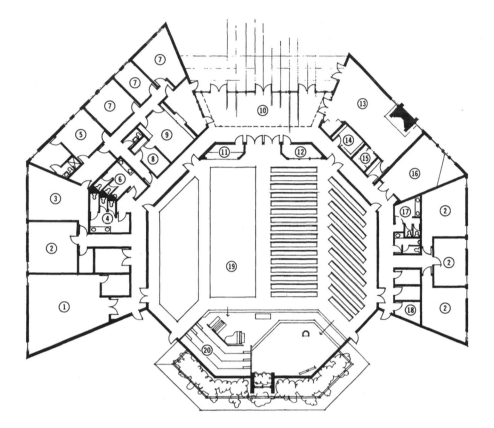

①	Choir Practice Room	⑪	Sound Control Room
②	Classroom	⑫	Cry Room
③	Conference Room	⑬	Fireside Room
④	Women's Rest Room	⑭	Library
⑤	Pastor's Office	⑮	Kitchen
⑥	Men's Rest Room	⑯	Chapel
⑦	Office	⑰	Women's Rest Room
⑧	Work Room	⑱	Sacristy
⑨	Receptionist/Secretary	⑲	Sanctuary
⑩	Narthex	⑳	Choir

Seating Schedule

Sanctuary	652
Choir	60
Total	**712**

FIG. 10-13

Octagon Sanctuary (Large)

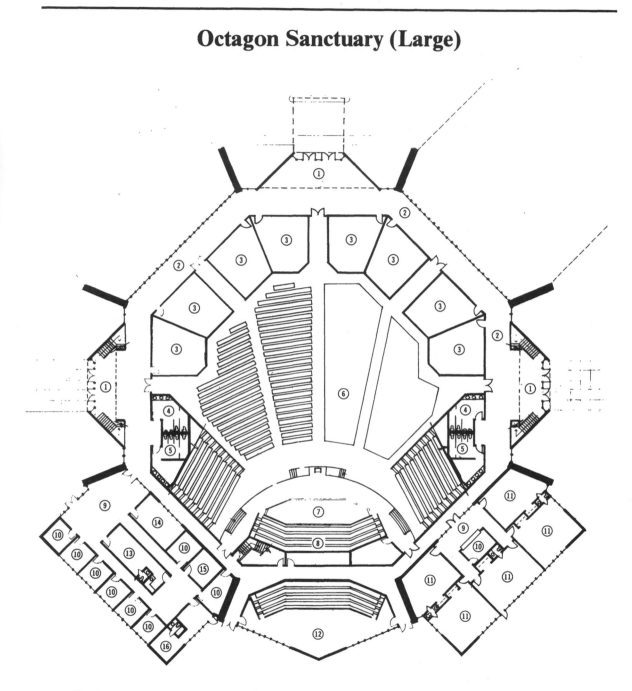

①	Foyer	⑨	Receptionist/Secretary
②	Concourse	⑩	Office
③	Classroom	⑪	Nursery
④	Men's Rest Room	⑫	Choir Practice Room
⑤	Women's Rest Room	⑬	Work Room
⑥	Sanctuary	⑭	Library
⑦	Orchestra	⑮	Conference
⑧	Choir	⑯	Pastor's Office

Seating Schedule

Sanctuary	1872
Future Sanctuary	986
Choir	155
Balcony	488
Future Balcony	1212
Total	**4713**

FIG. 10-14

Octagon Sanctuary (Large)

Balcony Floor Plan

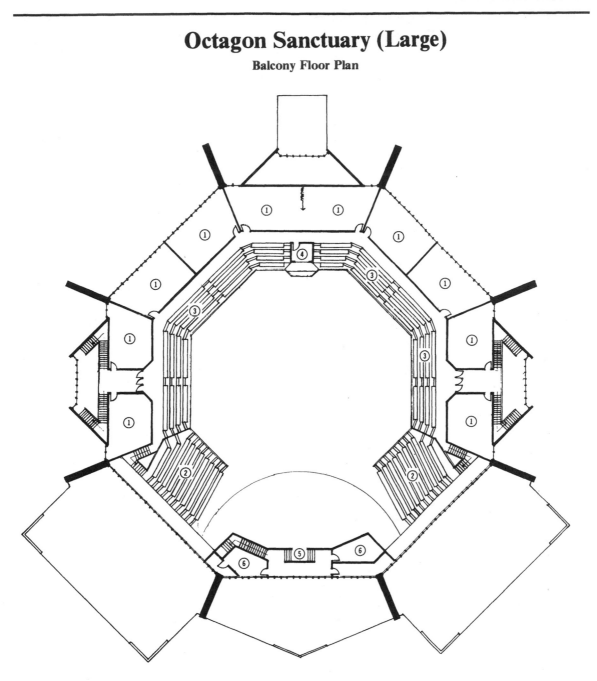

1. Classroom
2. Gallery
3. Balcony Seating
4. Sound Control Room
5. Baptistry
6. Dressing Room

FIG. 10-15

Rectilinear Sanctuary (Small)

First Floor Plan

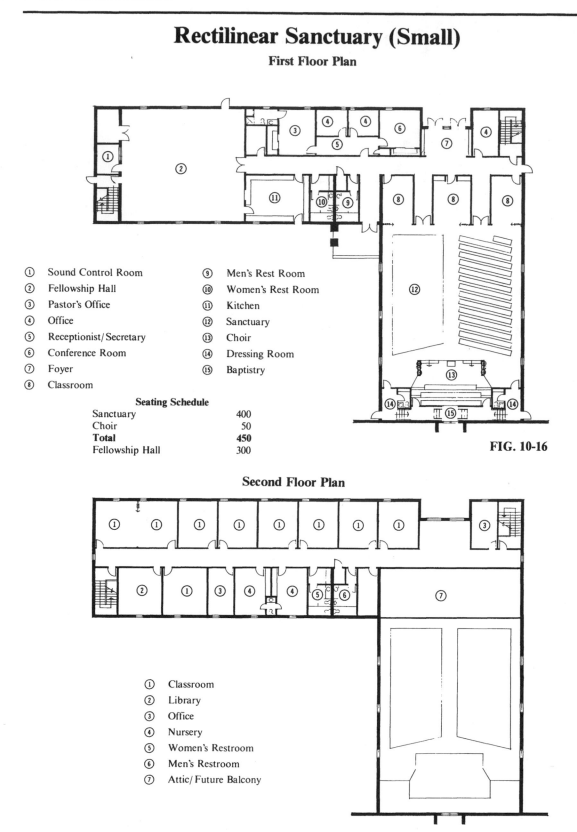

①	Sound Control Room	⑨ Men's Rest Room
②	Fellowship Hall	⑩ Women's Rest Room
③	Pastor's Office	⑪ Kitchen
④	Office	⑫ Sanctuary
⑤	Receptionist/Secretary	⑬ Choir
⑥	Conference Room	⑭ Dressing Room
⑦	Foyer	⑮ Baptistry
⑧	Classroom	

Seating Schedule

Sanctuary	400
Choir	50
Total	**450**
Fellowship Hall	300

FIG. 10-16

Second Floor Plan

①	Classroom
②	Library
③	Office
④	Nursery
⑤	Women's Restroom
⑥	Men's Restroom
⑦	Attic/Future Balcony

FIG. 10-17

Rectilinear Sanctuary (Medium)
First Floor Plan

① Platform
② Meeting/Dining Hall
③ Kitchen
④ Men's Rest Room
⑤ Women's Rest Room
⑥ Foyer
⑦ Receptionist/Secretary
⑧ Library
⑨ Pastor's Office
⑩ Work Room
⑪ Office
⑫ Colonnade
⑬ Courtyard
⑭ Sanctuary
⑮ Choir
⑯ Baptistry
⑰ Minister's Assembly
⑱ Dressing Room
⑲ Choir Practice Room
⑳ Communion Preparation

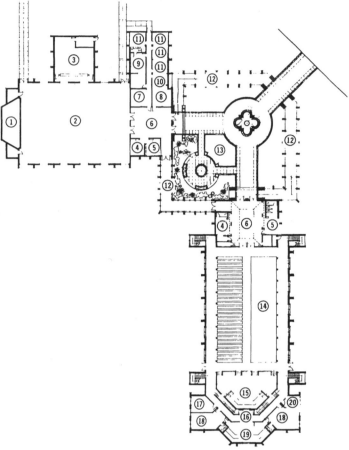

Balcony Floor Plan

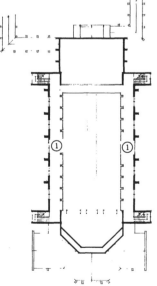

① Side Balcony

Seating Schedule	
Sanctuary	750
Choir	65
Total	**815**

FIG. 10-18

Rectilinear Sanctuary (Large)

First Floor Plan

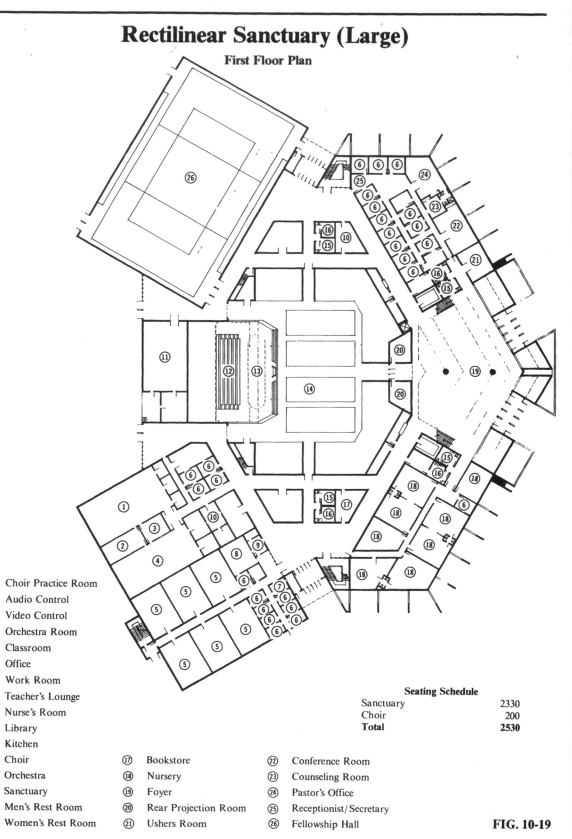

① Choir Practice Room
② Audio Control
③ Video Control
④ Orchestra Room
⑤ Classroom
⑥ Office
⑦ Work Room
⑧ Teacher's Lounge
⑨ Nurse's Room
⑩ Library
⑪ Kitchen
⑫ Choir
⑬ Orchestra
⑭ Sanctuary
⑮ Men's Rest Room
⑯ Women's Rest Room

⑰ Bookstore
⑱ Nursery
⑲ Foyer
⑳ Rear Projection Room
㉑ Ushers Room

㉒ Conference Room
㉓ Counseling Room
㉔ Pastor's Office
㉕ Receptionist/Secretary
㉖ Fellowship Hall

Seating Schedule

Sanctuary	2330
Choir	200
Total	**2530**

FIG. 10-19

Rectilinear (Large)
Second Floor Plan

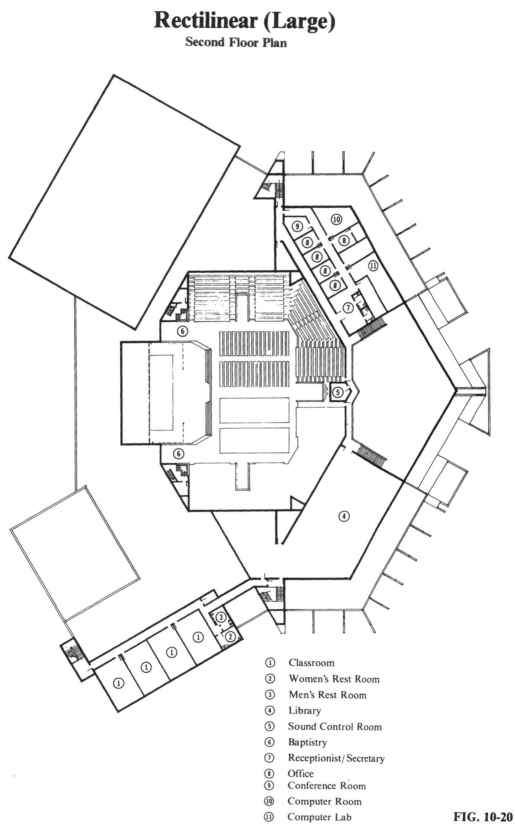

1. Classroom
2. Women's Rest Room
3. Men's Rest Room
4. Library
5. Sound Control Room
6. Baptistry
7. Receptionist/Secretary
8. Office
9. Conference Room
10. Computer Room
11. Computer Lab

FIG. 10-20

Fan Sanctuary (Small)
First Floor Plan

① Kitchen
② Classroom
③ Women's Rest Room
④ Men's Rest Room
⑤ Receptionist/Secretary
⑥ Office
⑦ Pastor's Office
⑧ Nursery
⑨ Choir
⑩ Sanctuary
⑪ Concourse
⑫ Foyer
⑬ Chapel

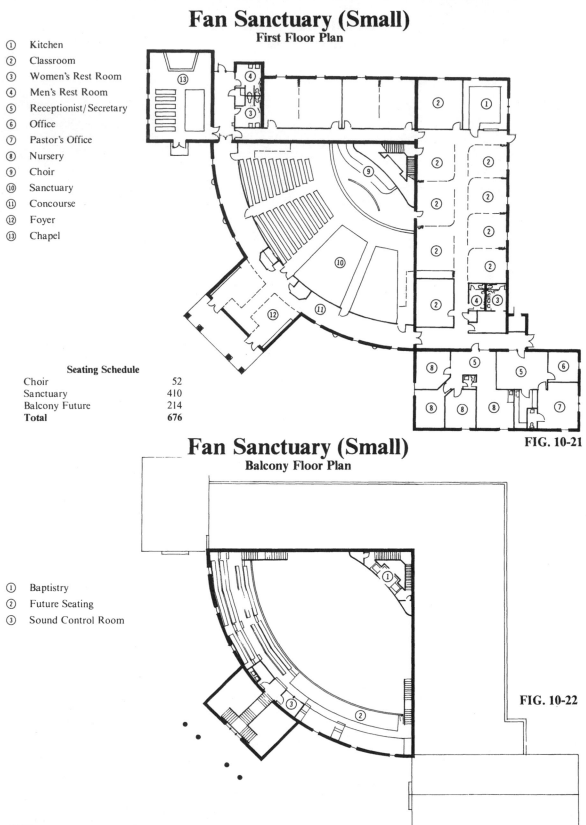

Seating Schedule

Choir	52
Sanctuary	410
Balcony Future	214
Total	**676**

FIG. 10-21

Fan Sanctuary (Small)
Balcony Floor Plan

① Baptistry
② Future Seating
③ Sound Control Room

FIG. 10-22

Fan Sanctuary (Medium)
First Floor Plan

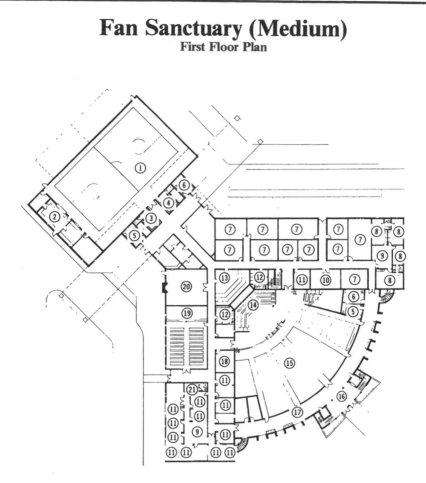

①	Fellowship Hall	⑦	Classroom	⑬ Choir Practice Room	⑲ Chapel
②	Kitchen	⑧	Nursery	⑭ Choir	⑳ Fireside Room
③	Men's Locker Room	⑨	Receptionist/Secretary	⑮ Sanctuary	㉑ Pastor's Office
④	Women's Locker Room	⑩	Library	⑯ Foyer	
⑤	Men's Rest Room	⑪	Office	⑰ Concourse	
⑥	Women's Rest Room	⑫	Dressing Room	⑱ Prayer Room	

Fan Sanctuary (Medium)
Balcony Floor Plan

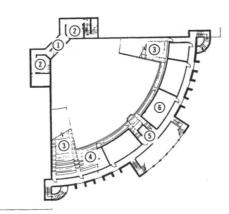

① Baptistry
② Dressing Room
③ Gallery
④ Future Seating
⑤ Sound Control Room
⑥ Classroom

Seating Schedule	
Sanctuary	890
Choir	100
Future Balcony	515
Total	**1505**

FIG. 10-23

147

Fan Sanctuary (Large)
First Floor Plan

1. Chapel
2. Prayer Room
3. Choir Practice Room
4. Orchestra
5. Choir
6. Sanctuary
7. Men's Rest Room
8. Women's Rest Room
9. Concourse
10. Audio-Visual Cassettes
11. Classroom
12. Receptionist/Secretary
13. Office
14. Nurse
15. Media Center
16. Kitchen
17. Fellowship Hall
18. Locker Room
19. Gym
20. Nursery
21. Work Room
22. Pastor's Office
23. Bookstore

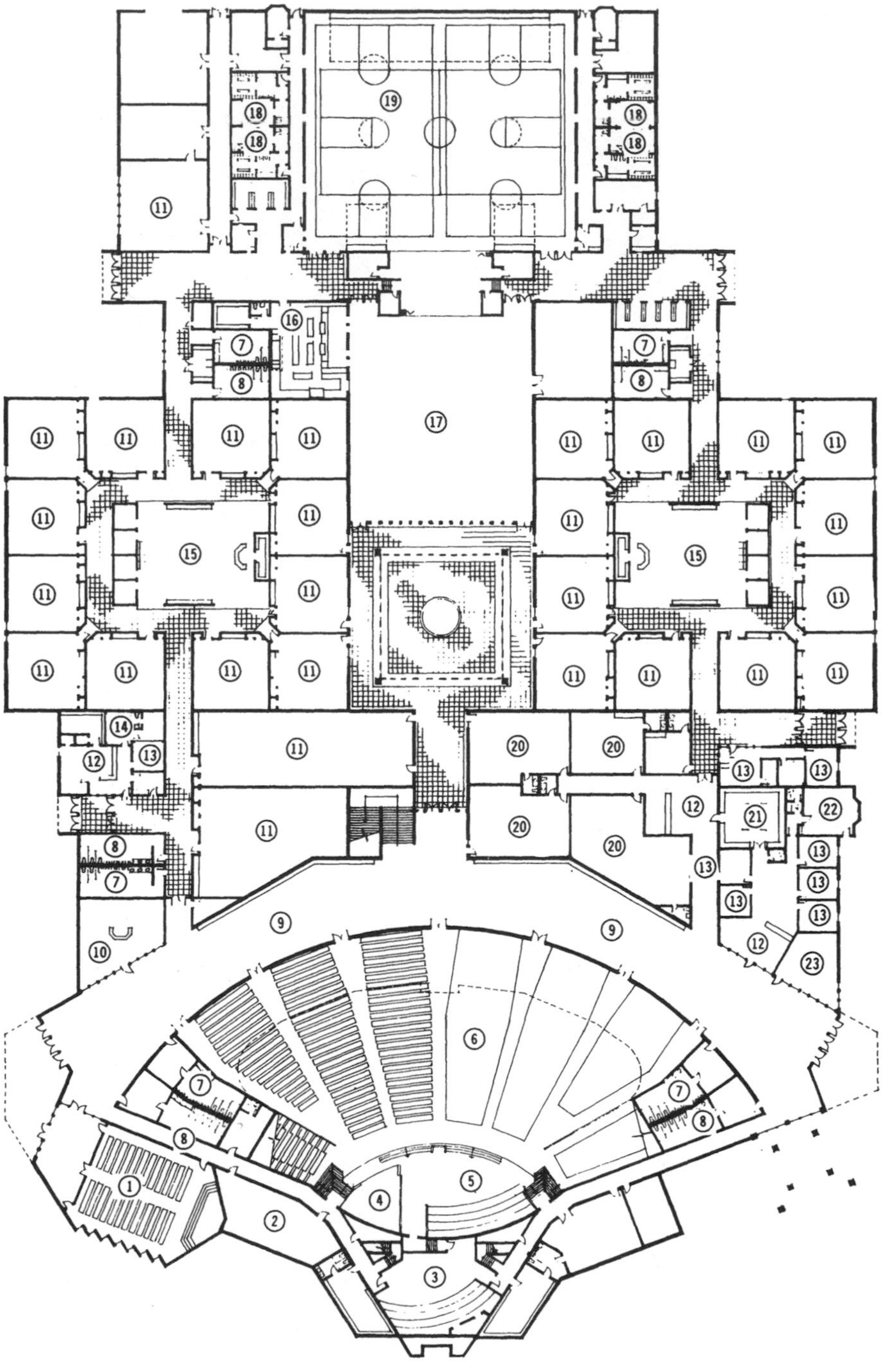

Seating Schedule

Sanctuary	2000
Choir	150
Balcony	600
Total	**2750**

FIG. 10-24

Fan Sanctuary (Large)
Balcony Floor Plan

① Dressing Room
② Baptistry
③ Gallery
④ Balcony Seating
⑤ Sound Control Room

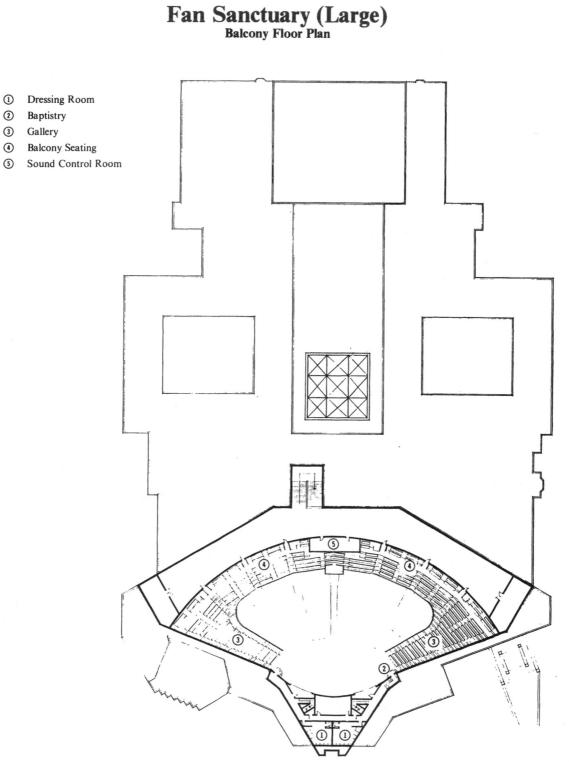

FIG. 10-25

Planning for Worship and Evangelism

The sanctuary, or auditorium, is an assembly space. Since most denominations are geared for a concentration of activity in the platform area, it is essential that the sight-lines are clear and unobstructed. But church worship, in every form and in every sense of the word, calls for active participation from the clergy, the congregation and the choir. The shape, arrangement and size of the sanctuary must provide the atmosphere and logistical components for total involvement.

Plans

The size of your auditorium and the number of people you need to accommodate will help determine the shape of your sanctuary. Also, the plan you choose must suit the minister's teaching style.

For a small congregation of 500 or under, a rectangular plan with one central and two outside aisles is a traditional option.

Some churches prefer to plan the worship room for symbolic significance, with the congregation seated in appendages of a cruciform and the chancel at the strategic head of the cross. The early architectural design of the Greek Orthodox churches is an example. There can be special problems of acoustics and uniformity with this arrangement, however.

The fan, or pie-shaped sanctuary has the capacity to solve most problems for a medium-to-large congregation.

Another plan locates the pulpit and platform area in the center of an encircling congregation, giving a resulting sense of intimacy and involvement. But with today's emphasis on communications concerns, this plan can be an acoustical challenge. There are many other plans that have been and could be utilized in church design and building to meet the needs of your congregation. But our goal is to recommend the most effective ways to face the challenge of the contemporary and growing churches.

The fan, or pie-shaped sanctuary has the capacity to solve most problems for a medium-to-large congregation. The premise of this design is to bring people "into" the pulpit and platform area. It eliminates the need for binoculars and takes a great strain off the ears and neck. Seating actually "fans" around the platform and avoids the spectator-performer syndrome, even in the largest of churches. It creates easy participation, hearing, seeing, entrance and exit, and the ultimately desired feeling of participation. (Easy does it, remember?) And if the sloping floor concept is utilized, it gets even better.

Balconies

Since we've been discussing the importance of participation,

Sanctuary Section

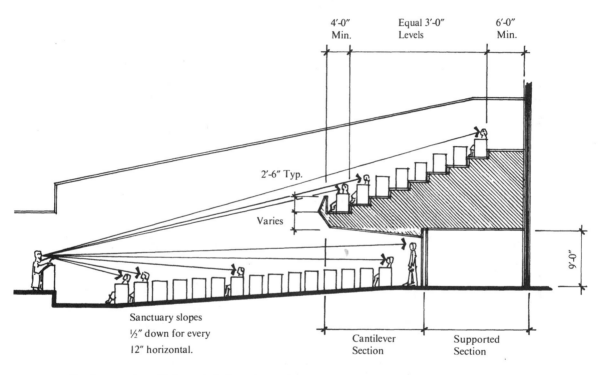

4'-0" Min. Equal 3'-0" Levels 6'-0" Min.

2'-6" Typ.

Varies

9'-0"

Sanctuary slopes
½" down for every
12" horizontal.

Cantilever Section

Supported Section

• Cantilever portion of balcony shall always be equal or less than the supported portion.

FIG. 10-26

communication and belonging, it should be obvious what the problems of balconies can create. A portion of the congregation are spectators. They may feel isolated, intimidated and inconvenienced when it comes to approaching the altar. What's more, balcony seating can be costly, per square foot, with the addition of steps, exits, ramps. and the structure it takes to hold it all up.

If you choose to incorporate a balcony, each row must step up 10 to 14 inches to give the best sight-lines possible. Although regional code requirements may differ, the minimum calls for two enclosed fire stairs to the exterior. Facing the facts, balconies are not recommended unless the congregation seating exceeds 1,000. That's the down side.

Now, for the up side. Balconies are the best overflow space you can provide. And there's an optional and effective way to provide seating for that growing congregation of yours!

The gallery concept is designed to take the balcony seating right onto the floor of the sanctuary. There is no separation from the rest of the congregation or the altar area, since the plan allows aisles that feed directly down to the chancel area. Although the congregation may be large, with the gallery design people can feel just as much a part of the total space as those sitting in the lower level.

Added bonuses: there can be better seating with better sight-lines. Galleries are an effective option for the larger churches. And, aesthetically, a balcony can be a positive feature of the sanctuary design since it provides a dramatic effect in the interior space.

The gallery concept is designed to take the balcony seating right onto the floor of the sanctuary.

Overflow

We've mentioned balconies as a good overflow space. But if your church is growing at the rapid pace you hoped for, you must provide even more space for seating on the lower level. Movable walls, or folding partitions, in areas adjacent to the sanctuary overflow areas always have been a design challenge. Generally, this space is used for educational purposes, but has been designated as a multi-use area for overflow. Folding chairs are readily available with comparable storage space. This technique has served many churches for many years. But there are built-in problems such as acoustics, sight-lines and the feeling of separateness.

Sometimes, even the concourse is utilized for overflow, which may – or may not – violate the fire codes in your area, plus having the drawbacks of acoustics and sight-line.

An option you might want to consider is to convert your fellowship hall into a worship area during these times of increased

Types of Platforms

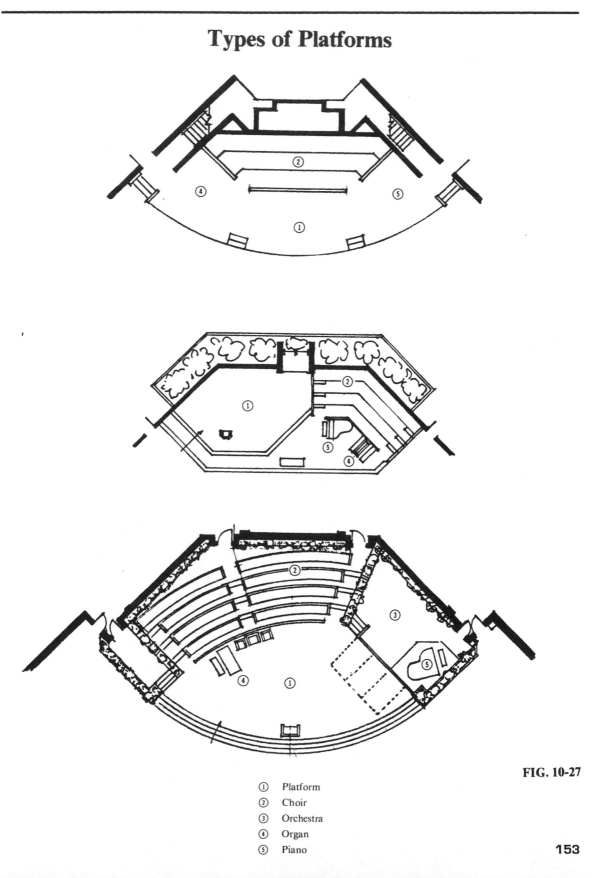

FIG. 10-27

① Platform
② Choir
③ Orchestra
④ Organ
⑤ Piano

Types of Platforms

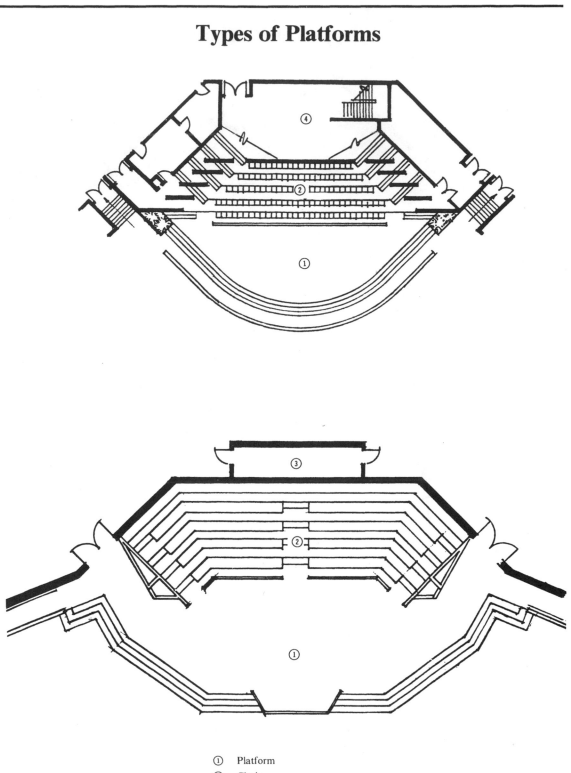

①   Platform
②   Choir
③   Mehcanical Room under Baptistry
④   Choir Robing

FIG. 10-28

Altar

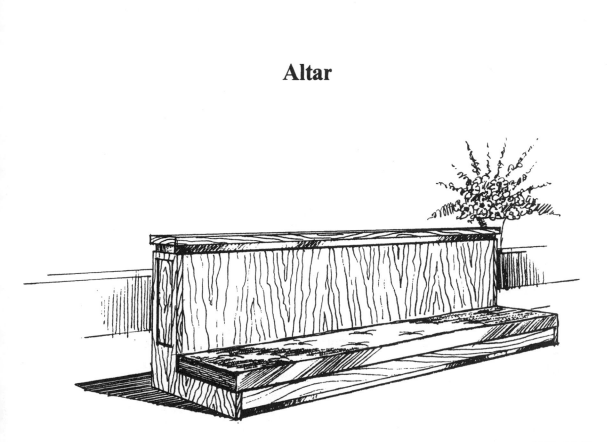

FIG. 10-29

attendance and overcrowding. A closed-circuit television system, along with a church leader for the personal touch, can offer your people a next-to-best participatory experience.

Platform

The center for ministering should be the focal point when designing a sanctuary. The chancel, as it's often defined, is the part of the church which contains the altar, pulpit and seats for the clergy and choir. Arrangements of the various parts of the chancel are discretionary. The customary practice, however, has church leaders ministering from this area, and it must be designed to edify Him while encouraging the congregation to participate.

The platform should be at least nine feet from the front row, with steps for access and elevation above the congregation. The main platform is flat, with an option of different levels for musical instruments and choir. It can be as large as your needs and checkbook allow. If your ministerial staff is large, you'll need adequate seating behind the pulpit. Your music and drama programs will dictate how much space you should provide for special presentations.

The platform should be at least nine feet from the front row, with steps for access and elevation above the congregation.

Pulpit

Although the platform is the focal point of the sanctuary, the pulpit - or lectern - is the main attraction. Designed as the place for ministry and exhortation of God's Word, the pulpit should be in close proximity to the congregation. If the church is very large, and has no sloping floors for good sight-lines, the pulpit needs to be elevated. The best plan is to bring the pulpit and pastor as near to the people as possible, or at least create that illusion. The feeling of rapport is very important for an effective ministry.

Altar

The altar is traditionally the most sacred part of the sanctuary. It is here that people come for confession, prayer, worship and participation of the ritualistic Last Supper. It is sometimes referred to as the communion rail. Located between the congregation and the pulpit, this is designed with denominational preferences in mind, and should be easily accessible to the entire congregation.

Choir

The music program of each church is as diverse as the

languages of Babel's Tower, so the platform area must be planned around your particular ministry.

In many of today's churches, however, the choir is a tool and an integral part of the worship service, rather than an antiquated "voice of the angels" component that is heard but not seen. The choir is used to lead the people in congregational singing and also serves as a performance group for worship music.

In many cases, the total musical ministry of the church includes not only a piano and organ, but an orchestra and area for drama. Whatever is unique to your church's musical thrust, and whatever the size of your choir, you should opt for the best possible placement and shape.

The sound system can make or break the quality performance of your choir. (See Chapter 11.)

The preferred arrangement for the choir is an arched, centrally-placed, behind-the-pulpit location. A good and workable alternative placement is to one side of the platform and pulpit.

Alcove, rear-of-the-church, in-front-of-the-altar, within-the-pews or divided choir seating are possible, but not recommended, options. It's important that the choir is visually and acoustically close to the congregation for effective ministerial and leadership impact.

Choir chairs should be lightweight, movable and stackable, yet comfortable and quiet. Chairs with arms are not recommended for space purposes, but a special place for music folders is a nice bonus for the singers.

The choir row must be three feet in depth, with rows progressively heightened by 12 to 18 inches. A modesty rail in front of the first row of the choir is an option that depends on the design and use of a particular sanctuary platform. It can be an attractive, yet functional, backdrop to the pulpit, while accenting and integrating the finish materials and furniture design.

The choir row must be three feet in depth, with rows progressively heightened by 12 to 18 inches.

Larger churches with choirs of 200 members or more need special considerations. It's no small matter to load and unload the choir loft with this many people, so you need to offer as many functional and aesthetically pleasing entry points as possible. One option is to plan entrances from both sides of the platform, with upper and lower level doors on each side for quick and easy access.

Instruments

The traditional placement of the piano on one side of the choir and the organ console on the other can be nothing short of a musical disaster if your platform is very large and your choir is sprawled out somewhere in-between. Hearing and communication between the musicians can be greatly enhanced in this case by establishing a centrally arranged location close to the choir for both instruments. This design allows the necessary rapport among singers, players and the choir director, with nothing to block vision or hearing.

If you have now, or are anticipating the incorporation of an orchestra in your services, the best space for the instrumental ensemble is in front of the choir to ensure ultimate communications among all the musicians.

An alternative for the orchestra location is between the front pews and the pulpit platform. Sight-line and acoustics are priority concerns in any arrangement and must be expertly addressed by designing engineers. Flexibility needs to be a part of the platform plan if your ministry involves a variety of musical or dramatic presentations. In this case, permanent platforms or risers should be avoided.

Many platform plans call for removable risers and partitions to provide a large, flat and open platform area for special programs. Platforms in many Family Life Center plans are used for storage, with doors placed on the face of the platform. Chairs, tables or any other items can be slid under the platform on portable rolling racks, and stored.

David S. Winkler, owner/director of Psalm 150 Publications, a company specializing in instrumental music for churches and Christian schools, says: "For best results, try to keep the orchestra in a centralized, fan-shaped arrangement as much as possible. In calculating the amount of space needed, plan on an area of at least four feet wide and five feet deep for each player. This will allow the extra space needed for a music stand in front of each chair, as well as the 'elbow room' needed for many instruments such as violins, guitars, and even flutes. In general, plan for space for at least 25 players. This number is based on a minimum instrumentation which would be required for a 'full' orchestra (two flutes, oboe, two clarinets, bassoon or bass clarinet, three trumpets, two horns, three trombones, tuba, four violins, viola, cello, bass, harp, and two percussion.) Remember to leave lots of extra space for percussion and for larger instruments such as harp and double bass."

When you're planning your sanctuary platform area for its various functions, be sure to install enough electric outlets for the microphones and instruments you'll be using.

Many platform plans call for removable risers and partitions to provide a large, flat and open platform area for special programs.

Baptistry

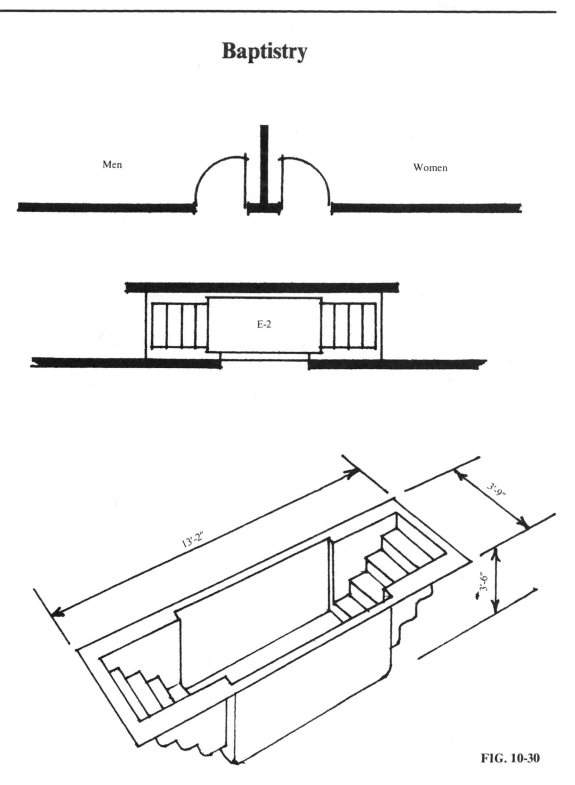

Men

Women

E-2

13'-2"

3'-9"

3'-6"

FIG. 10-30

Choir Practice Room

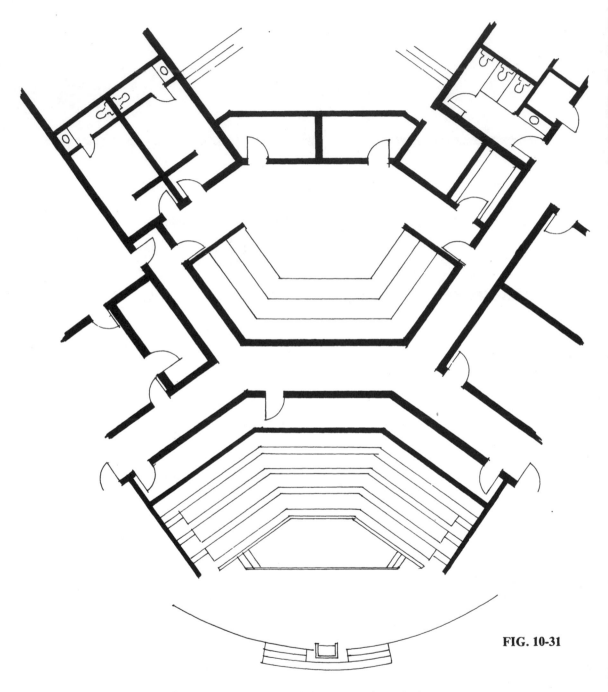

FIG. 10-31

- The configuration of the practice area should be similar to the choir area in the sanctuary.
- In this area there needs to be a room where choir music and robes are stored. When required, this is where a choir office could be located.
- The dressing rooms are where the choir changes into their robes. These areas usually have access to rest rooms.
- The choir should be able to move from the practice room to the sanctuary platform without entering from the front of the sanctuary.

Multi-media

The projection screen is an amenity that often is requested in new building projects and is a feature that adds a great deal to the presentations and flexibilities of the sanctuary. Modern technology offers progressively superior fabrics in screens for high quality viewing. Size and placement of the screen, however, should be determined by the size of your auditorium. Projection machines may be mounted in ceiling and operated from greater distances producing more sophisticated presentations. Lighting dimmer controls, audio provisions and viewing angles should be considered when you're planning for any visual media in your church. We recommend that you evaluate your presentation needs and techniques, and set your budget accordingly. Again, be sure to include electrical outlets for any and all of your multi-media needs.

Baptistry

A denominational option.

The baptismal font is an integral part of the liturgical service. It should be located close to the chancel and in view of the congregation. This unit can be a movable unit or permanently fixed, depending on your needs.

If water immersion is the practice for your denomination, a traditional location for the baptistry is above and behind the choir. The design of your focal platform area, however, can place the baptistry in another area. The main thing is that it's easily seen by everyone in the congregation. We recommend fiberglass baptistries. Why? The companies who manufacture these baptistries offer good service, flexibility, custom design and easy maintenance – plus an excellent guarantee. Participation from the candidate, the minister and the congregation is an important part of this sacred ritual.

An attractive feature for the minister is the baptistry that provides seating in the unit for the candidate while the minister stands behind the baptistry in a dry area. This particular model costs less for water and heating requirements, and allows the pastor to rejoin the church service expeditiously, without the trappings of a soaked, quick-change artist.

Special lighting, microphones and plumbing access should be part of the baptistry design. Your architect knows this, of course. But check on it.

More Support Systems

- Men's and women's dressing rooms should be located close to the baptistry. These spaces could conveniently include such amenities as toilets and safe storage closets for towels, robes

> *Special lighting, microphones and plumbing access should be part of the baptistry design.*

and private possessions. If you can afford the feature, it is much better to separate this function from the public restrooms of your church.

- The choir rehearsal room should allow approximately 14 square feet per person. This will be enough room for robing, robe storage, piano and seating which duplicates the area in the auditorium, including storage for music. The soundproofed choir room needs a separate space to feed in and out of the choir loft, to avoid jamming-up with parishioners on their way to and from church. The route from the choir room to the platform must be easy and direct. Many choir rooms are provided with a music office, music storage space and a library. The choir rehearsal room should be designed with details in mind - even down to the "pigeon holes" where choir members can find their music!

- The vesting room, or sacristy, can be adjacent to the sanctuary if not located in the foyer area. If accommodations require storage for clothing and preparation for communion elements, this space should have sinks, a refrigerator and cabinets. Proper plumbing, please.

- Good acoustics is a must for effective ministry and music in the sanctuary. It's such a big subject, in fact, that we've created a whole chapter for the subject. (It's coming up next.) Sound and lighting in the sanctuary can wreak havoc with your ministry if not properly installed and played out. It's nonsensical to attempt an intelligent explanation here in the planning stages; qualified engineers must be employed with the recommendation of your architect. This is an area, however, of which you should be aware. Make sure nothing goes wrong. Experts are at your fingertips. Use them.

- Sound and signal systems are two more items to put on your check list. These systems may include a nursery call into the sanctuary to signal parents that they should come to the nursery, or a bell and intercom for day care, elementary school and educational areas. Also included may be a five-alarm system and/or smoke detection devices. Requirements usually dictate that these systems are tied into the emergency lighting design. Again, your architect can help choose which system(s) will fit your operational plan and budget, while keeping in mind all national and local code requirements.

Keep the systems simple for operation and maintenance purposes. There should be no confusing signals, so make certain they are clear and audible. A clock system also is an option, and may be coordinated with a building security system. Plan for the church telephone system and equipment - and anticipate growth.

Other sound and signal systems we recommend including

The choir rehearsal room should allow approximately 14 square feet per person.

are television and computers, whether they are utilized for television production engineering or for learning experiences in the class room. Church administrative areas use computers for more efficiency in bookkeeping, mailings and member outreach. Provide cabinet space or mechanical/electrical closets or rooms to house the technical equipment. Design this space to be accessible, whether it is in conduit or in computer-raised floors.

All systems can be integrated with the church plans, and examined in closer detail as the architectural/engineering plans develop.

We have illustrated many individual elements within the sanctuary, each having its own vital importance. A successful and gratifying worship service is the goal. This can be achieved with clear, concise planning and placement of the all the "pieces."

Your growing church has proven that "getting together" is in God's plan. If delineations and demands are in line with your budget at this point, the plan for your future sanctuary should have His special stamp of approval!

Provide cabinet space or mechanical/electrical closets or rooms to house the technical equipment.

Bethel Church
Los Angeles, California
An example of gallery seating

11

SIGHT AND SOUND

State-of-the-art planning for acoustics and lighting

Good sight and sound in worship spaces can produce dramatic improvements in the ministry.

There was only one Man in time, during only one time in the ages, whose messages were meant to be, and often were, predictably obscure.

Through Isaiah, He said: "Though you hear my words repeatedly, you won't understand them. Though you watch...as I perform my miracles, still you won't know what they mean..." (Isaiah 6:9, TLB).

But Jesus Himself let us know in no uncertain terms that "All that is now hidden will someday come to light. If you have ears, listen! And be sure to put into practice what you hear. The more you do this, the more you will understand what I tell you" (Mark 4:22-24, TLB).

With pronouncements like these to assimilate, today's churches and preachers of the Word have enough to do without built-in design distractions for "watching" and "understanding!"

Good sight and sound in worship spaces can produce dramatic improvements in the ministry. Believe us, it won't matter how magnificent the sanctuary looks if its lost in the haze of poor lighting. And who wants to strain their ears – or cover them in self-defense – for even the most dynamic of messages?

The place of worship, praise and exhortation should provide a total, spiritual experience that will be both inviting and compelling. For full effectiveness, special acoustical and lighting attention must be directed to each room and all connecting spaces.

With professional planning and installation, your church's interior environment can be a real comfort to the soul – and the senses!

Acoustics

This suspicious-sounding word is quite innocent, basically. It has the nice qualities of determining the ability of an auditorium to reflect sound waves for clear, distinct hearing. It's well-meaning, too, since it defines the science of dealing with production, control, transmission, reception and effects of sound.

But don't be misled. There are rooms with good acoustics and there are bad ones. Acoustical culprits are waiting in the wings of nearly every church auditorium plan. Get rid of them now, in the designing stage! They have no place in the sanctuary where people must "listen, for the life of your soul is at stake" (Isaiah 55:3, TLB).

Proper acoustical design is a "must" in the worship center for proper reflection patterns, as well as appropriate noise levels and sense of reverberance. To achieve the balance you need, here are some up-front decisions to be made - in order - after you have determined the number of seats needed in your new auditorium:

1. Platform arrangement and design.
2. Distance to farthest listener, ceiling height, and volume.
3. Wall, ceiling and floor design (e.g. dimensions, shape).
4. Wall, ceiling and floor surface materials.
5. Organ and requirements.
6. Type of sound reinforcing system.
7. Location of speakers.

Before you begin to decide on any of these items, please read ahead, since answering one question affects the answers for the rest of the questions.

Acoustical culprits are waiting in the wings of nearly every church auditorium plan.

Direct sound

Direct sound starts at a source, such as a speaker, singer or instrument, and is transmitted by longitudinal pressure waves through the air. This type of acoustical radiant energy is measured by the decibel (dB). The intensity of sound ranges from 0 (absolute quiet) to 120 (for a large jet 200 feet away), and to 195 (for 50 pounds of TNT exploding 10 feet away). For comparison's sake, a comfortable level for normal speech conversation is 60 to 70 dB.

Direct sound predictably decreases in intensity as it travels from the originating source, creating obvious limitations in hearing at long distances. For example, sound pressure may only decrease 10 dB at 10 feet from a source, but decreases 30 dB at 100 feet from the same source. This is where reverberant sound comes into play. As you move away from a sound source in a room, direct sound decreases and reverberant sound increases.

Reverberant sound

In simple terms, reverberation time is the length of time (measured in tenths of seconds) it takes for a sound to decay, or die away, 60 dB in the room. Since reverberant sound may bounce several times from the ceiling, walls and floor before it ever reaches the ears of the listeners, it can produce a tremendous fullness of quality – especially in music.

But don't confuse reverberance with echoes. If reverberance hangs on too long, the innocent parishioner may hear an irritating repetition of sounds. Loud echoes reflecting into the seating areas indicate bad acoustical design. Echoes color the sound and raise the potential for feedback. To prevent this diabolical invasion, an acoustical analysis should be performed, taking into account the size, shape and coverings of the wall, floor and ceiling. The location of the speakers must also be considered to avoid creating electronic echoes. Many choices should be made early in the planning stage to ensure a natural reverberant field without causing damaging echoes.

A room with an abundance of hard surfaces, such as brick, stone, uncarpeted floors, or a very large interior volume will have a long reverberation time. This is known as a "live" room. Gothic-type cathedrals are examples.

A room with surfaces covered with carpet, acoustical tile ceilings and drapes naturally will have a shorter reverberation time. These "dead" rooms usually have less than one-second reverb time; recording studios are a good example.

So now, what?

Since a church service can offer everything from speaking, choir music, soloists, instrumental music and congregational singing to drama and televised programs, there are opportunities for great variety in your acoustical needs.

However, each single sound source has a desired balance of direct to reverberant sound that doesn't necessarily match the others. For instance, while long reverberation time will blur the sound of speech, it's great for music – especially the organ. It also adds a deep richness to the tonal qualities of your auditorium.

For pragmatic and problem-solving purposes, let's begin by establishing some "ideals" in reverberation time.

A room with an abundance of hard surfaces...will have a long reverberation time.

Speech:	Less than 1.5 seconds
Congregational singing	1.6 seconds
Choir	1.8 seconds
Instruments	1.4 to 3.0 seconds
Drama	.8 to 1.4 seconds
Organ	More than 3.0 seconds

Room Acoustics: Reflection, Diffusion and Diffraction

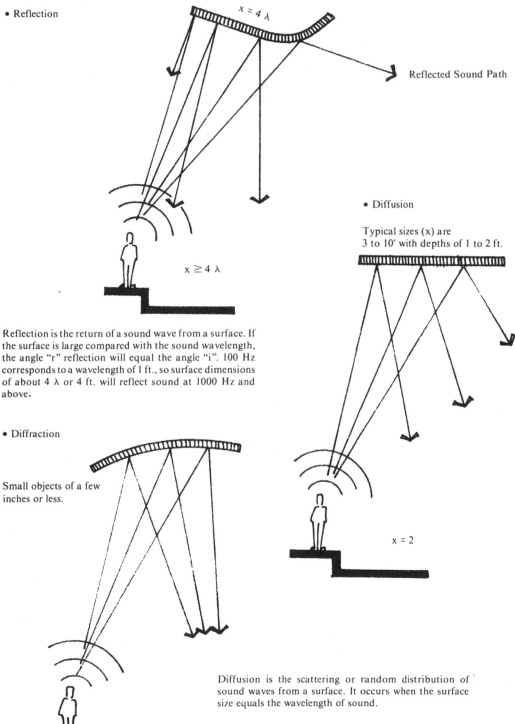

- Reflection

$x = 4\lambda$

Reflected Sound Path

$x \geq 4\lambda$

Reflection is the return of a sound wave from a surface. If the surface is large compared with the sound wavelength, the angle "r" reflection will equal the angle "i". 100 Hz corresponds to a wavelength of 1 ft., so surface dimensions of about 4 λ or 4 ft. will reflect sound at 1000 Hz and above.

- Diffusion

Typical sizes (x) are 3 to 10′ with depths of 1 to 2 ft.

$x = 2$

- Diffraction

Small objects of a few inches or less.

$x < 2$

Diffusion is the scattering or random distribution of sound waves from a surface. It occurs when the surface size equals the wavelength of sound.

Diffraction is the bending or "flowing" of a sound wave around an object (or through an opening).

FIG. 11-1

167

Optimum Reverberation at 500/1000 Hz for Auditoriums and Similar Facilities

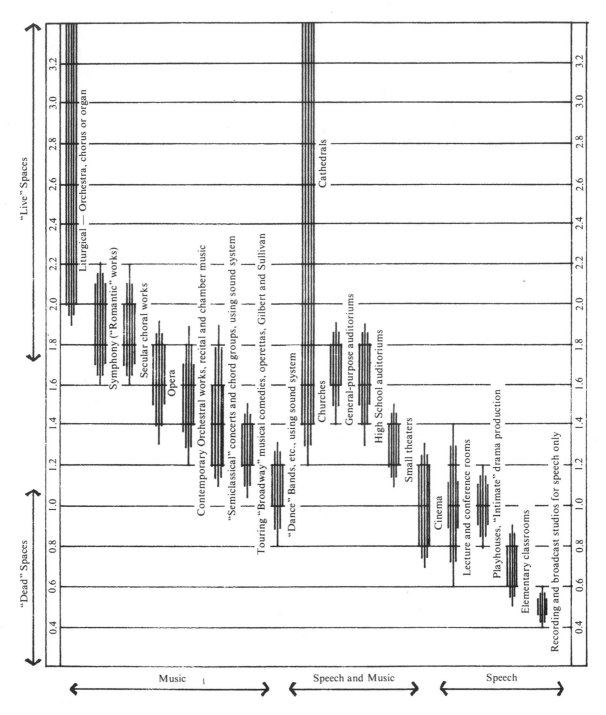

Note: In general, larger rooms should be nearer the top of the reverberation time ranges than smaller rooms of the same type.

FIG. 11-2

Which is best for your sanctuary? Looks like there is no one best answer. Not to worry. This is what acoustical consultants deal with every day – maintaining effective "liveness" for music while maintaining high speech intelligibility (ease of understanding).

Much of the acoustical planning depends on the "style" of your church's service. Evangelical fellowships are more inclined to combine platform performance with audience participation, which needs a careful acoustical balance. For instance, too much drapery and other heavy sound-absorbing materials may "deaden" what you had hoped would be at least "moderately live" church services. Communicate with the experts on who you are and what you want to achieve. They'll make it work.

Auditoriums, 500 or less occupancy

In a small sanctuary or any other room with highly reflective surfaces, the level of reverberant sound can surpass direct sound many times, causing a loss of speech intelligibility. So avoid straight, parallel walls at all costs. Why? They are reflecting – keeping the sound bouncing back and forth creating "flutter echo" and standing waves. Standing waves are sound waves of one frequency that sustain as the reverberant sound naturally decays. This occurs in a room where there is not an even diffusion (spreading) of sound. These standing waves cause abnormalities in the tonal quality of different areas in a room.

We suggest a hard-surfaced, uncarpeted choir loft.

We suggest a hard-surfaced, uncarpeted choir loft. Everything behind the speaker's position – walls, floors and ceiling – should be reflective also. In fact, the first two-thirds of the auditorium should be treated as areas to reflect sound energy into the rear area to help overcome distance and absorption loss.

Auditoriums, 500 or more occupancy

With increased volume comes an increased reverberation time. This means that due to the increased reverb time, acoustic speech intelligibility will lessen, and the installation of a reinforcing sound system is essential in order to maintain clear understanding of speech. To improve audio and visual communication, we suggest designing the auditorium to bring the audience "around" the platform so that the furthest seat is no more than 100 feet away. Galleries extending from the main floor up to the balcony should be used when the platform width exceeds 65 feet. Galleries will not only provide additional seating but also help to provide early reflections off the side walls to improve the reverberant field.

Room Acoustics: Distribution of Reflected Sound

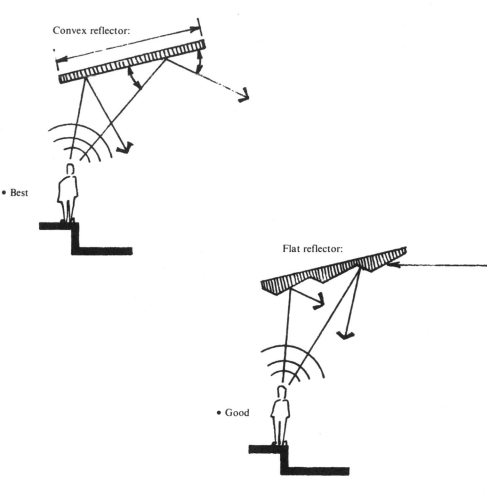

Convex reflector:

• Best

Flat reflector:

• Good

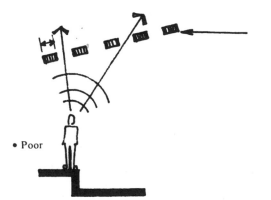

Concave reflector:

• Poor

Convex and flat-shaped hard-surfaced building elements can be effective sound-distributing forms.

Concave sound-reflecting surfaces can focus sound causing echoes.

FIG. 11-3

All auditoriums

The shape of the sanctuary plays a big role in the acoustical qualities of any church. Be sure to avoid buildings that are shaped like domes, circles and squares due to the inherent acoustical problems of these particular room designs. Proper blending of materials and wall surface designs will result in a good balance for sound reflection and dispersion.

In the platform area, a good basic rule is to design the walls, ceiling and surface finishes to reflect sound into all parts of the room except back onto the stage. An oak or tile floor, with carpet limited – at most – to the rostrum area, is ideal. The height of levels in the choir area should be a minimum of nine inches. Twelve to 15 inches is best. A lower ceiling above the stage is recommended. Excessive sound reflections and echoes can be prevented by applying acoustically-absorbent materials on the rear walls of the auditorium. Also, you may reshape the rear walls or ceiling for downward reflection of sound into the rear seats.

Pew seats and backs should be upholstered to help the room maintain a fairly constant reverberant field even when there are many empty seats. For even better results, use carpet or cork in the aisles, but put tile under the pews. Select carpet early since the fabric weight and color are important acoustical – and lighting – factors. For best results, we recommend a short, closely woven fabric with no backing, and glued down.

If the audience is seated on one level, not only is it difficult to see the speaker, but most of the sound is absorbed above and around the heads of the audience. A raised platform and raked or sloping floors in the auditorium are necessary for proper visual contact.

The balcony and the underbalcony need special acoustical attention. If the initial sanctuary design calls for a future balcony installation, keep the entire acoustical picture in mind when you're planning. Ideally, balconies should be only as' deep as the ceiling is high above or under the balcony. The maximum depth of a balcony should never exceed twice the balcony ceiling height.

Since these areas tend to make the parishioner feel as if he is in a much smaller area, the balcony and underbalcony area should be designed as "live" as possible. Hard ceilings with an upward slope toward the platform are essential. One also must be able to sit on the back row and have a clear line of sight from the speaker cluster to the middle of the podium.

Peripheral rooms

Audio production rooms, classrooms, multi-purpose rooms,

A lower ceiling above the stage is recommended.

171

Room Acoustics: Ceiling Shapes

Flat Ceiling

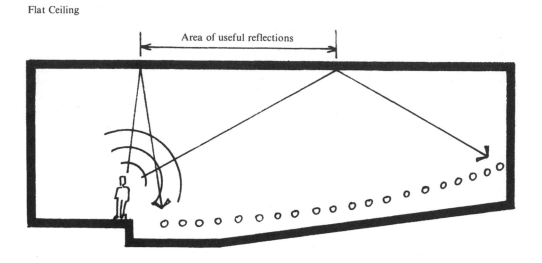

Reoriented Ceiling

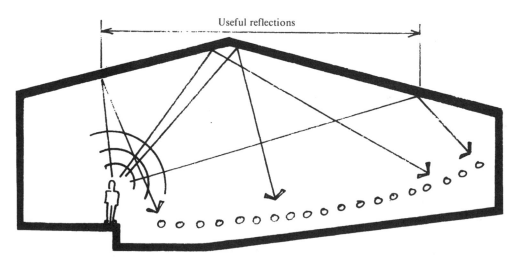

FIG. 11-4

Room Acoustics: Rear Wall Echo Control Treatments

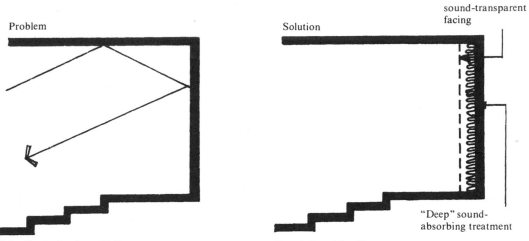

Problem

Echo Producing Rear Wall

Solution

Protective sound-transparent facing

"Deep" sound-absorbing treatment

Sound Absorbing Treatment

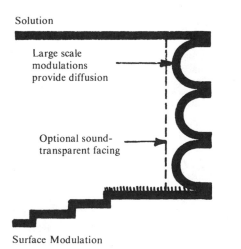

Solution

Large scale modulations provide diffusion

Optional sound-transparent facing

Surface Modulation

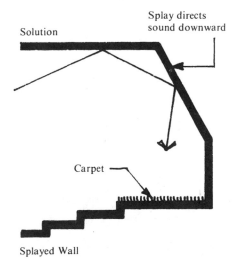

Solution

Splay directs sound downward

Carpet

Splayed Wall

FIG. 11-5

Room Acoustics: Audience Seating

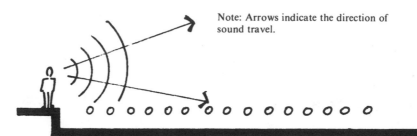

Note: Arrows indicate the direction of sound travel.

A. Sound level outdoors falls off with distance and from audience attenuation or grazing off the seated audience.

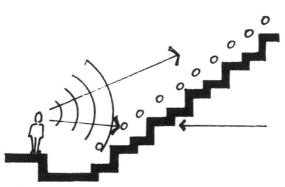

Sloped seating reduces audience attenuation, and provides good sight lines.

B. Sound level falls off only with distance.

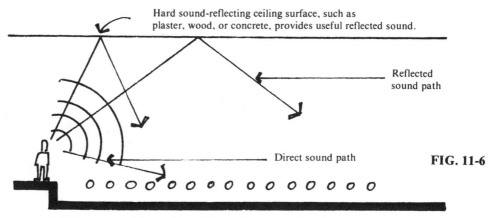

Hard sound-reflecting ceiling surface, such as plaster, wood, or concrete, provides useful reflected sound.

Reflected sound path

Direct sound path

FIG. 11-6

C. Reflected sound from ceiling reinforces direct sound level indoors.

Room Acoustics: Balcony Design

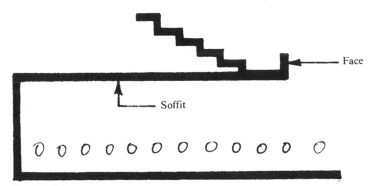

Poor Design

Persons seated deep under a balcony cannot receive
useful reflected sound from the ceiling and will hear poorly.

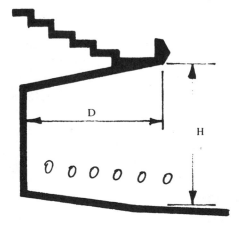

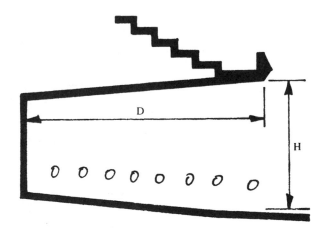

Designed for Music
   For best music sound D should not exceed H.
Symphony music requires considerable reveberant
sound as well as diffusion of the sound.

Speech and Music
   Distance D should not exceed 2H for best sound.
For both situations, soffits should be sloped and
faces should be angled to reflect sound to listeners.

In halls where there is a central loudspeaker system,
all persons should have a line of sight to speaker cluster.

FIG. 11-7

chapels, choir rooms and offices also need special attention to acoustical design. Achieving a correct and comfortable reverberation time or diffusion of sound waves is the goal in each case. The shape of rooms, acoustical walls, ceiling and floor coverings, adjustable panels and furnishings all will play a part in the ultimate acoustical design. One special consideration, however, is in the choir rehearsal room. This space, though different in volume, should acoustically approximate the sanctuary for obvious reasons. If the choir room is also used for recording, movable or adjustable wall panels can be installed to accommodate the varied room functions. Once again, rely on a consultant to design this room.

High noise levels

No matter how cloistered you think you'll be in your new church building, there are certain clamorous marauders that are bound to invade your space! Some of them are from the outside, such as airplane and automobile traffic noise. Others – air conditioners, organ blowers, motors, pumps, even hallways and foyers – come with the territory. Wherever these noisy nuisances originate, they have the potential of seriously effecting the ability of your audience to understand what they came to hear!

In the initial planning stages, there must be an acoustical design level for the maximum allowable noise. Specify a maximum noise curve (NC) of 30. However, a NC of 25 or – even better – 20, would be ideal for a church. This lets your engineer and architect know that you want a quiet auditorium.

Here are some practical suggestions for reducing noise:

> *Air conditioners should be placed on isolating pads.*

- Air conditioners should be placed on isolating pads. Ducts should be lined with an acoustically-absorbent material. Flexible duct connections should be used.
- Never allow rooftop units to blow directly into a room. Offset return air louvers from each other.
- Increase the mass of construction with thicker walls or, preferably, double walls with dead air space between them.
- Extend walls to the roof, or build sound dividers above the ceiling to avoid sound transmission over the top of a wall.
- Use precision fittings, solid-core construction, and by all means, no air louvers to prevent sound from traveling under or through a door.
- Prevent sound interference caused by too much "liveness" in hallways or stairwells by using carpet and acoustically-treated walls and ceilings.
- Double-glazing is a good deterrent to sound transmission. Use laminated glass or double glass with air space between to deter

Mechanical System Noise and Vibrations: Vibrating Equipment

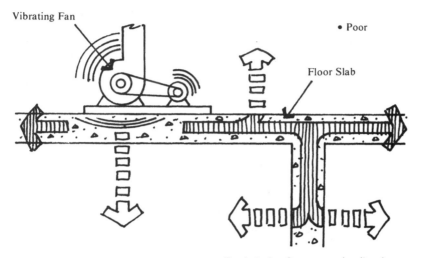

Vibrating Fan

• Poor

Floor Slab

Fan bolted to floor transmits vibrations directly into structure.

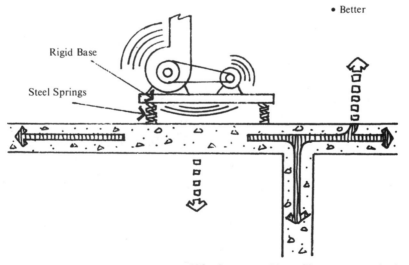

• Better

Rigid Base

Steel Springs

If fan is supported by resilient mounts and relocated close to structural column. Fan continues to vibrate, but "structure-borne" sound is reduced considerably.

FIG. 11-8

Sound Isolation: Ceilings

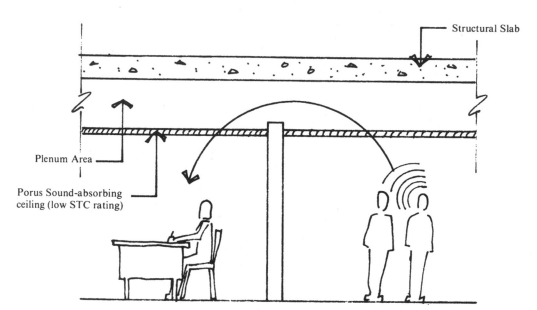

Structural Slab

Plenum Area

Porus Sound-absorbing
ceiling (low STC rating)

Ceiling Flanking

Prevent ceiling flanking by using high STC sound-absorbing
materials, or use construction details shown below.

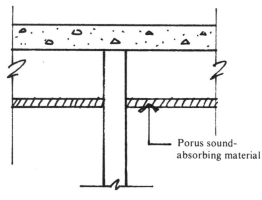

Porus sound-
absorbing material

A. Partition extended to slab

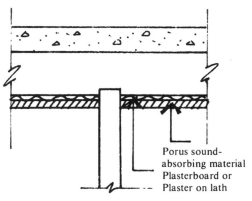

Porus sound-
absorbing material
Plasterboard or
Plaster on lath

B. Plaster backing

FIG 11-9

Room Acoustics: Echo Control

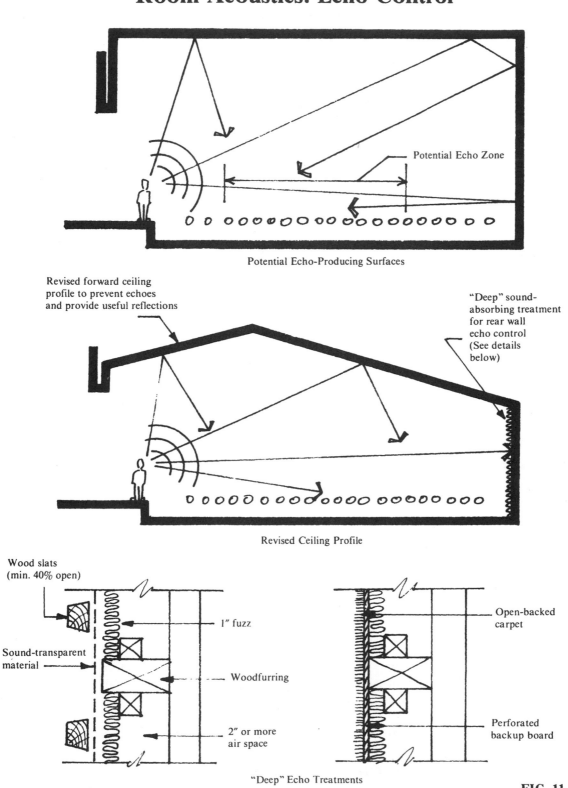

Potential Echo-Producing Surfaces

Potential Echo Zone

Revised forward ceiling profile to prevent echoes and provide useful reflections

"Deep" sound-absorbing treatment for rear wall echo control (See details below)

Revised Ceiling Profile

Wood slats (min. 40% open)

Sound-transparent material

1" fuzz

Woodfurring

2" or more air space

Open-backed carpet

Perforated backup board

"Deep" Echo Treatments

FIG. 11-10

179

sound transmission.

The best wall material for good sound absorption is a medium density fiberglass batt insulation (similar to Owens-Corning 703) with a decorative fabric stretched over it. Grill cloth or any porous material that will let the sound, trapping it by the fiberglass, can be used. This is a great solution for reducing reflections bouncing off the back wall toward the platform. Also, this can be used in equipment rooms to "trap" noise in those rooms. Sometimes these panels may need to be built out from the wall three to five inches to allow even more absorption.

Sound systems

No matter how elaborate or expensive a sound system you buy for the church, it may as well stay packed in the boxes unless the rest of the criteria for a good acoustical environment are met. Don't kid yourself. A state-of-the-art sound system won't always compensate for poor room acoustics.

A state-of-the-art sound system won't always compensate for poor room acoustics.

American Audio, Inc., based in Ruston, Louisiana, is a nationally-known firm, recognized for excellence in planning, designing and installing sound systems. The company is a consultant for R. Messner Construction and has also worked and consulted with a variety of acoustical design firms, including Coffeen-Anderson of Kansas City, Kansas, and Joiner-Rose in Dallas, Texas. Jim Young, president of American Audio, Inc. gives this advice:

"Four basic elements must be considered to help determine what is the 'best' sound system for a particular congregation. They are:

- Style of worship
- Auditorium acoustics and configuration
- Flexibility desired in system operation
- Budget constraints

"Let's look into each of these areas for more detail.

"The basic requirements of the sound system vary from denomination to denomination. Each one of us has his own style of worship and praise. Some may have a full orchestra with a 500-voice choir, while others have a pipe organ with a 25-voice choir. Others may have more contemporary instrumentation with drums, electronic instruments, and separate microphones for each singer on the platform. Some have ministers who prefer to stand behind the podium to deliver their message, while others prefer to use a wireless hand-held mic while ministering in the congregation.

"Each of these (methods) may require different features of operation and sound pressure capability. For example, a church with organ-type music may only require an average of 80-85 decibels, while a more contemporary service with a full band may hit peaks of 105 decibels, or more. A consultant or experienced contractor will be able to help determine your exact needs.

"The next element is not always the easiest question to answer. The acoustics and configuration of the sanctuary are the elements that are the hardest to 'fix' with the sound system. As we stated earlier, 'A good system doesn't fix a poor room.' Extreme care should be taken when designing all aspects of your sanctuary, or you may never enjoy the full potential of worship in your building.

"Central cluster systems are still the first choice for any building where the understanding of speech is the most important need. A central cluster is a group of speakers normally located at the ceiling in front of the pulpit. Each speaker, or group of speakers, is then aimed and balanced, to provide even sound coverage of the seating areas while trying to avoid 'splattering' sound on the walls. As you can see, it is easier to adjust the sound system design to allow for 'live' sanctuary acoustics and not harm speech when using a central cluster.

Central cluster systems are still the first choice.

"Low ceilings are a poor choice for optimum acoustics in most buildings. If the ceiling is too low, a split cluster or several clusters may have to be used. In a very deep building –100 feet or more – time-delayed clusters or ceiling speakers may be needed for consistent sound levels in the rear of the sanctuary. Remember, in order to keep the sound associated with its source, a cluster should never be more than 40 feet above the platform floor.

"If your sanctuary has a long reverb time, larger speakers with high directivity (Q) may have to be used for the best speech intelligibility. Speakers with a medium or low Q may be used if your room have a low reverb time. Speaker type and location may also be influenced by items suspended above the congregations such as chandeliers or decorative objects. Light paths for platform lighting must also be taken into consideration when designing the system; however, it is usually less detrimental to move lights than to move the sound system.

"One of the sometimes-easier, yet more involved, elements in system design is the flexibility of operation. When you complete the description of your type of worship to the consultant, you should also list the capabilities, options, and flexibility that you want in your system. You might call this your 'Wish List.' This list should include the number and type of microphones and monitors (platform speakers) required by different individuals on the stage. Each person – whether he is the minister, music leader, choir member or

Sound Control Room:

One-Story Churches

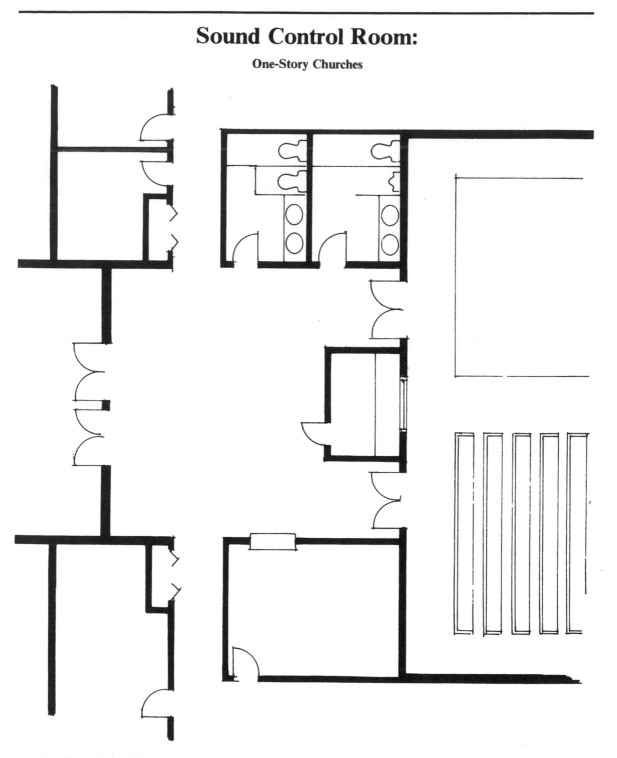

1. **Sound Control Room**

    For one story churches or fellowship halls the sound control room is usually located at the back of the sanctuary, with access into the entrance foyer. This allows access to the sound control room without disturbing the sanctuary.

FIG. 11-11

Sound Control Room:

A Church With a Balcony

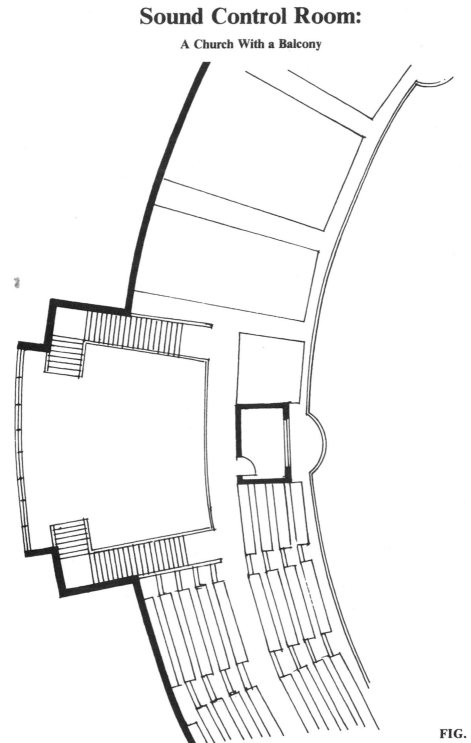

FIG. 11-12

1. **Sound Control Room**
   In a church with a balcony the sound control room would be located on the balcony. This would allow an overview that would help in the monitoring of the sanctuary below.

2. **T.V.-Sound Station**
   At various points along the edge of the balcony there would be T.V.-sound stations.

instrumentalist – has special, yet different needs. The most difficult problem to resolve is the difference between the 'Wish List' and the bottom-line budget.

"Be sure to involve your sound operator in this process since he may have a very valuable insight. He will be able to determine the number of microphones that are used at the same time to decide the number of inputs needed for your mixer. Also, you need to have a diagram showing optimum locations for your mic and monitor uses in your building. The number of different monitor 'mixes' and changes required during a service will determine if you need a separate monitor mixer located near the stage, or if you simply need more monitor mixes on the sanctuary mixing console located in the sound room or booth.

"Other considerations to be made include requirements for broadcast (television) audio, recording rooms, choir rooms and remote rooms such as the fellowship hall and gymnasium. Separate isolated mixing consoles are usually required when broadcasting or doing studio-type recording. Audience mics, multi-track recorders, and compressors are other possible needs. If you are building a room designated for broadcast audio or recording, be sure to have the consultant design it for proper acoustics also. The costs will be far offset by the difference in quality of the audio mixed in these rooms."

The bottom line

"Probably the one problem that all of us have had to deal with at one time or another is budget limitations. When a system design exceeds the financial capacity of the church, most well-meaning people look for a 'cheaper' bid. The truth is, 'You get what you pay for.' If you find your church in a situation like this, work with the consultant to see if there are any 'frills' that are not essential to the proper operation of the system. Look at the frequency with which you use things such as wireless mics, digital effects and large mixing consoles. Sometimes these items are needed only once or twice a year. If this is the case, it is best to rent these items instead of buying. Also, a $16,000, 32-channel mixing console may work just as well as a $34,000, 32-channel console, but without all the bells and whistles. The best rule is to use your - and your consultant's - best judgment.

"Now that you have answered all of the consultant's questions, it is time to place some specification requirements in the perfor-mance capability part of the design. Following are some generally accepted standards for system performance:

1. "There must be even distribution of the reinforced sound

The most difficult problem to resolve is the difference between the "Wish List" and the bottom-line budget.

throughout the entire seating area, typically plus or minus three dB front-to-back, and side-to-side for the one-octave band centered at 4,000 Hz. Total variation from the worst to the best seat should not exceed plus or minus four dB. (This guarantees that everyone will have the same sound volume, no matter where they sit in the auditorium.)

2. "Provide uniform frequency response (tonal quality) throughout the seating area. Typically, plus or minus three dB across the main seating area as measured with one-third-octave bands of pink noise. System response should basically be flat from 50 to 10,000 Hz while rolling off at two dB per octave above that. The system should be capable of 50 to 20,000 Hz.

3. "Provide high intelligibility of speech and music at each seat with no more than 15 percent ALcons (articulation loss of consonants). This means that the system will enable you to understand every word that is spoken or sung over the system.

4. "Provide adequate dynamic range at an acoustic distortion level sufficiently low enough to ensure minimum listening fatigue. The system should be capable of delivering *dB-SPL average program level with an additional 10-dB-SPL peaking margin to any seat in the audience area at an acoustical distortion level below five percent total harmonic distortion (thd). (This provides you with clean, undistorted sound even at the loudest part of your service.) Insert the correct level for your church:

> 80, for light organ music and small choirs;
> 85, for traditional music with piano, organ, and
>   medium-sized choirs;
> 90, for large choirs with full orchestra or a small band;
> 95, for charismatic services with full bands.

Provide uniform frequency response (tonal quality) throughout the seating area.

5. "The system must provide the specified volume before 'feedback,' commonly called potential acoustic gain (pag). This ensures that the system will not go into feedback before the congregation is able to clearly hear the program. The acoustical consultant will be able to calculate the 'pag' needed based on the acoustical design of the sanctuary.

6. "Alignment of the loudspeaker array(s) shall be performed physically, and then converged electronically using the Tecron TEF analyzer or comparable test equipment. The electronic delay unit shall be adjusted so that no signal delay greater than 20 microseconds shall exist at any seat within the minus six dB coverage pattern of any two speakers in the array. In other words, all parts of the cluster work together for a uniform sound. This reduces feedback potential and increases speech intelligibility.

7. "Further convergence of the array shall be performed, using the same test equipment in conjunction with the electronic delay to provide maximum phase coherence between the low-frequency and high-frequency components of the array. (This is similar to six, except this refers to speakers generating different parts of the audio spectrum.)

8. "The system should be free of noticeable noise, hum, ground loops, short circuits, parasitic oscillations, and instability of any form, including RF interference.

"If this seems complex - it is! Sound and acoustics is an exact science. There is no guesswork. This is why you must have an experienced consultant work with you to design the system that will best fit your needs.

Sound and acoustics is an exact science. There is no guesswork.

"Look for firms who stay up with the times, and who are members of professional organizations such as Synergetic Audio Concepts, the National Sound and Communications Association, and the Audio Engineering Society. Also, make sure that they have at least one experienced consultant working on your project who is familiar with your specific needs. Be wise, and check with their previous clients who had needs similar to yours before you engage a consultant or contractor."

Lighting

Now here is a word we can all understand. But don't be fooled. A comprehensive lighting design for your entire church should come from the drawing board of a qualified electrical engineer who has done many church designs and, in turn, will work cooperatively with the architect, designers and building contractor.

Utilitarian and architectural lighting must complement each other. There should be a blend of accent aesthetic lighting with actual necessary functional lighting. Keep in mind, however, that 'the degree' of lighting changes from room to room shouldn't be drastic, although they will vary according to the rooms' functions.

There is a wide range of criteria to consider, also, such as scalar and working range illuminance, surface brightness, glare limitations, directional emphasis and, of course, maintenance.

But lighting engineering should be kept simple. Lighting is energy. Energy moves in wave lengths, and these wave lengths have color characteristics. Standard fluorescent lamps have white light; mercury vapor lamps have clear-blue; and sodium lamps have a yellow hue. This is important to remember when selecting wall, carpet and pew colors, since the type of light which shines on those colors and finishes will affect how the colors are perceived.

Foyer, concourse, hallways, stairways and exits

In these areas, the possible uses for lighting are:

■ General. Recessed down-lighters or surface-mounted lights can be installed in a relatively low ceiling. For a higher ceiling, as in the foyer, a suspended multi-lamp luminary (chandelier) can be utilized.

■ Highlighting structural design features and signs. Upward directional spot lights, wall washes, underlighting and luminaires (wall lamps) are options.

■ Display and exhibition. Use tracklights or swivel fittings at an approximate 40-degree angle.

■ Functional. Any communication areas, such as information or telephone booths, should be serviced with higher local intensity, downward spots or floodlights with an approximate 70-degree angle.

■ Safety. Install emergency lights at exits, stairways, steps, in the foyer and along the concourse or hallways.

Just as sound and acoustical quality can be measured and identified, so can light – and light quality. Color temperature is measured in degrees Kelvin. Light is reflected just as sound waves are reflected. However, instead of the hard and soft surfaces we're concerned with in acoustical design, black and white surfaces measure the quantity of light being emitted, transmitted, or reflected in lumens. A foot candle is the basic unit of illumination arriving at a work plane. One foot candle is equal to one lumen per square foot. The following is a list of accepted standards by the industry for proper lighting in certain areas:

Just as sound and acoustical quality can be measured and identified, so can light – and light quality.

Task	Minimum footcandles
Auditoriums	
Social activities	5
Assembly	15
Exhibitions	30
Basketball	
Regulation	50
Recreation	30
Ordinary reading	30
Study areas (long periods)	70
Sunday School classrooms	30
Offices	50-70
Kitchens	50-70
Corridors	20
Outdoor parking lots	.5 to 1

Offices and classrooms

Lighting should be soft, glare-free, evenly distributed and adequate for reading and studying. Fluorescent lighting can be used in nurseries and toddlers' classrooms.

Sanctuary

Up front, we recommend that fluorescent lighting should not be used. Otherwise, the lighting design for a church auditorium should meet several requirements:

We recommend that fluorescent lighting should not be used.

- Illumination must be at a level that avoids contrasts and claustrophobia, while at the same time is conducive to concentration. Beware of "the mego factor." (Mego is an acronym for "mine eyes glaze over" and can easily produce a dazed boredom in the beholder!) Sanctuary lighting should have the capabilities of being dimmed or increased, according to the activity in progress. If dimming equipment is not properly shielded and grounded, it could cause trouble with the sound system.
- Avoid glare and reflection from any surfaces, windows or light fixtures. Maintain a good balance between lighting, surfaces and color coordination.
- Install the required emergency exit lighting.
- Certain types of air-handling luminaires can remove lighting heat for energy-saving purposes.
- The sanctuary's total design should include specialized stage lighting for music and drama productions. Television broadcasts or video recording systems also require theatrical lighting and controls which allow variation of light colors, intensity and direction. Racks for hanging the fixtures can be incorporated in the ceiling design with a moderate degree of inconspicuousness. All specialized stage lighting must be equipped with a dimming control. A word of caution: do not confuse the quality of lighting with the quantity of lighting. The quality has to do with the ratios of diffusion, uniformity and chromaticity of lighting.
- The larger the sanctuary, the more important it is to have a high ceiling reflectance to aid in diffusing light. Also, ceiling decoration in large auditoriums comes more naturally into the field of vision, so the design and installation of fixtures is important. To avoid glare, or reflection of light from any other specialized lighting source, the ceiling decoration should have no mirror-like, or specular, qualities. There is a variety of luminaires, or light sources. They all can be used to create effective and aesthetic lighting design. Light distribution can occur through indirect, semi-direct/general diffusing/direct and focal direct. These light fixtures may be selected based on elements including task,

ceiling height and wall dimension.

- Wall surfaces are an important consideration in the effect of lighting and atmosphere. In a smaller sanctuary, a high chroma paint or wall covering should be avoided, since it tends to have the effect of dominating, and at the same time diminishing the size of the room, as well as altering the distribution of light. A large auditorium can handle bolder wall decorations with less irritating effect on the eyes and the illumination. If indirect lighting is used on sanctuary walls, they must have a well-finished, non-specular surface for a balanced shading effect.

- In general, visual performance increases with object brightness. A great deal depends on the background against which an object is viewed, and the consequent contrast in brightness between the object and its surroundings. Ideally, the brightness of the task should be the same as that of the background. A person behind the pulpit should not be silhouetted by a light background, or brightened by a black background.

Good lighting and acoustical systems in your church are a productive pair. For a reasonable amount of wisely-invested dollars, they'll work for you every time – with big results. After all, so goes the old German proverb, "The eyes believe themselves; the ears believe other people."

A person behind the pulpit should not be silhouetted by a light background, or brightened by a black background.

Deliverance Church
Philadelphia, Pennsylvania

12

Business ...
As Usual

Blessed for success with proper administrative space

In other chapters, we discuss the process of creating spaces that best serve people – the ones who come to your church for learning, listening, worship and fellowship. And justifiably so, since the primary purpose for building anything is to facilitate the functions for which the structure is designed.

No less important, however, is the designated space in the building for administration of business.

"Business?" you ask, askance. "Just how much room do we need for record-keeping and pastoral consultation? We'd rather spend money on sanctuary and educational space. Besides, we really don't think of this as a business."

Well, think again. The operation of a church is a business – God's business. And you can't afford not to have adequate space for professionals to do His job.

Many church leaders (too many, in fact) view the daily business operation as a breather – an unadorned window between the open doors of the sanctuary or Sunday School. Only heavy traffic signals the big event, and audience participation is perceived as what really counts.

In the grand scheme of things, only symmetry – a harmonious balance of the different parts – will get your act together.

The church's administrative office should portray the same eight-to-five scenario that's acted out in any efficiently-run company. The lyrics may be slightly different, but the score is the same. The players know their lines of expertise and are front and center in making it all happen. The face your church presents on

The operation of a church is a business – God's business.

Administration

Floor Plan A

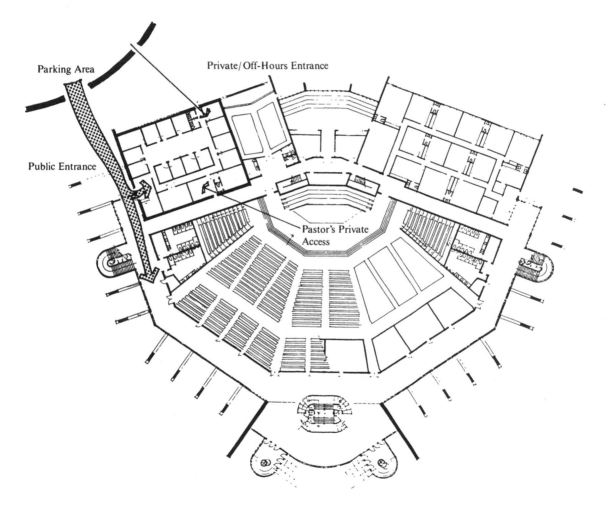

- Concentration of administration into a complex is desired for security and resulting ease of interaction.
- This administration complex is located near a foyer/public entrance.

FIG. 12-1

Sundays depends on maximum daily performance, with a minimum of hassle, by the church staff. A work environment created by specialists, for specialists, can set the stage.

Location

This is a matter of choice.

Some churches prefer to have the administrative offices close to the auditorium. Others opt for the office suites to be away – isolated from the mainstream of activity.

Whichever location you choose, outside and inside entrances should be identified easily with signage indicating "Office/Administration."

Remember, signs tell the story and make life easier for people who will be coming and going every day of the week. Diminishing the need to read between the lines, good direction also lends a professional ambience to the work area.

A "pastors' assembly room" located next to the auditorium and leading directly onto the platform can eliminate the need for close-by office space. This specially-designed area is ideal for pastors to meet before services for discussion, meditation, preparation and prayer.

Since the Sunday school offices must be close to the educational facilities, you may want to consider designing the space accordingly, with other administrative offices adjacent, but farther away from the flow of traffic. In most cases, you'll find it undesirable and inconvenient for the pastors' offices to be too accessible to the larger Sunday morning crowds.

If your church has, or is planning to have, an elementary or K through 12 school program, the corresponding offices should be totally separate from the main administrative areas. Although the school will be utilizing some of the Sunday school space, it is important to design a special office complex apart from the regular church business operation to accommodate the steady stream of children and parents throughout the week.

A reception area is an indispensable requirement, and should be separate from the other offices.

Size and Arrangement

Waiting room

A reception area is an indispensable requirement, and should be separate from the other offices.

The dimensions of this room depends on the size of your church. For smaller churches, the receptionist may be serving double-duty as the one-and-only secretary. In churches that employ two or more

Administration

Floor Plan B

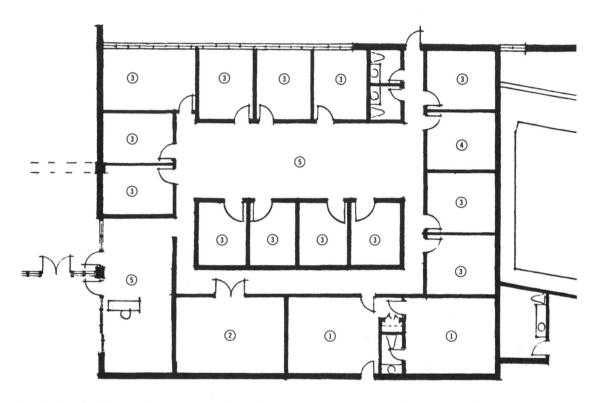

① **Pastor's Office** usually consists of an office and a connecting study with attached rest room. The location within the administration complex varies according to the pastor's needs. Sometimes an exterior view with private entrance is required. Other times there is a need for locating on an interior wall for private access to the pulpit and platform in the sanctuary.

② **Conference Room** is an area large enough to support a conference of the administrative personnel. This room is usually centrally located for easy access from the general offices and the pastor's office.

③ **Offices** usually are a standard 10x12 or 12x15 size. The number of offices varies with the programs of the church.

④ **Work Room** consists of a working area and if desired a lounge for staff. This room would be located for ease of access from the receiptionist/secretary area.

⑤ **Receptionist/Secretary Area** is where one would come for assistance, thus there is a need for this area to be orientated towards a foyer or entry.

FIG. 12-2

staff members, the receptionist's singular role may be Keeper of the Gate.

In either case, the space and the attendant are equally important. In the church office, as in any business office, the entrance area makes a statement to the public, and the first person seen should be friendly and able to make almost anyone feel welcome and at ease. Thoughtful placement of the receptionist's desk can minimize the stark "gate-keeper" impression.

The arrangement of the reception room must allow for adequate and comfortable seating. A coat rack, books and magazines project a nice image. Good reading, good lighting and yes, even good music can help lower stress levels during the waiting game. Restrooms and a drinking fountain should be located conveniently close by. Ideally, the reception area should be a minimum of 200 square feet in size. Wallpaper, carpeting and tasteful artwork throughout the administrative space is recommended to create a pleasant atmosphere for both staff and visitors.

A handy addition to the total reception area is one or two small conference rooms with a table and four chairs in each. Why? A private meeting room at the front can eliminate unnecessary traffic through the other office areas. Also, staff members can come to these rooms for short-term consultations or for potentially disturbing sessions with visitors. If you can afford it, this arrangement will be beneficial for everyone concerned.

Thoughtful placement of the receptionist's desk can minimize the stark "gate-keeper" impression.

Pastor's office

The senior minister should enjoy the largest space in the administrative area. The best plan includes two rooms: an outer office and a study, or work room.

A pastor's front office must create a favorable first impression. The aim of any staff member is to put visitors at ease, of course. But appropriate furnishings and amenities in this area should be visible evidence of the senior pastor's status. Designed with sensitivity and finesse, a suitable environment can be accomplished handily without undue pretention. Everyone's happy. We suggest planning for a minimum of 250 to 325 square feet.

Directly behind, or beside, the main office is the study/work space. This room might be as small as 100 square feet since some senior ministers have an additional study in their home for convenience and undisturbed privacy.

Normally, the pastor's study is an insular area for work and prayer. It should include a desk, bookshelves and credenza. A large room could include a work table, depending on how much time

Pastor's Study

FIG. 12-3

Pleasant Valley Methodist Church
Wichita, Kansas

actually is spent at the church.

Because of busy schedules that leave little free time between appointments, a private restroom in the pastor's office/study combination – with a shower and closet for an extra set of clothing – is convenient if the budget can bear it.

Windows

As in all church administrative offices, we recommend plenty of windows with a clear and unobstructed outdoor view. Even a glass connection to the world can help eradicate the foxhole feeling, maintain a better perspective and definitely enhance working conditions.

As a matter of fact, it's a good idea to have a window, approximately 10 by 10 inches, on the entry door to the pastor's office. (The world of micromanagement has its own vistas!) This feature eliminates potential problems while creating a further feeling of openness and camaraderie. The lines of demarcation must be precise, but permeable.

Staff offices

The offices for associate ministers and other paid staff members should encompass the secretarial pool area. The suggested dimensions for each room are an approximate 150 square feet. All the amenities – desks, storage space, bookshelves, carpet, wallpaper, adequate lighting and ventilation – are recommended.

By the way, fluorescent lighting is the more economical way to operate. It costs about 50 percent less than its incandescent counterpart, while dispensing the same light level with half the energy.

Now, how many offices do you need? Let's figure it this way:

One pastor (i.e. one staff member) should suffice for membership of 250 people. With each additional 200 members, hire an assistant. A large church may employ several associate pastors; music, educational and recreational directors; counselors; and, a business administrator. But everything depends on the size of your church and that zinger – The Budget!

Your best bet in planning office space is to allow for growth potential by figuring a multi-year schedule. For instance: With a 10-year plan, estimate – then factor in an eight percent annual growth pattern. This should keep you on track and fully prepared to parcel out offices as the needs arise. You may want to build some educational rooms near the administrative area, keeping an eye on

The suggested dimensions for each (staff member) room are approximately 150 square feet.

potential conversion to office space.

Considerations for Cordiality

Music

Many senior ministers prefer to have their entire staff close by and within easy-reach distance.

To those not so adamant on the subject, however, we recommend that the music director's office be located next to the rehearsal room, and apart from the main office complex.

The specialized job of the minister of music calls for obvious audio reverberations that could be disturbing to the other staff members, and equally unsettling to the director in question! Instrumental practice, arranging and planning are an integral part of this staffer's job description. The director needs full rein to carry out his or her ministry without the worry of being a noisy nuisance. This means a separate office with commodious space for storage, a library, instruments – and convenient proximity to the musicians. Selah.

We recommend that the music director's office be located next to the rehearsal room.

Financial records

The history of financial record-keeping in small churches reads like a book. It's predictable and it's O.K. But it's also under the treasurer's bed – along with the records!

When a church begins to grow and develop membership roles that stretch beyond 75 people, it's time to leave home. The treasurer's books need to assume their rightful place in the church office where they are accessible to the pastor and other staff members. The mentality of a church should match the physical bulk.

The moral of this story: create a home away from home for the treasurer and all the financial records. With proper nurturing and a sound business mind, you can avoid stunted relationships during your growing years.

Secretarial pool area

As we mentioned before, this space should be a pivotal point in the administrative area. Surrounded by staff offices, the secretaries are in the mainstream of activity and highly visible to the senior minister and his associates. Likewise, the arrangement affords easy accessibility as roles of communications are reversed. No secretary enjoys searching high and low for a boss who chooses to hide in the hinterlands of the office complex.

This physical placement is preferred for economical reasons, also. You'll save money if one secretary can handle duties for four staff people, as opposed to each minister having his own personal clerk. Cooperative clerical help is good, sound business.

Most churches have a willing well of volunteers in the congregation, so it's a good plan to supply a couple of extra desks and typewriters/computers. When your secretaries need some helping hands to put out a fire or a church bulletin, everything's in place. No strain. No pain. The work area itself has become a science of efficiency and maximum output. Buy quality furniture both in function and appearance.

Conference room

A space for staff and board meetings should be adjacent, or at least conveniently close to the pastor's offices.

Since this room is especially allocated for administrative sessions, it needs to be large enough to seat your projected number of decision-makers. Don't skimp on the square-footage, since you'll probably want to include a large conference table and chairs, bookshelves, storage space, a built-in cabinet with coffee bar, and room enough for a chalkboard, projector and screen. A telephone and at least four electrical outlets are suggested for the conference room, which must be a minimum of 200 square feet. Four hundred to 500 square feet should be ample. Restrooms located near by – or even in the conference room – are appreciated during important, but sometimes lengthy working sessions.

Work/supply room

You should plan on no less than 200 square feet for this room. Add more (approximately 100 square feet) if you include a mail room. You'll need plenty of space for shelves, cabinets, sink and countertop, typesetting and production equipment, depending on how ambitious are your goals. Well-stocked work areas are vital links between paid staff, parishioners and the public.

A Final Note

As a member of God's work force, the church office staff member should enjoy comfortable, convenient and personalized facilities. The appearance, arrangement and location of each person's work station can be an important factor in relationships and productivity.

Although space and budget restrictions will dictate the final

You should plan on no less than 200 square feet for the work/supply room.

decision on most design plans, ask for input. Including employees during the planning phase is a win-win situation. Not only will you glean some rational and creative ideas, you'll gain the solid support you need to carry out God's business plan for your project. It's symmetry at work, in the Highest sense!

Conference Room

FIG. 12-4

13

EDUCATIONAL SPACE FOR THE GROWING CHURCH

Planning effectively for the three R's of God's Word

The growing church must emphasize family participation, along with the constant challenge of practicing what we preach.

Christian education does not start or stop in the sanctuary. The time allotted in the worship room, however necessary and meaningful for enlightenment from spiritual leaders, or even for the blessed celebration of the sacraments, is still only a time – and limited, at that.

The growing church must emphasize family participation, along with the constant challenge of practicing what we preach ("The kingdom of God is not just talking; it is living by God's power" (1 Corinthians 4:20, TLB). And for effective congregational ministries – in every sense of the term – supplemental educational facilities are a "must" for thorough training in God's Word.

If we know this: "Teach a child to choose the right path, and when he is older he will remain upon it" (Proverbs 22:6, TLB), then we also must know that all believers – young or old – "Should behave like God's very own children, adopted into the bosom of his family, and calling to him, 'Father, Father.' ...And since we are his children, we will share his treasures..." (Romans 8:15,17, TLB). His children – of all ages – must learn that the Bible "is useful to teach us what is true and to make us realize what is wrong in our lives. It is God's way of making us well prepared at every point, fully equipped..." (2 Timothy 3:16,17, TLB).

We're all students; some are teachers as well. Receiving good *instruction, representing Him to others and reaching out with the confidence Paul exuded in his messages to the church at Colosse, is our commission. A vital educational program is the feeder for those new sanctuary pews. And with good planning, your learning facilities can be the "gift that keeps on giving" in an enlightened church of today!*

As you may have guessed, we're high on building churches through the educational departments. Our Southern Baptist friends – among other growing denominations – have proven this theory over and over, and who are we to knock success? But if you and your church have found another effective way of reaching people and boosting the numbers, keep up the good work (and let us know your secret)!

Acquiesce to us now however, if you will, for some solid advice on program space needs in educational planning.

First of all, let's talk about what really makes up "educational spaces." Programs that utilize these facilities can include the Sunday school, weekday school, licensed day care, church library and resource center, clubs for men, women, boys and girls, music, recreation, vacation Bible school and hobby/vocational training rooms.

Careful scheduling centered around multiple-use educational space is an efficient way to stretch your dollar. You know what your church needs and goals are, so in planning, don't overlook any facet of your total program. Remember, however, that the success of any or all of these components will depend on the amount of space provided. And space costs money.

A good measure for calculating total educational space is 30 square feet per person. Calculate 35 to 40 square feet per person for educational and worship space if you plan for multi-utilization of the total area. The variety of programs in a very large church may call for as much as 45 square feet per person. These are estimates we have developed over the years. (Each church, however, has its own educational emphasis, so good communication between the architect and the church will result in a good solution.)

In most cases, Sunday schools are departmentally divided. Each department may be more or less self-contained – if you can spend the money – with a larger assembly room and smaller classrooms with doors leading directly to the large-group area. (But classrooms do not spell c-u-b-b-y-h-o-l-e-s!)

Of course, each area should be well ventilated with good temperature controls for optimum comfort. The heating/ventilation/air-conditioning system (HVAC) chosen for this area may

A good measure for calculating total educational space is 30 square feet per person.

Education
Floor Plan A

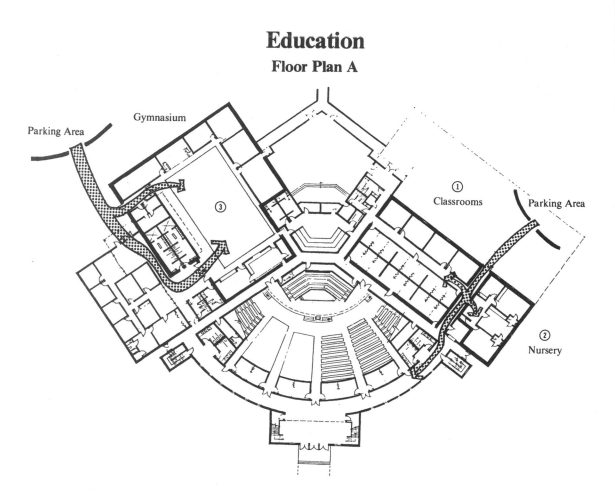

- Education is usually made up of three major components. These are ① classrooms, ② nursery, ③ gymnasium.
- All components of education should be located near a foyer/public entrance for ease of access.

FIG. 13-1

depend on the overall system chosen. A forced air system effectively creates the proper number of air changes required. Keep in mind that zoning of areas is also efficient. Plenty of windows and good lighting can enhance the space and make a difference between a pleasant or unpleasant experience. Attractively painted or vinyl wallpapered walls, acoustical tile ceilings, sound-resistant floors and appropriate furnishings should be selected with easy and low maintenance in mind.

Carpet for educational use may be either cut pile or loop. Carpet comes in an array of nylons or olefins; it also comes in a variety of weights, such as 28, 34 and 42 ounces. Color, texture, wearability and maintenance should be the considerations when floor finishes are chosen.

Allow space for adequate supply and coat storage, along with enough electrical outlets for department needs. Electrical outlets for Sunday school classrooms typically are placed one per wall. In a licensed educational classroom, the architect/engineer must follow appropriate local and regional codes. All electrical outlets must be child-proofed. Lighting levels in Sunday school classrooms should maintain at least 30 footcandles throughout the room. In licensed registered state educational classrooms, 60 footcandles is typical. (An architect/engineer has approximately 100 to 150 footcandles at his drafting desk.) Again, codes and common sense will provide a solution.

Since music is an important part of most churches, it's wise to provide room for a piano in each department. Portable folding or stackable chairs and tables for flexibility are the best investment. And remember to have restrooms conveniently located and easily accessible to each area.

Clearly, the planning for individual departments should keep the "students" in consideration, with relevant provisions for the age groups you're serving.

Now, let's break it out.

Children's Division

Preschool Department

For the little folks and their teachers, you should allow at least 20 to 35 square feet per person. The room itself should be a minimum of 200 square feet with walls no less than 12 feet long.

We recommend that these areas are located on the ground floor near an entrance/exit, with obvious access to the main foyer or concourse. Window sills should be approximately 18 to 24 inches from the floor, with the amenities of clear glass windows with

Portable folding or stackable chairs and tables for flexibility are the best investment.

Nursery

FIG. 13-2

Education

Floor Plan B

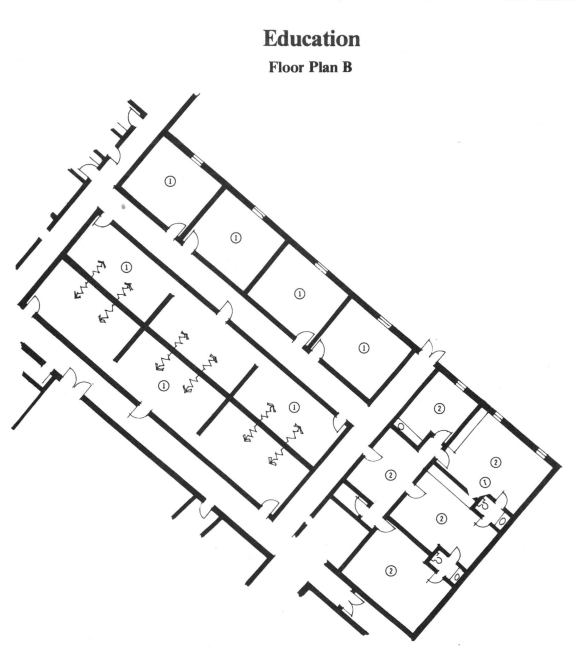

① **Classroom** sizes vary according to the number of students per classroom desired. They can be single rooms, or a large room with movable partitions that allow flexible usage. In addition, classrooms can be used to utilize space that would in the future be used for additional seating, such as in the back of the sanctuary or in the balcony.

② **Nursery** rooms are where pre-school children/babies can be left during services. These rooms usually open onto a common reception area. This allows monitoring of the children while they prepare to be picked up or dropped off. It is desirable to locate the nursery rooms near a foyer/public entrance for ease of access with minimum disturbance to church services.

FIG. 13-3

screens. Because of the clamoring clientele in these rooms, the wear-resistant walls and acoustical ceilings, along with floors of a long-wear and easy-care material are a necessity.

Separate storage and cabinets should be built-in to keep supplies for each room. We recommend adjustable-shelved cabinets, wall-hung 50 inches from the floor, with a depth of 18 inches and a width of 36 inches. Storage units may be provided near the doorway. Provide cubbyholes or slots to accommodate diaper bags or other personal items which may be left and picked up handily by parents of the children.

Infants and toddlers will require tables for diaper changing. The measurements should be 24 by 30 inches high, topped with plastic laminate and a four-inch upturned edge for safety purposes. You may want to install a flush-valve water closet nearby for rinsing soiled diapers. A large disposal container for Pampered and Luved ones will be an appreciated addition. Toddler-sized furniture should be utilized in this area.

We recommend a toilet for each room, or at least one that is accessible to two adjoining rooms, with water closets 10 inches high. Lavatories should be 24 inches high and include a faucet/drinking water combination. A small kitchenette with a combination stove/sink/refrigerator is a nice addition if it's handy to all preschool rooms.

Beginner, Primary and Junior Departments

If possible, the space provided for these children should, again, be located on the first floor – close to an outside entrance/exit, and easily accessed from the main concourse. The classrooms are similar to the preschool rooms.

Allow 20 to 25 square feet per person, with ceiling heights of eight to 10 feet. Each room should have wall-hung cabinets 50 inches from the floor. They should be 18 inches deep, and 36 inches wide with adjustable shelves for versatility. One storage room for all rooms is acceptable, although you may choose to include a small area in each room for this purpose.

Windows should be placed 30 inches above floor level with screens and clear glass, allowing for good light and visibility. By this time in a child's life, audiovisuals have big impact. If your program includes this type of media ministry for the children, be sure to include windows with the capability of darkening the room.

Once again, walls should be covered with washable materials and ceilings must have acoustical qualities. One long wall is preferable for storage cabinets, bulletin boards, chalkboards and any other child-sized furnishings you may need.

Each room should have wall-hung cabinets 50 inches from the floor.

Education

Floor Plan C

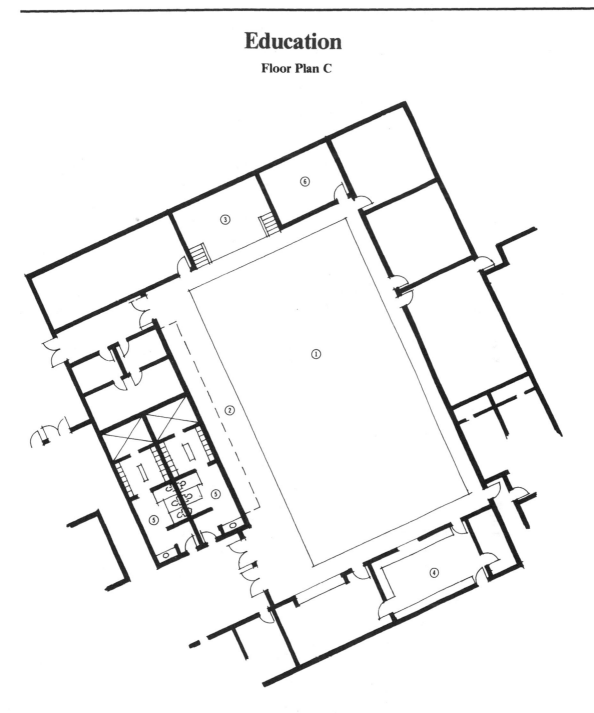

Gymnasium will usually consist of a standard basketball ① court size with ② bleachers on the side. A ③ platform is available for stage type productions. For serving church related meals a ④ kitchen would be available. In some cases a ⑤ locker room, with showers would be required. ⑥ Be sure to provide plenty of storage.

FIG. 13-4

Youth Division

Intermediate and High School Departments

The area planned for the Youth Division may have both a large assembly room and smaller group classrooms. At least eight to 10 square feet of space per person must be allowed for the large-group room; and a minimum of 10 square feet per person for the classrooms. If your plans call for a youth department that requires only an open assembly room with no smaller classrooms, allow approximately 20 square feet per person. More, or less, is an option. But we don't recommend going under 18 square feet. The department placement of this area, and its relationship to other departments, is flexible. The intermediate and high school classrooms may be in an annex. They also may be on upper floor levels and/or adjacent to the gymnasium/fellowship hall area. Pin-up boards and/or chalkboards, and other education devices that can be used for flexibility and creativity by the students will be effective. An expansive, unbroken front wall is preferred to create space for a worship/study atmosphere that relates to youth programming.

You're almost sure to incorporate audiovisuals in this department, so don't forget window-darkening provisions and plenty of electrical outlets. Storage cabinets should be built-in and wall-hung as in the other departments.

Many medium-to-large churches have youth ministers. Their input toward the design of this area is important.

In the Youth Division, at least eight to 10 square feet of space per person must be allowed for the large-group room.

Adult Division

Requirements for adult educational space are much the same as for the youth department: a large assembly room, with a minimum of eight to 10 square feet per person with smaller classrooms, or one open-spaced room with at least 20 square feet per person. Again, the entrance should be at the rear of the room and accessible from the main concourse. Young adults may feel more comfortable being close to the preschool department, so keep that in mind when planning. Older, or senior adults' space must be built on the auditorium level unless elevators are provided.

Weekday Programs

The total scope of your church program will determine what space you'll need in this department. But for informational purposes, the options in this category can include adult training, day care, nursery school, or even a complete Christian school, grades K-12. All of these activities increase the impact of your church's outreach in the community by providing much-needed services.

Some of these programs can be accommodated in the planned Sunday school educational rooms, maximizing the space and saving money. On the other hand, special codes and requirements demand uniquely-designed areas for certain programs. If the weekday activities are important extensions of your ministry and you intend to utilize Sunday School space, it is necessary to design the former according to weekday needs, or the maximum space required.

For example:

As a rule of thumb, 30-40 square feet per person is required for weekday programs.

Building codes may call for additional restrooms.

Departmental storage space could need to be increased, with perhaps even separate structures.

A room containing first-aid supplies, a bed or cot for separating an ill or injured child from the other students is recommended.

Depending on the number of children enrolled, an additional kitchen which is close to the department rooms may be required. The rooms themselves can serve as a dining area. Care should be taken, of course, to meet all code and sanitation regulations.

The janitorial supply and utility room could be the same space serving other church activities, if all programs are included in the planning.

A fenced outdoor play area must be incorporated for the weekday program, allowing 75-100 square feet per child, and located close to the classrooms for safety and easy accessibility. The area itself should be comfortable, functional and attractive, with good drainage and sufficient trees for at least partial shading. Creative landscaping in the play area can complement the play equipment, and help provide a good balance between hard and soft surfaces.

Administrative areas are discussed in the previous chapter. However, we must mention here that a full-scale school, grades K-12, will require its own offices for record-keeping, conferences and other activities, and should be anticipated in the initial planning stages.

As a rule of thumb, 30-40 square feet per person is required for weekday programs.

Media Library and Resource Center

This area of the educational system can put a big, shiny star of stewardship in your crown!

How many times have you or your teachers had to buy a reference book, a map of the Holy Lands, music materials or even a chalkboard – when the items in question were already somewhere in the church. But where? Duplicating purchases can skew your budget. Frustrations from endless searches through cluttered storage closets can skew your brain.

With accountability, proper identification, organization and utilization of all educational tools of your trade, the investment in your total ministry will be more efficiently disbursed for the maximum blessing.

Inventory

It's been said that in times past, the Sunday school library was the forerunner for the modern public library. In fact, that influence may still apply to some public libraries that offer a wide variety of religious books and other materials. But it's our opinion that every church should have its own resources to check out, available for teachers and students alike. The criteria you use to select materials should be weighed carefully and applied with standards to honor Him who inspired the Book of all books.

From a practical standpoint, you should consider durability, size of print, illustrations, price, relevance and versatility. Fiction, as well as nonfiction, reference and study books, give a nice balance to your collection. Selecting the books is only the first step. Classifying, cataloging, storing and dispensing them is another job for a qualified employee or church volunteer.

Other resources can include audiovisual materials and equipment, music and music equipment, drama materials and props, microfilm capabilities, viewing and study tables, maps, charts, posters, magazines, teaching aids and, of course, a card file with up-to-date records on what's available to church leaders and teachers.

Size, Location and Arrangement

If your library and resource center is planned as a full-service program, you should allow approximately two square feet for each person participating in the educational process of your church. Certainly, no less than one square foot should be attempted, even in the smallest program.

The ideal situation is to locate a single facility on the main floor close to the educational space, and with easy access from the main concourse. But because of the diverse resources being offered, it may be more convenient to separate some of the material for storage in more than one location. For instance, you may want to put all the music materials and equipment in an area close to the music, or choir room. Educational materials and equipment can be stored near the classrooms where they'll be utilized. Some equipment can be heavy and unwieldy; hauling it up stairs or down long corridors is no fun.

There should be an area available for teachers to experiment with equipment and preview audiovisuals. This space needs the

Your resource center should allow approximately two square feet for each person participating in the educational process of your church.

capability for darkening and either a permanent screen or wall for projection purposes. Plan for acoustical walls and plenty of electrical outlets. Allow space for the projector and several chairs. And if you're going in for the more sophisticated processes of film development and processing, you'll need a separate room with a sink and work table, and perhaps even a lighted art table.

A separate room or designed space within the media/resource room should be available for tape listening and recording. Naturally, the equipment must be included, along with appropriate furnishings.

The media library and resource center should be planned, as are all educational rooms, for those who will take advantage of the space and materials. In this case, both children and adults will be served, so appropriate furnishings and space must be provided for all age groups.

Promoting the Learning Resources

No matter how extensive or impressive you've developed your media library, if people are unaware of its service, you'll come up with a white elephant - and an expensive one at that.

The best way to get the word out about your wealth of materials and equipment is to keep people informed, through bulletins, memorandums to teachers from the librarian, announcements from the pulpit, satisfied customers and a lot of enthusiasm from the library personnel.

The service and ministerial advantages of a well-stocked, well-kept, well-publicized and well-used media library and resource center can help leaders and parishioners alike as they are "looking unto Jesus the author and finisher of our faith..." (Hebrews 12:2, KJV).

The architect and client must consider the priorities of space, quality and cost when planning for educational space. These three factors are the parameters for design and construction, and must be in perfect balance for a project to be successful.

Plan for acoustical walls and plenty of electrical outlets.

14

BUILDING FOR FELLOWSHIP AND RECREATION

How to plan space for social gatherings

There is a time for everything. Solomon knew it then; we know it now. The brotherhood that is inherent in the Body of Christ calls for times of relaxation, play, laughter and friendly repartee. These activities are healthy opportunities for friendly interaction among folks of all ages. And welcoming strangers can have some pretty heavenly results!

The concept of a genuine "Christian community" has fostered a sense of fellowship for a long, long time. Many of the early-day churches had meetings around the dining table. A sense of informality was the order of the day. It worked well in that setting.

Today, however, with memberships running well into the hundreds, even thousands, a great deal can be lost in the translation. The bonding that held together church participants in those times has become just another sticky situation.

The challenge now is to cement that spirit of fellowship. A church that is growing must grow as a family. In planning a new church to meet the overall needs of the ministry, it is absolutely necessary to design a substantial portion of the building – inside and outside – for fun, fellowship and recreation.

A church that is growing must grow as a family.

Indoor Recreation

A church with a large congregation and matching budget figures

Fellowship Hall Youth Activity Space

FIG. 14-1

Oak Cliff Assembly of God
Dallas, Texas

may prefer to build a separate activities building. Otherwise, there are many effective ways to provide space in and around the educational area of the church. Just keep in mind all the activities you want to offer.

Fellowship hall

Probably the most important and versatile community facility of the church, this area should be planned to accommodate approximately 25 to 50 percent of the anticipated educational enrollment. (This percentage can vary, depending on the church's educational emphasis.) Add a kitchen to the fellowship hall; it can be a dining room. Put in a stage; it is suitable for drama, speakers and musical presentations. Remove tables and chairs; it is adequate for basketball, volleyball, shuffleboard and other games. Keep it flexible!

If movable partitions are incorporated, adult and/or youth department classrooms may be utilized as part of the total space when the whole area is opened up. Or they may be reserved as overflow space.

Here are some points to consider in planning:

Plan about 12 to 15 square feet per person for table seating.

- To determine the size room you need, allow approximately eight square feet per person for folding chairs in row seating. Plan about 12 to 15 square feet per person for table seating. Aisles from the dining tables to the kitchen area should be at least five feet wide, with a four-feet space between tables. Seating arrangements are optional, of course, but for conversational purposes and flexibility in handling, tables for six or eight are preferred. Round tables are another choice. Then, again, you may want to mix and match the two to create a less institutional look.
- A first-floor location is suggested, with an easily accessible outside entrance. Restrooms must be close by.
- Separate multi-purpose classrooms located nearby can be used for small-group meetings or lounge areas.
- A specially-designed church parlor close to the fellowship hall provides a small but comfortable meeting place. This room – sometimes referred to as a "fireside" room – can be carpeted, decorated and furnished to lend a warm, "living-room" atmosphere.
- The height of the fellowship hall is not just a sports consideration. If it is too low, basketball and volleyball activity can damage the ceiling, of course. But more importantly in a large, multi-use space, the ceiling height and design must be high enough to avoid a heavy and closed-in feeling, or the "tunnel effect."

Floor Plan

Gym Seating 800

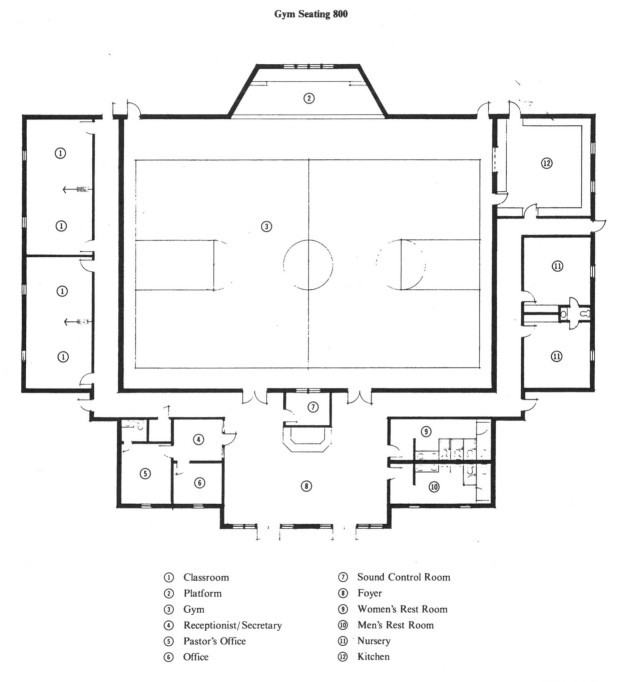

① Classroom	⑦ Sound Control Room
② Platform	⑧ Foyer
③ Gym	⑨ Women's Rest Room
④ Receptionist/Secretary	⑩ Men's Rest Room
⑤ Pastor's Office	⑪ Nursery
⑥ Office	⑫ Kitchen

FIG. 14-2

Floor Plan
Family Life Center

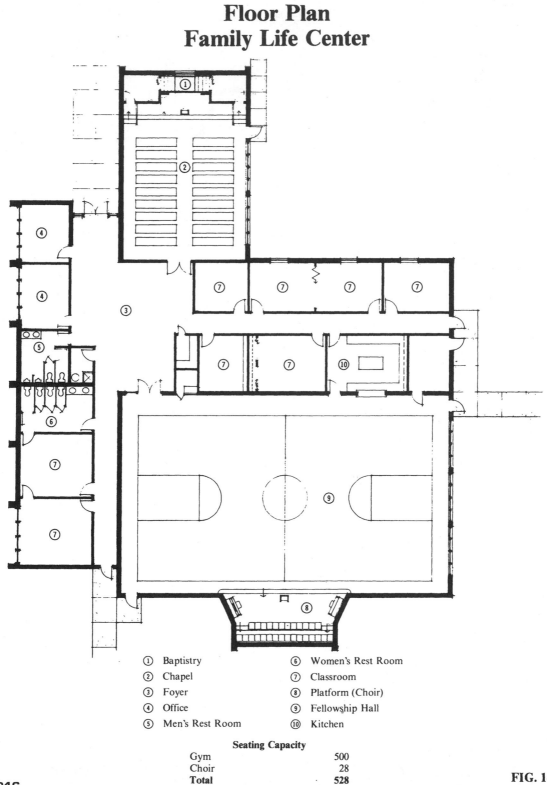

①	Baptistry	⑥	Women's Rest Room
②	Chapel	⑦	Classroom
③	Foyer	⑧	Platform (Choir)
④	Office	⑨	Fellowship Hall
⑤	Men's Rest Room	⑩	Kitchen

Seating Capacity

Gym	500
Choir	28
Total	**528**

FIG. 14-3

- Allow for ample storage space. Tables, chairs, props and sports equipment must have a secure home of their own when not in use.
- Design the room to include space for musical instruments and audio visual equipment, depending on your needs.
- Consider acoustical treatment for floors, ceilings and walls.
- Window treatment must be planned to handle light control for audio visual or drama productions, as well as physical activities within the hall. If you anticipate too much of a light problem with this multi-purpose room, a good case can be made for a windowless facility.
- A durable, easy-to-clean finish for walls, floors and furnishings should be selected. The color scheme can be coordinated, then, to give the entire area an inviting appeal.

Kitchen Facilities

Adequate and adjacent, obviously. In size, the kitchen should take up about 20 percent as much space as does the entire fellowship hall, or three to four square feet for each person to be served. It should have its own outside entrance with an optional dock and parking area for personnel and deliveries.

To avoid traffic jams within the kitchen, each work area should be given ample space. A good flow pattern is essential – from the arrival of bulk food, accessibility to dry and refrigerated storage, pre-preparation, preparation, cooking, baking and washing. Top-notch equipment, plenty of storage space, proper lighting and ventilation will make happy people of those who have kitchen duty. The result is maximum efficiency and participation.

For serving purposes, a counter between the kitchen and hall is one option. This way, the people waiting tables can pick up and deliver plates without ever having to enter the kitchen.

Another possibility is to have a small serving room, located between the kitchen and dining room. Double doors with kick plates, one for entrance and one for exit, separate the two main areas. Both options are reasonably suitable for screening the irritants of noise and clutter.

If you're concerned about kitchen noise (too many cooks can not only spoil the broth, they can obliterate a good after-dinner speaker), you might consider locating the kitchen across the corridor from the main fellowship hall. The only way this will work, of course, is to cordon off that area to traffic during serving times.

The main issue to consider here is accomplishing the objective of creating a pleasant and enjoyable atmosphere, both for kitchen

To avoid traffic jams in the kitchen, each work area should be given ample space.

Kitchen

FIG. 14-4

Gymnasium

FIG. 14-5

personnel and the fortunate diners who reap the benefits!

Separate Recreation and Activities Building

If you're thinking about going this route, remember to consider extra costs of construction, utilities, equipment and maintenance. Also, if your program is large enough to require a separate activities building, you'll probably need to hire a full-time recreational director. It all adds up.

For planning purposes, however, the building space might include:

- A junior high school-size gymnasium, approximately 42 by 74 feet; a high school-size gymnasium, approximately 50 by 84 feet; or a college court-size, approximately 50 by 94 feet.
- A reception area or lobby.
- Office space for the director and other church personnel, depending on your program needs.
- Special activities and/or educational meeting rooms. The size of these rooms may vary from 15 by 15 feet to 30 by 30 feet. Allow for adequate storage and cabinet space in each room.
- Carpeted lounge area or fireside room for informal gatherings, reading and relaxation.
- A kitchenette for serving refreshments. Any big meals could be prepared in the larger church kitchen and catered to the activities building. Remember, though, that locker room odors can kill an appetite in short order.
- An eating area next to the kitchen with several tables and chairs. Snack and beverage machines are suggested for this space.
- Gymnasium. Plan for at least 6,000 square feet, since general area requirements for basketball – a common denominator in a gymnasium – averages 60 by 100 feet with a ceiling height of no less than 20 feet. Space for spectator seating will add another three to four feet per row. The floor of the gymnasium may be delineated for volleyball or any other sports you want to offer.
- Auxiliary gymnasiums. For a more extensive (and expensive) indoor recreation program, you may want to plan for a 25-meter swimming pool, a bowling facility, a couple of tennis courts, handball/racquetball courts or a 1,500-square-feet weight-exercise room. Bowling requires a length of about 83 feet plus seating, and approximately 11 feet for each lane. The official size of a handball court is 20 feet wide by 40 feet long by 20 feet high.
- Shower and locker rooms should be adjacent to the gymnasium and accessible from the front lobby. Give equal thought to

For a gymnasium, plan for at least 6,000 square feet.

From Conceptual Drawing
to Master Site Plan

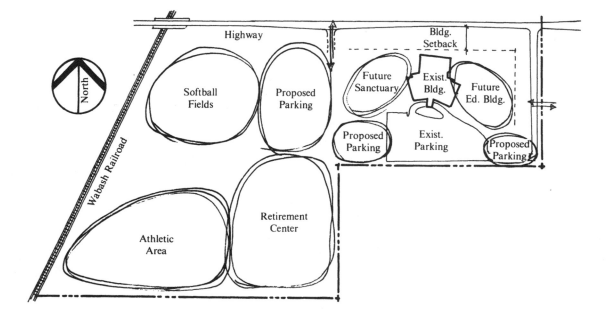

FIG. 14-6

maximum function, good lighting, temperature control, plumbing, ventilation, and finishes for walls and floors.

Outdoor Recreation

If your church is fortunate enough to own enough real estate to afford a good-sized recreational area, count your blessings! For people of all ages, "playing" together out-of-doors is a healthy complement to the ministry. In fact, recreational facilities are a major element in many site complexes including church, school, residential and industrial developments.

You should master plan the outdoor recreational area as carefully as you script your entire ministry's program. Once you've decided what activities you want to include on the property and before you actually map out the land, think on this:

1. Since each activity requires a specific layout, the site must be properly planned with considerations for orientation, topography and access.
2. It is not advisable to utilize even part of the church parking lot for recreational activities. The problems of surface hazards and scheduling hassles, not to mention the inherent dangers of automobiles homing in on their rightful habitat, are not worth the money you might save.
3. A designated parking area near the recreational areas will be appreciated by both participants and spectators.
4. Each area also will need to have access roads or paths for maintenance purposes.
5. Consider designing barriers between the recreational areas and any surrounding facilities, such as residential or commercial properties.
6. Plan for restrooms, drinking fountains, shelter areas and equipment storage space unless you incorporate the activities building for these services.

Area requirements for games and sports

Specific information on size, surface and layout is available through your architect. Generally speaking, however, if your game plan includes an average 350 by 350-feet area for baseball, you can feel secure that you'll have enough room for any other field sport – unless, of course, you're into polo or golf! For instant edification, here are the total area dimensions for several popular games:

■ Basketball – 42 by 74 feet; 50 by 84 feet; or 50 by 94 feet, with north-south orientation. The surface should be a bituminous

You should master plan the outdoor recreational area as carefully as you script your entire ministry's program.

Basketball

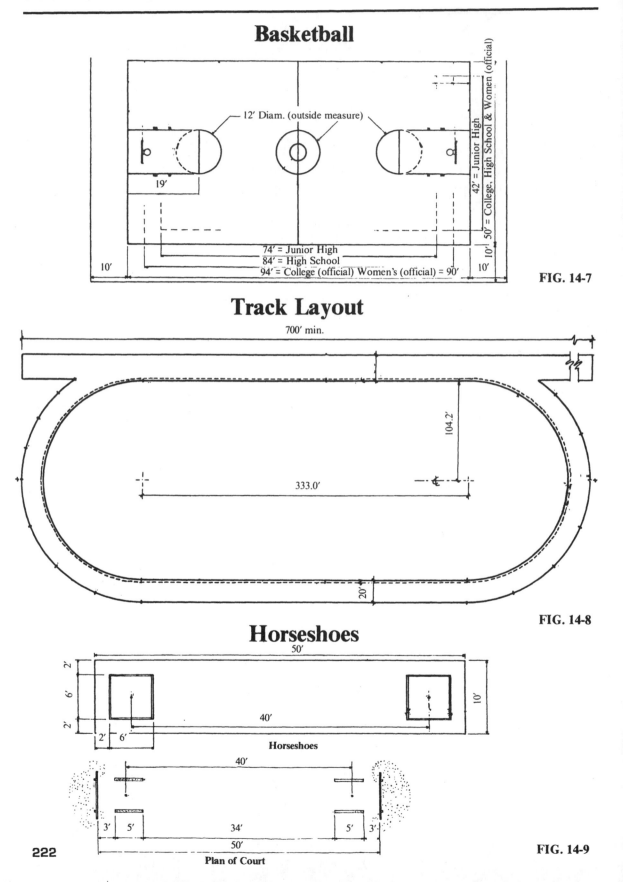

12' Diam. (outside measure)

19'

42' = Junior High
50' = College, High School & Women (official)

10'

74' = Junior High
84' = High School
94' = College (official) Women's (official) = 90'

10'   10'

FIG. 14-7

Track Layout

700' min.

104.2'

333.0'

20'

FIG. 14-8

Horseshoes

50'

2'
6'
2'

10'

40'

2'   6'

Horseshoes

40'

3'   5'   34'   5'   3'

50'

Plan of Court

FIG. 14-9

Softball/Little League

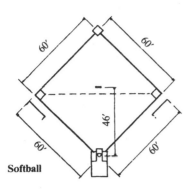

Softball

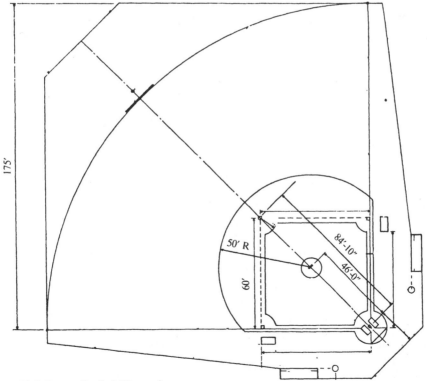

Little League Baseball Diamond

FIG. 14-10

Baseball/Slo Pitch

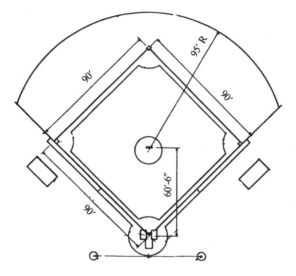

FIG. 14-11

Tennis Court

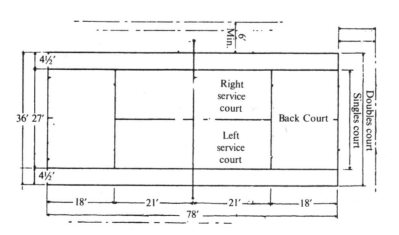

FIG. 14-12

Handball

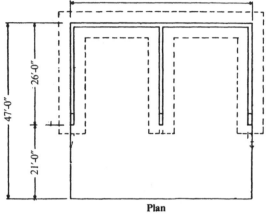

Plan

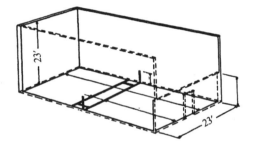

Isometric

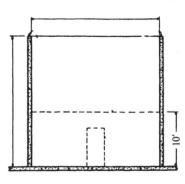

Section

FIG. 14-13

material or concrete.
- Bowling (lawn) – 120 by 120 feet for eight alleys; one alley is 20 by 120 feet. Surface should be sand-clay or bent grass, closely cut.
- Croquet – 30 by 60 feet for two to eight players.
- Football – 195 by 480 feet.
- Horseshoes – 10 by 50 feet; 40 feet between stakes.
- Quoits – 25 by 80 feet.
- Shuffleboard – 10 by 64 feet for two to four players; concrete surface and north-south orientation.
- Soccer – 240 by 360 feet, average, or 86,400 square feet.
- Softball – 175 by 175 feet, minimum, with a 60 by 60 feet diamond.
- Tennis – 7,200 square feet for doubles play; 6.000, singles. The base size is 60 by 120 feet. North-south orientation with concrete or bituminous material surface. Ten-feet high fencing is recommended.
- Volleyball – 50 by 80 feet, with north-south orientation. Bituminous material, concrete, sand-clay or turf surface, depending on the use.

Picnic areas and play lots

A valuable asset to the church is an outdoor area for cooking, eating and relaxation.

A valuable asset to the church is an outdoor area for cooking, eating and relaxation. The area should have at least partial shading and be located close to the other recreational areas. Permanent tables, benches and barbecue pits may be installed, and outdoor lighting should be provided for maximum usage. Restrooms, step-up drinking fountains, trash receptacles, a shelter and storage area must be nearby. (These may be the same facilities that service the entire outdoor recreational area.) Trees, flowers, shrubs and berms can add an aesthetic touch while lending a park-like atmosphere. Sidewalks or paths can be included for strollers, tricycles, wagons or even pedestrians who are inclined to walk or jog.

A playlot for children should be located close to the picnic grounds. The area should be approximately 21 square feet per family, or at least 70 square feet per child, to accommodate the very minimum of play equipment. Some of the elements you may want to include are: swing sets, slides, climbers, merry-go-round, parallel and horizontal bars, playhouses, a sand area, a wading or spray pool, and a separate area for group games and running. Natural turf is considered the best surface for playlets, since it has a low initial cost, a high-safety softness and a pleasing appearance. Around and under the play equipment, however, your options include sawdust, sand, and wood chips.

Swimming pools

Since each outdoor activity should complement the others, a master plan of the entire outdoor recreational area should be a design priority. If you are building a swimming pool now or later, it should be planned in conjunction with the rest of the activities for accessibility and maintenance. Other planning considerations are:

- For good drainage, don't build your swimming pool in a low spot.
- Trees on the property are a nice "dressing" but if they're too close to the swimming pool, the falling leaves will play havoc with the filtering system. And, since the pool area is not one that needs shade, too many nearby trees blocking the sun defeat the purpose of an outdoor pool.
- A good filtering system is essential for good water conditions. If your pool is located too close to the street, dirt and blowing debris are other annoyances.
- If you don't plan to build a separate activities building, a bathhouse is recommended. A design that includes a roof for temporary shelter will be appreciated by parents with infants, or anyone else who is sun-shy.
- Surveys tell us that only about one-half of the participants in the area are actually in the pool at the same time. This means that a large deck area should be provided for lounging and sunbathing. If you have the room, plan for a deck that is twice the size of the water area, and elevated no less than six inches above the water surface.
- You must surround the entire pool/deck area with a fence at least six feet high, for the obvious reasons of safety and control, equipped with gates that can be locked.
- Provide nearby storage space for equipment, supplies and mechanical equipment. The rectangular pool is economical, easy to supervise and can accommodate competitive swimming with at least a 25-yard short course with a 45, 60 or 75 feet width. The drawback is a limited shallow space for younger children. A T-shape, L-shape or Z-shape can handle all these needs adequately, including an area for diving. Whichever design you choose, estimate a maximum load, then plan for approximately 25 square feet of water surface space for each swimmer. An adjacent wading pool, with a depth of up to 18 inches, is recommended. This area should be separated from the larger pool by a three to four-feet fence, and can have permanent seating built for those supervising the children. The depth of the pool depends on whether you want to include diving facilities. A three-meter board, installed 10 feet above the water surface

A master plan of the entire outdoor recreational area should be a design priority.

and five feet beyond the edge of the wall, requires a minimum water depth of 12 feet. A five-meter platform needs to be 16V2 feet above the water with a 14-feet depth. Excluding diving, a swimming pool should have a minimum depth of two to three feet; we recommend five to six feet, with a uniform slope from three feet to the five or six feet.

Golf course

For the church who has enough land and enough money to support it, you may want to consider a par three or even a par five golf course. But the size of the property is important, since you'll need at least 50 acres for a nine-hole course and 110 acres for an 18-hole course. Another factor is the condition of the soil. Sandy loam is the ideal golf course soil in order to grow a good stand of grass. The availability of water and power is an absolute necessity; and, the costs of both the connections and power must be included in your plans. Finally, the land should have some natural golf features such as a slightly rolling terrain, trees and ponds. Most of these elements can be replaced by artificial hazards, if necessary, but this is a costly proposition. A good golf course architect may be employed if you are considering this possibility.

Your indoor and outdoor recreational facilities should make merry the hearts of parents and kids of all ages! It's a perfect mix for the total ministry of your church, and definitely good medicine for everyone.

> *Your indoor and outdoor recreational facilities should make merry the hearts of parents and kids of all ages!*

15

EXTERIOR SPATIAL DESIGN

Considerations for parking, planting and other fringe benefits

D*avid said it. "The Lord pours down his blessings on the land and it yields its bountiful crops. Justice goes before him to make a pathway for his steps" (Psalm 85-12,13 TLB).*

Justice, yes. And a qualified landscape architect! In today's world, the entire design of a church starts with the site. The building itself, although planned to a T for indoor functional quality, just won't hold seed if there is no well-plumbed relationship to the surroundings.

Beginning with the inherent environmental and visual characteristics of a site, a trained planner will tie the exterior design of the church – and any adjacent structures – to the functions needed to occur around it.

Natural vegetation, as well as geographic and topographic features, can be an artist's inspiration to create an aesthetic blending with land use requirements. Water, one of the basic natural components of human existence, may be a very important building element. Whether it is a quiet waterfall over a rock structure, or a noisy and vibrant spray shooting into the air, water fountains can create an exciting entry to the parking area or church. Even trafficways, parking, signage, fences, utilities, service, storage and recreational areas require an expert's understanding of the spatial structure.

> *A trained planner will tie the exterior design of the church...to the functions needed to occur around it.*

Why make such a fuss as long as the church has enough square-footage for an adequate auditorium and educational space?

A pleasing blend of the interior/exterior factors sends a

message to church members and visitors: "Come to Christ, who is the living Foundation of Rock upon which God builds" (1 Peter 2:4, TLB). And when Peter said: "Be careful how you behave among your...neighbors" (1 Peter 2:12, TLB), he must have known how the folks who live next to your property would appreciate a first-rate church building and grounds. Another piece of advice, "Fear God and honor the government" (1 Peter 2:17, TLB), makes us wonder if the old apostle ran up against some building codes of his own!

Working with the architect, the church building committee and various regulatory groups, landscape architects and civil engineers will design the total site area for growth. They can provide a plan for spatial enclosure around your new church with an inviting and open pathway to the people. You're inviting people to come to your church and stay a while! Do everything you can to make their visit easy and pleasant enough that they'll want to come back.

Outdoor Signage

Information

First of all, the primary sign for your church must be seen easily from the freeway or street. Following the primary sign should be clear directional signs to the various facilities on the site. One-way streets, pedestrian crossings and other regulatory messages must be indicated. You may even want to include a general organizational sign for the entire campus. You must have signs to indicate accessible entrances to the church and other buildings, as well as an informative sign on each structure.

Readability

Choose a consistent format and design for your signs, then stick with it. A clear, concise and readable message will keep people moving in the right direction. Signs for visually and physically handicapped people should be considered. Raised letters, braille strips and graphic symbols are a few useful techniques.

Placement

Excepting those created for the blind or partially sighted, all signs should be set in locations that would not conflict with pedestrian traffic or vehicular operation. For aesthetic purposes, you may want to combine signage with lighting fixtures. This way, you can avoid additional posts and illuminate your signs, all at the same time. Please check into the building codes and regulations for

You're inviting people to come to your church and stay for a while!

Fountains

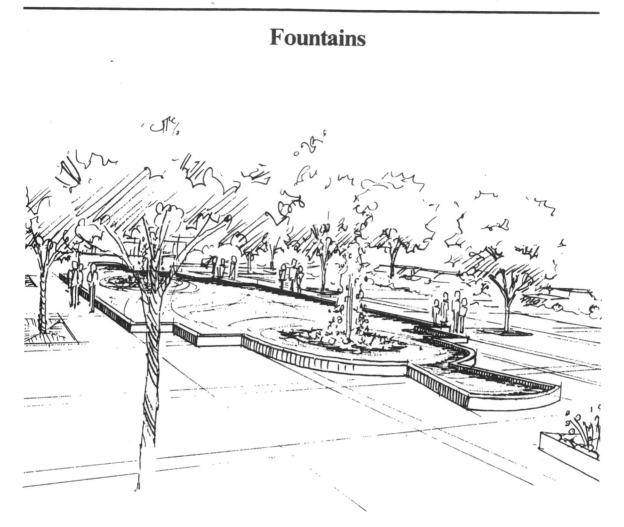

FIG. 15-1

Lighting Fixtures

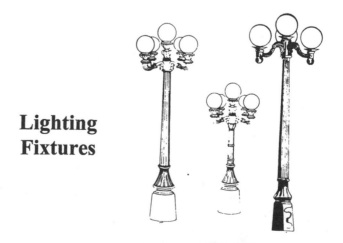

FIG. 15-2

guidelines in this area.

Lighting

Adequate exterior lighting is essential in creating awareness. Properly designed and well-placed, lighting will feature the architectural character of your facilities and blend it effectively with the surrounding environment. Concealed, upward, downward and symmetrical illumination can be combined with floodlighting for the ultimate service on your site.

There are functional considerations. Parking lots, entrances, walkways, access roads and recreational areas must be well-lighted for optimal use and as a deterrent to vandalism. Use fixtures with baffled lenses so the light source is not seen directly, and spill-over light is controlled. Again, regulatory codes spell out your assignment in no uncertain terms, varying degrees of intensity are required for different areas. And when you're choosing fixtures and illumination techniques, consider their day-time appearance for coordination with the architectural theme and signage. Durability should be taken into account, also, to cut back on replacement costs.

Drop-off and Pick-up Zones

Obviously, these areas should be as close to the building entries as possible, preferably with little or no variation in the road surface and adjacent walkway grade. If there is a grade change that requires stairs, include alternative provisions for wheelchairs or strollers. Depending on the climate in your area, you may want to consider a sheltered waiting area. Allow at least nine-and-a-half feet of vertical clearance. If you plan for a drive-through canopy, allow at least 19 feet clearance for buses.

To avoid traffic jams, allow enough length on your approach drive for cars waiting on embarking or disembarking passengers. And for safety purposes, it's recommended that the drive is plotted for one-way traffic, with passenger unloading always close to the church entrance.

Then, since many parking lots are a good hiking distance from the church, adequate directional signage leading to the area must be installed.

If you get started off on the right foot by being considerate and making it comfortable for folks to get to church, you're halfway there!

Parking Lots

We're not going to discuss parking garages here. On purpose. Unless your church has an inner-city location (where a parking

Depending on the climate in your area, you may want to consider a sheltered waiting area.

Parking Lot Landscape Concepts

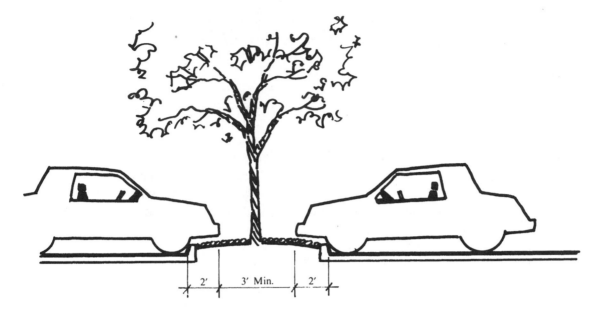

2′   3′ Min.   2′

- Trees are needed for shade to cool hot parking areas.
- Large expanses of paving can be softened by planting islands.

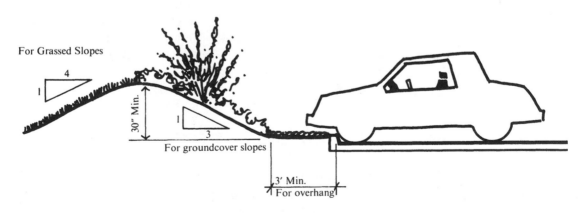

For Grassed Slopes

4
1

30″ Min.

1
3

For groundcover slopes

3′ Min.
For overhang

- Screen parking lot perimeters with combination of grassed berms and shrub plantings.

FIG. 15-3

garage may be your only choice), you're better off – budget-wise – going with a parking lot. (By the way, most cities require a certain amount of off-street parking. The typical people-to-parking ratio is three, four or five to one, depending on the regional location.)

Any good parking lot must meet several criteria:

Design

Following our "inherent spatial characteristics" theory, a parking lot should be designed to fit into and harmonize with the entire site layout and development.

Since it will get 12 months of use, the grading and surface materials are important considerations. Proper grading will give you adequate drainage throughout the year, regardless of the surface you choose. Crushed stone, gravel, concrete and blacktop are all possible choices.

Fences, walls, curbs or hedges can give a nice "finish" to a parking lot. They're also good safety measures, since it will keep automobile activity limited to the lot. You may want to incorporate more than one of these features. As you plan your enclosure, allow a car bumper overhang of about two feet for head-in parking. Three feet is the average allowance for back-in parking.

Entrance/exit, signs and lighting

We can't stress these features enough. Proper information on the location of the parking lot must be posted at all entrances. Entrance and exit signs should be no less than 50 feet from intersections. Also, if the church is accessed by a busy freeway or major street artery, separate entrances and exits are suggested. Single-lane entrances must be no less than 14 feet wide; exits, a minimum of 12 feet. For a combination entrance/exit, allow at least 26 feet. If possible, provide extra space for vehicles as they are entering and exiting to avoid backups in traffic lanes on entering, and easy access to street traffic lapses during the exit phase.

Inside the parking lot, one-way directions and pedestrian walkways should be identified clearly. Since you'll be having evening activities at the church, adequate illumination on the parking facility can provide security, avoid pedestrian and vehicular accidents, and definitely encourage participation with a sense of safety.

Lot size and arrangement

Generally, a church parking lot must provide 300 square feet of

> *For a combination entrance/ exit, allow at least 26 feet.*

45° Parking Dimensions

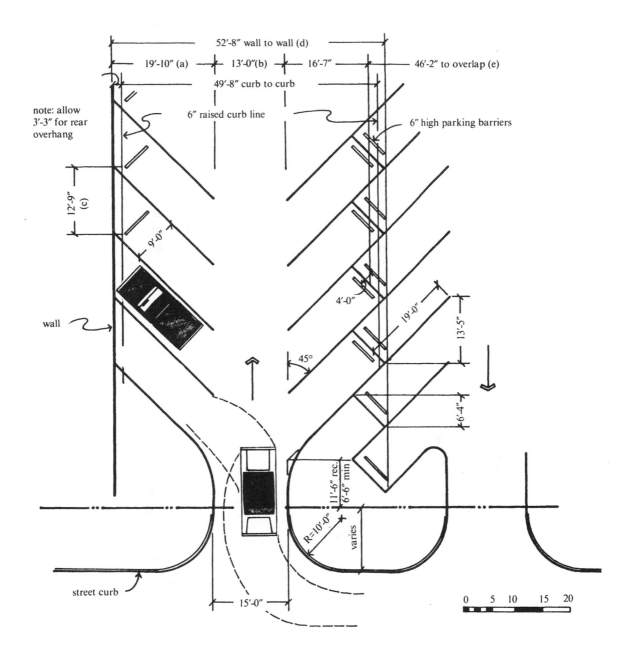

FIG. 15-4

stall width	(a) stall to curb	(b) aisle width	(c) car curb length	(d) wall to wall	(e) overlap to overlap
8'-0"	19'-1"	14'-0"	11'4"	52'-2"	46'-6"
8'-6"	19'-5"	13'-6"	12'0"	52'-4"	46'-4"
9'-0"	19'-10"	13'-0"	12'9"	52'-8"	46'-2"
9'-6"	20'-1 "	13'-0"	13'5"	53'-2"	46'-6"
10'-0"	20'-6 "	13'-0"	14'1"	54'-0"	46'-11"

60° Parking Dimensions

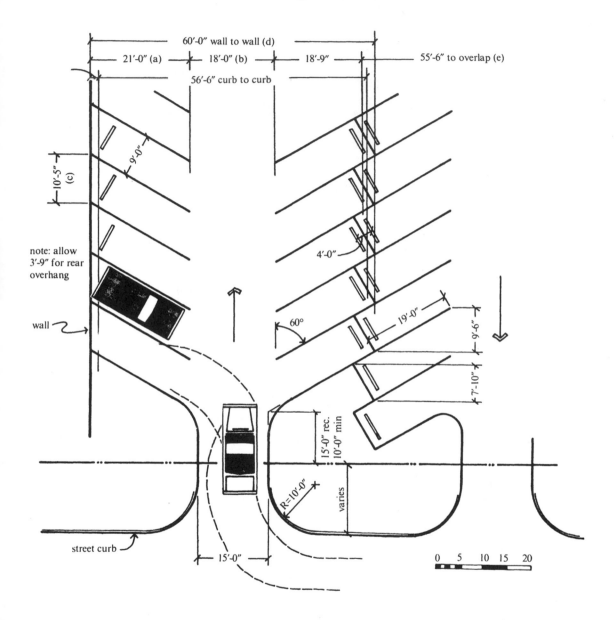

stall width	(a) stall to curb	(b) aisle width	(c) car curb length	(d) wall to wall	(e) overlap to overlap
8'-0"	20'-5"	19'-0"	9'2"	59'-10"	55'-10"
8'-6"	20'-8"	18'-6"	9'10"	59'-11"	55'-7"
9'-0"	21'-0"	18'-0"	10'5"	60'-0"	55'-6"
9'-6"	21'-2"	18'-0"	11'0"	60'-5"	55'-7"
10'-0"	21'-6"	18'-0"	11'6"	61'-0"	56'-0"

FIG. 15-5

90° Parking Dimensions

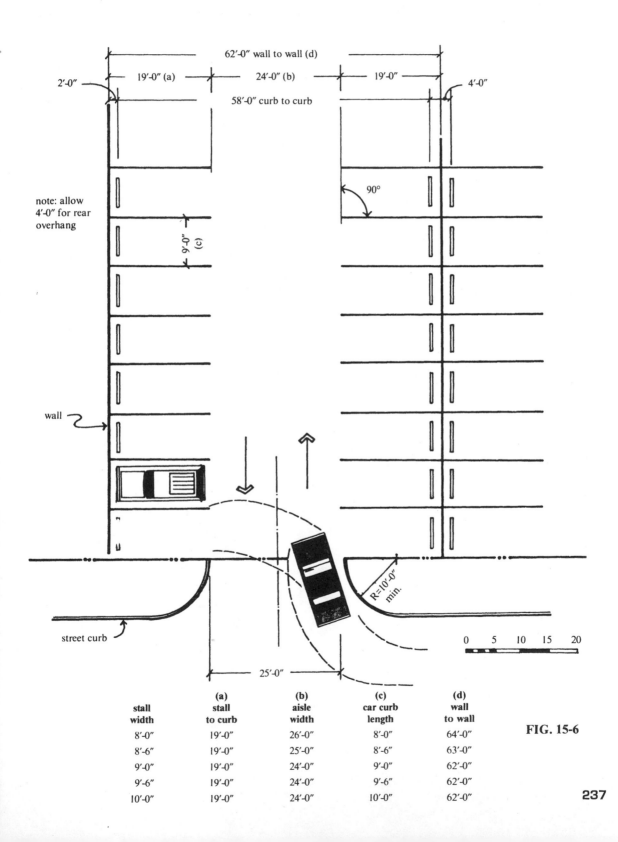

	(a)	(b)	(c)	(d)	
stall width	**stall to curb**	**aisle width**	**car curb length**	**wall to wall**	**FIG. 15-6**
8'-0"	19'-0"	26'-0"	8'-0"	64'-0"	
8'-6"	19'-0"	25'-0"	8'-6"	63'-0"	
9'-0"	19'-0"	24'-0"	9'-0"	62'-0"	
9'-6"	19'-0"	24'-0"	9'-6"	62'-0"	
10'-0"	19'-0"	24'-0"	10'-0"	62'-0"	

standing or maneuvering for each car, but this will vary according to the planned parking-angle layout. Under no circumstances should a stall be less than 18 feet long and nine feet wide, unless identified as compact car spaces. As for lot aisles, the bigger the better. Wide aisles will keep the traffic moving and aid in easy, quick parking. Lot aisles generally are 22 to 24 feet wide. Local building codes undoubtedly will help you decide the necessary dimensions for your area. In any case, parking stalls must be marked clearly by painted surface lines.

One space for each 20 cars, or whatever is required by local codes, must be allocated for those who need wheelchairs or other mechanical aids. These spaces should be as close to the main entrance as possible, or a maximum of 100 feet away. If your site plan calls for the parking lot to be at a greater distance, the unloading area at the main entrance will serve you well.

Schools must provide at least one off-street parking space for each two employees, and one off-street parking space for each 20 students in junior and senior high school. Day care centers must provide one off-street parking space for each staff member and one space for each 300 to 350 square feet of floor area. Your architect must check on local regulatory codes, since they may vary.

Good circulation should be the goal in your parking lot.

If your church has an active and good-sized bus ministry, you must allocate a percentage of the parking lot for these vehicles. We recommend a separate entrance and exit for buses and a custom-designed loading and unloading area, as we mentioned before.

Good circulation should be the goal in your parking lot design. A 90 percent parking angle is the most efficient, but whichever you select as the best parking angle will depend largely on the size and shape of your property.

Landscaping

We have already determined that a landscape architect is qualified to do more, much more, than design a neatly-packaged plan for plantings. So, when your architect comes up with a complete master plan for the church site, the considerations for trees, shrubs, plants and grass should be included.

The questions to ask when you're working with your architect are:

1. Can you show us how to fully utilize the site and its natural features?
2. Can you incorporate plantings that will assist natural barriers?
3. Are you familiar with indigenous plantings?
4. Will you plan for low-maintenance in the design?

Elements of a Preliminary Landscape Site Plan

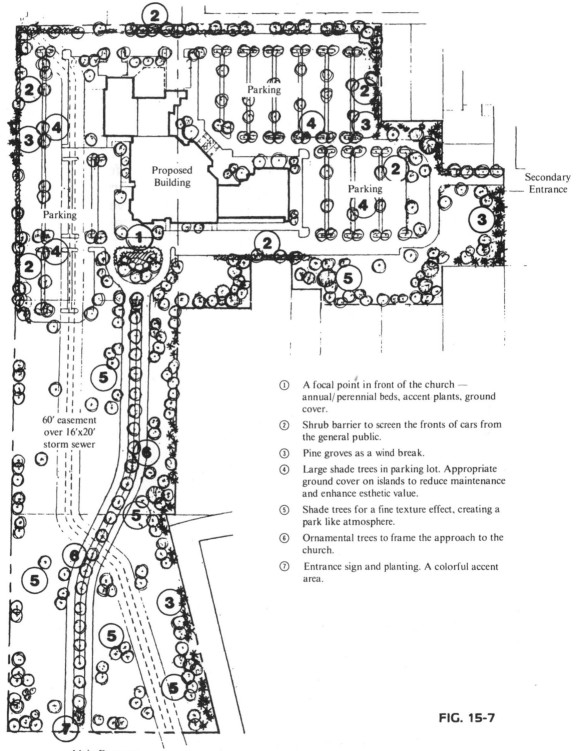

① A focal point in front of the church — annual/perennial beds, accent plants, ground cover.

② Shrub barrier to screen the fronts of cars from the general public.

③ Pine groves as a wind break.

④ Large shade trees in parking lot. Appropriate ground cover on islands to reduce maintenance and enhance esthetic value.

⑤ Shade trees for a fine texture effect, creating a park like atmosphere.

⑥ Ornamental trees to frame the approach to the church.

⑦ Entrance sign and planting. A colorful accent area.

FIG. 15-7

The Dos and Don'ts of Landscaping

DO

DON'T

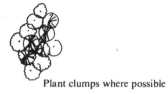

Plant clumps where possible

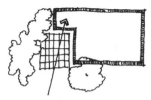

Use to define entry space

Reinforce drives & roads

Form exterior activity areas

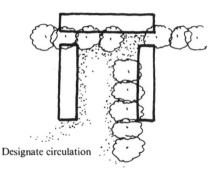

Designate circulation

Plantings act as sound and wind buffers

FIG. 15-8

5. Are you aware of the local greenbelt regulations?
6. Are you creative?
7. Are you familiar with hillside ordinances, height limitations and zoning ordinances?
8. Can you assist the church in re-zoning and land-use studies to local government?

It makes no sense to waste your time or ours at this point in discussing installation and care of regional vegetation. The secret is in having full confidence in the architect, thus the landscape architect, both of whom will present plans indigenously compatible to your locale and site. Landscaping can be functional as well as beautiful. And, it must complement and enhance the architectural styling.

The total plan for your church will help yield the bountiful crops to match those of His choosing, and provide a walkway of justice preceded only by Him. With a professional exterior design, a modern-day interpretation of an age-old message can give timely direction!

With a professional exterior design, a modern-day interpretation of an age-old message can give timely direction.

Calvary Church
Charlotte, North Carolina

16

BUILDING FOR THE PHYSICALLY CHALLENGED

Barrier-free provisions for the disabled and elderly

As early as 1974, the American Institute of Architects (AIA) Conference on a Barrier-Free Environment issued this statement: "...it shall be national policy to recognize the inherent right of all citizens, regardless of their physical disability, to the full development of their economic, social, and personal potential, through the free use of the man-made environment." Since then, the statement was endorsed by the President's Committee for Employment of the Handicapped, the National Easter Seal Society for Crippled Children and Adults and other groups.

A hefty percentage of this country's population has mobility problems due to temporary or permanent disabilities.

This edict definitely was a step in the right direction, since a hefty percentage of this country's population has mobility problems due to temporary or permanent disabilities. And the recent increased attention to the needs of the physically challenged has generated city, state and federal regulations for buildings, requiring easy accessibility and usability. All well and good. But several problems still exist.

Variations in codes and regulations among the states indicate different standards. Many of the mandates do not cover entirely the needs of the disabled population. Some architects and designers tend to plan facilities for the majority of the population – those whose capabilities are similar to their own. Why?

What may appear to be confusion or a lack of empathy is really the process – albeit slow – of understanding. If one has never been confined to a wheelchair, or had a vision problem, or suffered with arthritis, it's difficult to plan with complete comprehension. Yes, codes and regulations are a start. Beyond *those, creating an environment where everyone will be safe, comfortable, productive and independent is the humane thing to do, and is part of God's plan.*

Jesus gave instructions to "bring them here...," then, "...feed them" (Matthew 14:18,16, TLB). Healthy, sick, young and old. No bias. No partiality. And from Peter: "Show deep love for each other, for love makes up for many of your faults. God has given each of you some special abilities; be sure to use them to help each other, passing on to others God's many kinds of blessing..." (1 Pet. 4:7-11, TLB).

"Isn't that special," is not just a caustic and condescending portrayal of The Church Lady on Saturday Night Live. Unfortunately, it inadvertently personifies an underlying attitude toward the physically disabled and their needs.

Churches – especially churches – should "lead by good example...feed the flock of God; care for it willingly, not grudgingly; not for what you will get out of it, but because you are eager to serve the Lord" (1 Peter 5:2, TLB).

The guidelines in this chapter for accommodating the physically challenged are not "special." They are the basic environmental criteria intended for all of God's people.

Designing a barrier-free church facility and site does not mean a simplistic compliance in one or two areas. There must be a total relationship in design elements throughout the complex. Otherwise, you'll be defeating your purpose. To meet the needs of the physically disabled, the plan should take them easily on and off the site, in and out of the facilities and throughout the interior elements with a minimum of hardship.

If you're building a new facility, obviously it will be easier to include functional requirements as a part of the overall design. Remodeling and adding on to an existing building can be more difficult. However, it is possible and must be done to comply with current regulations. The American National Standard for Making Buildings and Facilities Accessible to and Usable by Physically Handicapped People (ANSI A117, 1-1980) is a result of the growing social concerns for the disabled. Intended to "achieve uniformity in technical design criteria." The standard applies to;

1. The design and construction of new buildings and facilities, including both rooms and spaces; site improvements; and public walks.
2. Remodeling, alteration, and rehabilitation of existing construction.
3. Permanent, temporary, and emergency conditions.

Designing a barrier-free church facility does not mean a simplistic compliance in one or two areas.

Stair Details

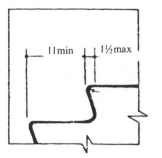
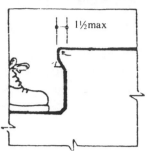
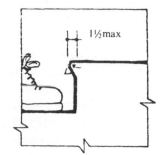

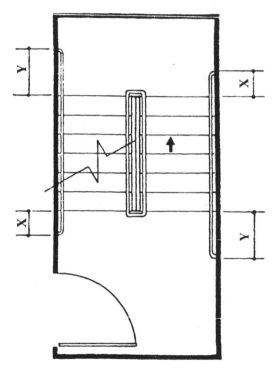
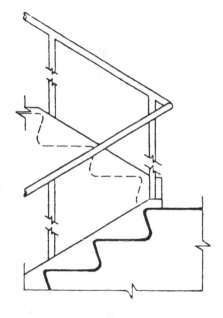

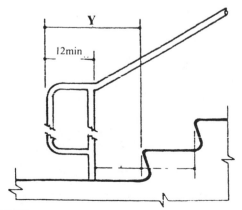
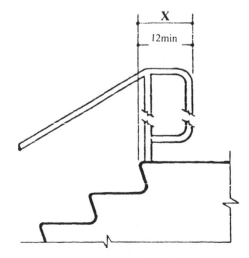

FIG. 16-1

When planning your new facility, obtain a copy of this standard from your architect.

The Physically Challenged – Who Are They and What Are Their Needs?

Those we define as physically challenged have sensory, manipulatory or locomotor handicaps, or a combination of these problems. In other words, they may have vision or hearing disabilities, impaired function in the arms and hands, or need walking aids and wheelchairs. The condition of some elderly people – or those with extremes in physical size – could fit into one or more of these categories, so any provisions to create easy accessibility naturally apply.

More, and sometimes different, specifications are required for the chairbound, but generally they also will apply to others who are disabled. Those with vision and hearing impairments do need some special aids, however, to help them move throughout the building.

The Blind or Partially Sighted

Approaches to entryways should have very little grading variation. Sloping curb cuts must be designed with a warning surface that contrasts with the surrounding surface. Curbs on sidewalks can be a tactile device on their own. If there are no curbs or other detectable elements to separate pedestrians from vehicular traffic, the walkway needs a three-foot width of textured surface to denote a hazardous area. In fact, any exterior and interior walking space that approaches traffic, pools, stairways or other elements that could endanger a person with severe visual disability should be specially surfaced. Raised strips or grooves, rubber, plastic cushioned surfaces or exposed aggregate concrete are some of the warning textures that can be used. Whatever surface you select, make it standard throughout the complex.

Handles or other operating hardware on doors leading to off-limit or dangerous areas should be identifiable by touch. Whether you knurl, roughen or apply a special material to the surface, it's an inexpensive and valuable warning.

Since many blind people are guided through a facility at least once, they tend to rely on memory and familiarity. Be careful not to place unexpected barriers in foyers or hallways. Avoid any obstructions, free-standing or overhanging objects, and protrusions that would reduce the clear width of an accessible route or maneuvering space. Although guide dogs are trained in detecting and avoiding hazards, most visually impaired people use a long cane as a maneuvering aid and will notice obstructions only if they can be detected by the cane. Hallways, walks, aisles and any other

International Symbol of Accessibility

FIG. 16-2

circulation areas should have at least 80 inches of clear head room.

Stairs should be planned with safety in mind for everyone, but especially for the disabled. Open steps or those with nosings projected more than one-and-a-half inches are an invitation to accidents. All stairways should have continuous hand-rails on both sides of the stairs. If they're not continuous, they should at least extend one foot beyond the top riser and the same distance, plus the width of one tread, beyond the bottom riser. Railings for support and guidance also may be used by the semiambulatory.

Signs and other methods of communication are a special problem for those with vision disabilities. Raised and large symbols are options for short messages, but braille characters are recommended for lengthier parcels of information. Recorded instructions or tactile maps can be developed to help increase independence on the grounds and in the church. Also, for those with limited visual acuity, light-colored characters against a dark background offer the best contrast for readability. We suggest that elevator buttons be identified by both raised numbers and braille. A combination of both visual and audible messages is the ideal situation, especially in determining an elevator's direction of travel and which car is answering a call.

Finally, since those with vision disabilities develop and depend on a heightened sense or hearing, good auditorium acoustics are essential. You may want to consider preferred seating in the sanctuary and classrooms.

The key to effective provisions for those with vision disabilities – or anyone, for that matter – is consistency. Once a person becomes familiar with an environment that is standardized, they should be guaranteed it won't change!

The key to effective provisions for those with vision disabilities – is consistency.

The Hearing Impaired

Again, sound quality is important to these people. Since most of the hearing impaired are not totally deaf, special planning in the auditorium can create a comfortable and comprehensive environment. Many churches today recognize the need for a sign language ministry. In this case, a designated area close to the platform, along with a signing minister, will enable the hearing impaired to participate actively in the service. Listening systems within a specific seating area can benefit those who have a slight hearing loss. People with hearing aids need custom and carefully designed equipment that must be properly engineered. To date, audio loops seem to be the best alternative for those with hearing aids equipped with inductive pickups. A special section in the pew seating may provide head phones.

Visual as well as audible signals, warnings and directions must

Curb Cut Ramp

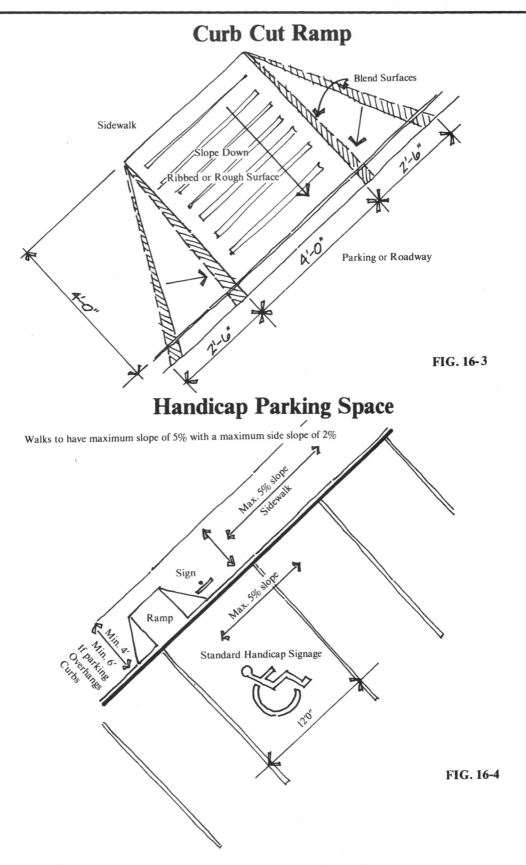

Blend Surfaces

Sidewalk

Slope Down

Ribbed or Rough Surface

2'-6"

4'-0"

4'-0"

2'-6"

Parking or Roadway

FIG. 16-3

Handicap Parking Space

Walks to have maximum slope of 5% with a maximum side slope of 2%

Max. 5% slope

Sidewalk

Sign

Max. 5% slope

Ramp

Min. 4'

Min. 6'
If parking
Overhangs
Curbs

Standard Handicap Signage

120"

FIG. 16-4

Ramp Cross-Section

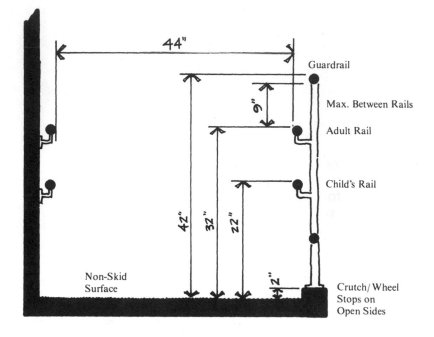

- Access should be provided to all major building levels by ramps.
- Ramps to have smooth, non-skid surfaces. Carpet is not recommended.
- Ramps to have intermediate landing when the rise of the ramp is greater than 36". If intermediate landings are required the rise between landings should be a maximum of 30".
- Upper and intermediate landings should be 5' in length. Bottom landing should be 6' in length.
- Clearance between wall and handrails should be not more than 2".
- Ramps should have a 2" crutch/wheel stop on open sides.

Handicap Ramp

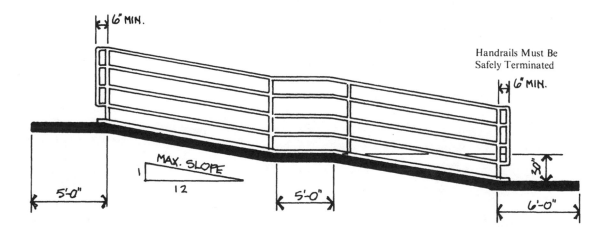

FIG. 16-5

be included on telephones and other communication systems. A few well-identified telephones should be equipped with receiver amplifiers and volume controls. Emergency signals with appropriate intensity and frequency can get the attention of those with a partial hearing loss.

Create visual messages throughout the facility that are obvious and easily understood. This will eliminate confusion and the need to ask questions, even among those with no physical limitations.

Chairbound, Manipulatory and Ambulant Disabled

Site and Building Accessibility

The first hurdle for a physically disabled person is getting from the parking lot into the church facility. Well-planned parking and drop-off locations, safety features and peripheral site designs will remove most barriers and allow a maximum of mobility and ease.

The access symbol for the chairbound disabled must be predominantly posted in designated exterior areas of parking, entrances, ramps, paths and other spaces on the site with the appropriate accommodations, interior areas, such as restrooms, communication systems, seating areas and elevators also must be clearly identified.

Parking stalls for the physically disabled must be at least 12 feet wide. A minimum of one handicapped-designated parking space for each 50 standard spaces is required. These parking areas should be close to accessible building entrances that have been adapted for special use, such as curb cuts, ramps and handrails. The surface of the handicapped parking space must be level, paved and preferably sheltered. People who are chairbound and have other manipulatory disabilities should not have to travel behind other parked cars to access the building. As for passenger loading and unloading zones, an access aisle of four feet wide and 20 feet long must be parallel and next to the pull-up zone, with ramps when applicable.

From the parking lot to the main church facility, you must have one accessible route with a maximum gradient or slope of not more than five percent, or one foot every 20 feet. An approach with more slope than this is classified as a ramp, which can be used to connect levels into and throughout the building. Typical ramps may not exceed one foot in every 12 feet. The surface material of the route should be stable and firm, but not slick in any weather condition. The minimum width can be three feet, but we recommend wider paths. Permitting a wheelchair to make a tight 180-degree turn requires a five feet diameter.

Parking stalls for the physically disabled must be at least 12 feet wide.

When an accessible route crosses a curb, provide a cut with a minimum of three feet clear width. Level landings at the bottom and top, also must be provided. A curb cut needs to have the least possible slope. Edges on a curb cut should be sloped, or flared, to prevent tripping. A non-skid material on the entire surface is required. If there are no curbs to separate pedestrians from automobile traffic, you must apply a special warning surface.

Building entrances and ramps

The area leading to the church entrance should be as accessible to the disabled as to anyone else. Since ascent and descent can be a long and tiring journey for the chairbound especially, ramps must be kept at a maximum slope of 1:12 with an occasional level rest platform and top and bottom levels that equal the width of the ramp. They should have curbs or railings to prevent slipping off the edge, and be designed so water does not accumulate on the surface. Install handrails on both sides of ramps to aid those in wheelchairs and others who need help in walking. The landing, or level space at the front entrance should be approximately 60 square feet with about 18 inches of extension on the door-opening side.

Install handrails on both sides of ramps.

Door details

All building entrances and doors designated for the disabled should have a minimum clear opening of 36 inches. If heavy traffic in this area is anticipated, allow more space for wheelchair maneuverability and to avoid congestion. If your church design calls for front entry doors leading into another set of doors, make sure you allow about seven feet of vestibule space for full wheelchair clearance of any swinging doors.

Door opening force should be kept at a minimum for everyone, but especially the disabled. The accepted maximum opening and closing pressure for general usage is about eight pounds. Sliding doors or automatic doors with delayed timers may not be as aesthetically pleasing as you'd like for your building, but they certainly are more convenient for those with certain disabilities.

Door hardware must be shaped for easy grasping with one hand, and not require any excess strain. Lever-operated, push-type or u-shaped handles are acceptable. Any hardware should be installed at a height of no more than 42 inches. Any hardware, whether it's door handles, switches or controls, should be within easy reach to a standing person without stooping. This guideline is acceptable for the chairbound, since it's comfortably within their reach.

Typical Rest Room Layout

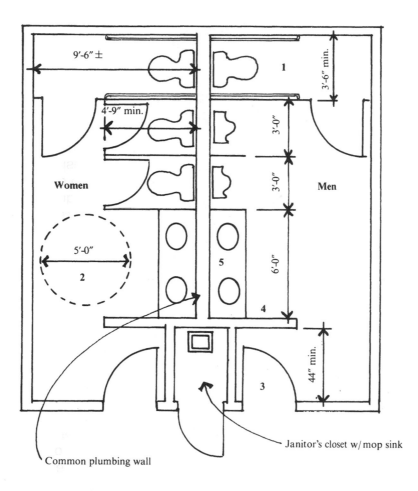

FIG. 16-6

• Special size handicap water closets (stalls) are usually located in the back due to their extended length requirements. This allows ease of access for a wheelchair. At least one chrome or stainless steel handrail 54″ long, 1½″ diameter must be mounted on the wall 33″ above the floor.

• Handicap restrooms are required to have a 5′-0″ turning radius for a wheelchair.

• Restroom doors should provide privacy. Doors to toilet rooms must have 32″ door openings.

• Lavatories must be mounted with bottom of apron 29″ min. A.F.F. with a 34″ max. rim top. A.F.F. waste piping must be insulated to protect the wheelchair person.

• Mirrors and shelves shall not be more than 40″ A.F.F. Towel racks and dispensers shall not be more than 40″ A.F.F.

Note: For worship places of assembly, plumbing codes require 1 water closet fixture per 150 women; 1 w. c. fixture per 300 men; 1 urinal fixture per 300 men; 1 drinking fountain per 75 people

Check local codes for adherence or exceptions.

Since most people tend to push against a door with the wheelchair or walker, we recommend the installation of kickplates on doors with closers. If they cover most of the door's width and reach to a height of 15 inches, you'll see a marked reduction in maintenance requirements.

Stairs

Any stairs that connect levels in your church facility should have uniform height risers with tread widths no less than 11-inches and non-projected nosings. The underside of the nosing must have no less than a 60-degree angle from the horizontal alignment. As we discussed in the section in this chapter concerning the visually impaired, all stairways should have handrails on each side. The space between the handrail and the wall needs to be about one-and-a-half inches, and 30 to 34 inches above the stair nosing.

Landings are a nice device to minimize the length of stair flights. Also, good lighting is mandatory. If the size of your church and your budget can stand it, and if you have a real concern for meeting everyone's need, it's a good idea to offer an alternative to stairs. Depending on the local building codes, you may have no choice.

> *Landings are a nice device to minimize the length of stair flights.*

Elevators

To be totally accessible, elevators must have visual and audible signals, inside and out. Inside the car, buttons must be 42 inches above the floor, and, as previously mentioned, comprehensible in raised letters and/or braille.

For the hearing impaired, a light to signal the car direction and floor destination is required. Requirements call for a 20-second door reopening device when the passageway is obstructed. After that amount of time, the door may begin to close but can be stopped easily by a minimum of force.

The door opening should be a minimum of 36 inches. Operational design must guarantee automatic leveling so there is no difference between the floor and car surface, and there should be no more than a one-half-inch gap between the two.

The floor plan of the elevator cars must include handrails to assist those who are unsteady on their feet, and enough space for wheelchairs. Regulatory codes call for a minimum width and depth of 68 and 51 inches to allow for turning 180 degrees.

Restrooms and lavatories

Doors to the restrooms and toilet stalls must have at least a 31-

inch clear opening width, with a lever handle installed at 42 inches from the floor. Stalls with a front access should have at least 36 inches of clearance in front of the water closet and be a minimum of 36 inches wide.

Urinals must have a 31-inch clear access width. To facilitate closing the stall doors, special closers, spring hinges or pull bars mounted on the inside can be installed.

Grab bars must be sturdy enough to support at least 250 pounds for transfers from a wheelchair to the toilet seat, usually either from the front or side. They should be installed at a height of 33 to 36 inches with no less than one-and-a-half inches of space between the wall and the handrail. The diameter should be about one-and-a-half inches with a good gripping surface. Both vertical and horizontal grab bars should be provided since they serve two different functions: pulling up and pushing.

Whether the toilet is wall or floor mounted, there must be a 42-inch minimum clearance of floor space to allow for footrests and comfortable maneuverability. The height of the toilet seat should line up with the seat of the wheelchair. The flush control and paper dispenser must be within easy reach. If possible, the ideal situation is to have a lavatory within easy reach of the toilet for those who are chairbound.

Lavatories must allow space for knee clearance of no less than 27 inches high, 30 inches wide and 19 inches deep beneath the sink. There should be also approximately 48 inches of clear floor space in front of the sink for an accessible approach. Any exposed pipes or surfaces under the sink must be insulated or covered to prevent injuries. The sinks and faucets must be in clear reach. Other accessories such as soap and towel dispensers should be installed at no higher than 40 inches above the floor. Mirrors should accommodate everyone, children included, so why not provide a single full-length mirror? Otherwise, mirrors should be installed so those in wheelchairs can see themselves.

If you're planning a recreational facility, you'll need to include a reasonable number of showers for the disabled. A three by three-feet stall provides the most safety, since grab bars (vertical and horizontal) and walls are within easy reach. However, a unit 36 inches by 60 inches, with no curb, may give better maneuverability to those in wheelchairs.

A shower seat – about 18 inches from the floor – must be installed in the smaller stall, and extend along the entire wall opposite the controls. The unit must include a shower spray with a 60-inch hose that can be hand-held or used as a fixed shower head. The minimum opening for a shower stall is three feet.

If you're planning a recreational facility, you'll need to include a reasonable number of showers for the disabled.

Drinking fountains

It is important that people in wheelchairs have knee space under the fountain, so allow at least 27 inches clear space from the floor, 30 inches of width and about 18 inches of depth. The spouts should be no more than 36 inches from the floor to outlet. They should be located closest to the person drinking and have a trajectory of water flow running parallel to the front of the unit. We recommend both hand and foot controls.

Telephones

Plan for a reasonable amount of public telephones that are within reach of the wheelchair disabled. The highest operable point on the telephone should not be any higher than 54 inches; the same applies for telephone directory storage areas. Enough clearance must be allowed for an easy approach and knee space. As we mentioned before, provisions must be available for the vision and hearing impaired.

Wheelchair-designated areas must be integrated with the fixed seating and have clear access to entrances and exits.

Table seating

Design aisles in the dining or work area of approximately 36 inches in width for wheelchair passage. Allow a minimum height of 29 inches with a width of 31 inches under the table.

Assembly areas

The sanctuary and education areas of your church should have specific areas with connecting accessible routes for the physically challenged. Aisles leading into the seating areas shouldn't be sloped more than one foot for every 12 feet. Wheelchair-designated areas must be integrated with the fixed seating and have clear access to entrances and exits. The viewing positions must be comparable to others in the auditorium. A minimum of 66 inches should be allowed for two wheelchairs which constitutes one viewing position. A good rule of thumb to follow is to provide four to six positions for every 500 people that will occupy the auditorium. Wheelchair positions require a level surface.

Generally accepted standards to make your new church building accessible and barrier-free are excellent guidelines in planning for the entire congregation. With increased understanding and sensitivity to the physically challenged, yours can be a pioneer church for total and active fellowship!

Assembly Seating for Wheelchairs

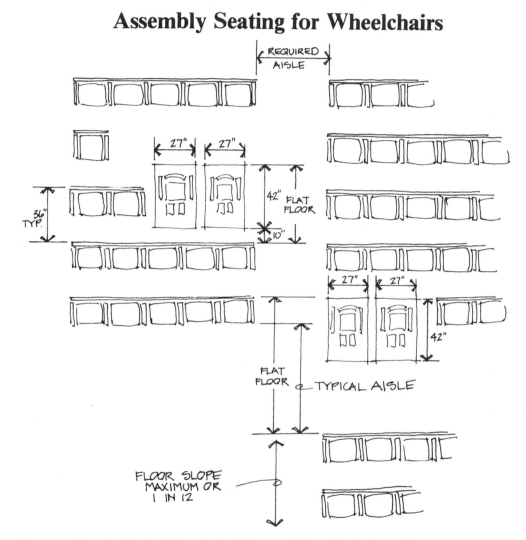

- A room with occupant level of 500 or less should have a minimum of 4 viewing positions.

Seating of 500-1,000: 12 positions

Seating of 1,000-1,500: 16 positions

Over 1,500 seats: one additional position for each additional 500 seats.

- Each viewing position to be accessed by ramp, walk or elevator via a principle entrance. The slope of any surface to not exceed 1 foot in 12 feet.

- Viewing positions should be located in pairs and on main level, not balconies or tiers.

FIG. 16-7

17

ENERGY SOURCES AND SOLUTIONS

Designing the church for responsible environmental control

Creature comfort has become an all-too-familiar way of life in today's society - inside and out. With technology available for environmental systems to warm us when we're cold, cool us when we're hot, light up our lives and keep the water running, human expectations have soared to a lofty perch between the best of both worlds.

This isn't a naughty-but-nice moral judgement that should send us over the edge on a paranoiac guilt trip. On the contrary. Improving the standard of living is a progressive and desirable evolution for mankind. But when, in the process, technological development generates costly wastefulness and unnatural possibilities for abusing – or even destroying – elements that are life-perpetuating, things change.

Gone are the days when building designers – and clients – can doze in the lap of luxury, dreaming of inexpensive and endless energy sources fueling mechanical equipment. In fact, the nightmarish reality is that the building industry itself has been one of the biggest perpetrators of creating long range inefficiency in energy-use patterns. In the blink of an eye, high energy costs and depleting sources have teamed up for a rude awakening.

There's only one source of energy.

"The Lord who gives us sunlight in the daytime and the moon and Stars to light the night, and who stirs the sea to make the roaring waves – his name is Lord Almighty" (Jeremiah 31:35, TLB).

"...Whatever is good and perfect comes to us from God, the

> The building industry itself has been one of the biggest perpetrators of creating long range inefficiency in energy-use patterns.

Creator of all light, and he shines forever without change or shadow" (James 1:17, TLB).

He's doing His job. It's up to us to do ours as we design for the construction and maintenance of His churches. Contemporary technological solutions are available, as well as practical alternatives to energize our built environment. And, according to federal and local regulations, there is no choice now but to act upon some of these options – especially if you want your building permit!

But forced compliances aside, the church has even more exciting opportunities to be good stewards in our concern for the earth, its people and the environment we create.

The Professionals

The interrelationship of church leaders, architects, contractors, engineers and consultants is at the heart of building a useful, energy-efficient and beautiful facility. This allows for a free exchange of information and suggestions regarding the plans, construction, review and maintenance, and ensures code compliance from Day One.

First, the church must communicate to the architect what it wants to build. Then (you can be sure), federal and regional regulatory groups will tell you what is needed to accommodate mandates for efficient energy consumption.

Most areas of the country have energy conservation standards which require that the total amount of energy consumed annually matches the allowable energy budget for the projected building. (To encourage utilizing the manifestations of the sun's energy – solar, wind and other natural energy sources are not a part of the energy budget.)

Don't hedge your bets. Without strict compliance to codes and laws, the financing for your church's building project will dry up faster than you can say "fossil fuels."

Since energy consumption is a broad heading for lighting, heating, cooling, ventilation, electrical systems, and the related construction activities, only qualified professionals can determine a total energy package according to directions of design and occupancy.

Every single component of the project must be taken into account to come up with the most efficient system that is both effective and economical over the long haul.

The participants essential in implementing conservation requirements of a building program are:

> *The church has...exciting opportunities to be good stewards in our concern for the earth, its people and the environment we create.*

Generalized Climate Regions of the United States

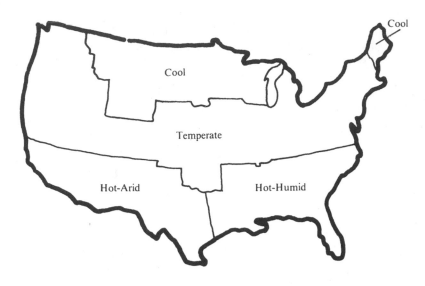

FIG. 17-1

Cathedral of the Holy Spirit
Decatur, Georgia

- Structural, electrical, mechanical and civil engineers
- Architects
- Building contractors
- Landscape architects
- Utility company representatives
- Alternate energy-source consultants
- Equipment suppliers

The Statement

The consumption of energy is determined by many elements in your total church building program. For purposes of assessment, design, and development of energy-saving techniques, you can rely on the professionals to consider several features:

Region and project site

- Location
- Size, boundaries and public easements
- Natural features of the land, topography, and water bodies
- Geological features, soil types and groundwater
- Vegetation
- Quality of air
- Climate
- Seasonal temperatures and precipitation
- Seasonal and daily sun angles
- Seasonal and daily wind patterns
- Sounds and smells
- Demographic and socioeconomic features
- Utilities and ordinances

Project and environmental interfacing

- Proposed facilities on site
- Functions of proposed facilities
- Facilities' design
- Occupancy
- Requirements for water and energy
- Projected waste materials
- Ability to meet air and water quality standards
- Ability for sound and smell control

Project assessment

- Determine environmental "fits" by matching requirements with

The consumption of energy is determined by many elements in your total church building program.

resources during construction and operation
- Determine environmental conflicts during construction and operation
- Consider positive alternatives for project goals
- Enumerate unavoidably adverse environmental effects

With a realistic statement like this – full of information about your site, your project and your understanding of the whole picture – any red-flag issues can be addressed early on and allow you to proceed in confidence and good conscience.

The Adjustable Environment

Some factors that affect human comfort in a built environment include:

- producing and regulating heat in the body
- heat and moisture losses in the body
- mean radiant temperatures (MRT)of surrounding surfaces
- stratification and relative humidity (RH) of air
- ventilation and movement of the air dust and odors

The ideal scenario in a building program shows a reduction of energy consumption and the unnecessary depletion of nonperishable sources.

Of this list, the last four factors can be regulated for thermal comfort and equilibrium. But they all relate to the total energy consumption in a building, as does interior design, construction, selected methods of air conditioning (heating and cooling), lighting and acoustics, and any related mechanical equipment.

The ideal scenario in a building program shows a reduction of energy consumption and the unnecessary depletion of nonperishable sources. This means that all the players – designers, engineers and consultants, in order to take full advantage of alternative natural sources – need to pay close attention to:

- the building's orientation on site
- climatic information
- coordination with the environment
- building form, windows, doors, insulation, mechanical and electrical systems.

For immediate purposes, we are directing the discussion toward the design and construction of new church facilities. If your building program calls for remodeling or enlarging already-existing structures, relax. There are plenty of effective modifications that will update your building to comply with today's energy-saving mandates. Additional insulation, window glazing, storm windows and doors, weatherstripping and caulking, air lock entrances, landscaping with berms, deciduous trees and evergreens, interior lighting, and mechanical equipment repairs or replacement can all improve energy conservation. Many energy-related suggestions in this chapter can be applied to an existing church for updating and redesign.

Space Conditioning

We've come a long way from the early ages when humans used natural growth of the land to heat and cool their sheltered spaces. Civilization and its demands for energy sources eventually turned us on to the use of water and fossil fuels (gas, oil and coal) which – in some instances – generate electricity for heating and cooling. The use of fuel sources vary, of course, depending on which part of this country you live and the proximity of predominantly-produced fuels. Fossil fuels, which are actually concentrated forms of the sun's energy, are not infinite. So it makes good common sense to turn to longer-term sources.

In recent years, the two most promising energy sources at our disposal have been nuclear and solar energy. The high-cost, high-technology and high-risk factors in nuclear energy are tending to raise some eyebrows as we look at alternative sources. Solar energy, although currently hampered by expensive integration with conventional systems for backup – depending on your geographical location – still offers the best ray of hope.

Any energy system incorporated in a church building needs to be combined with good and standard energy-saving techniques. To avoid costly energy losses, the design and construction phases of the building project should incorporate all necessary conservation measures.

To avoid costly energy losses, the design and construction phases of the building project should incorporate all necessary conservation measures.

Heat Gains and Losses

The four main causes of excessive heat gain and heat loss are inadequate insulation, wasteful ventilation, high rates of air infiltration and too much fenestration, or window areas. But there are several ways to minimize heat gains and losses in a building.

Location

Placing heavily-occupied spaces along the south, southeast and southwest sides of a building will minimize costs of space conditioning and lighting since the sun's energy can be utilized. Spaces requiring lesser amounts of energy requirements, including lighting, should be located along the north face of the building. During a 24-hour period, higher afternoon temperatures – due to the sun's intensity – makes the west side of a building a bit warmer than the east side. With this information, common sense tells us that interior spaces in a building that have certain requirements are placed in the appropriate locations according to the sun. That's only part of the program. Computerized calculations for thermal control should handle the rest of a large building project.

Insulation

The main purpose of insulating a building is to impede the inward and outward flow of heat. For economical consumption of fuel, all walls, floors, ceilings, roofs and every exposed outdoor space below must be built to resist the rapid transmission of heat. How efficiently this can be accomplished depends on thermal properties of the insulating materials, the thickness of materials, the method and quality of construction of spaces where insulation is placed, the interpositioning of air spaces, the use of reflective linings in these spaces to reduce radiant transfer, and the variance of inside and outside temperatures.

Total coefficients of heat transmission

- BTU (British thermal unit): the unit used in measuring quantity of heat.
- U value: the number of BTU's flowing through one square foot per hour of roof, wall, floor, or any other building component where there's a one-degree F difference in temperature between inside and outside air. The U value relates to materials, either a single one such as glass, or a combination, and is the reciprocal of the R factor.
- C (thermal conductance): the number of BTU's flowing through one square foot of material in one hour with a one-degree F difference in temperature between exterior surfaces. The C value measures heat flow through a specific thickness of material.
- E (emissivity): the property of surface thermal emission, or absorption.
- a: air-space conductance, or the number of BTU's flowing through one square foot with a one-degree F temperature difference between surfaces. The a factor depends on surface E values and position.
- f: film or surface conductance, or the time rate of heat flow in relation to air motion on the surface.
- k: thermal conductivity, which relates to the ability of a material to allow heat flow through one square foot of a homogeneous material with a thickness of one inch and one-degree F temperature difference between surfaces.

> *For economical consumption of fuel, all walls, floors, ceilings, roofs and every exposed outdoor space below must be built to resist the rapid transmission of heat.*

In computation, the overall U-coefficient value of transmission will be less than any of its components. This translates into a lower overall transmission coefficient with more parts, insulation, thickness and air spaces. It's actually more useful – in calculating heat loss in the building – to talk in terms of the U value, rather than the reciprocal R value.

R values can range from .78 to infinity, depending on the type and method of insulation used in ceilings, walls, floors and other parts of the building. Recommended values will relate to your church's geographical location. The forms of insulation are variable also, and include materials such as foamed-in, batt or blanket, blown or poured and rigid boards.

Air spaces and vapor barriers

Air spaces of an approximate 3/4-inch width can be effective insulating factors, particularly with the application of reflective foil on adjacent surfaces. This process will retard heat radiation by bouncing heat waves back toward the warm inner areas while simultaneously reducing heat loss.

The reflective foil also serves as a vapor barrier. A vapor barrier is a designed construction component that resists the flow of moisture and air and helps to prevent condensation in the walls and any other insulated areas.

Ventilation

Good ventilation is a breath of fresh air. In any occupied space, it is absolutely necessary for the overall comfort and well-being of people using the building.

Fresh air is a requisite for the reduction of odors, dust, carbon monoxide or any other nasty by-products of the human environment. It's also a great deterrent for drowsiness, and can do wonders in keeping Deacon Brown awake through the whole sermon! This can be achieved by an efficient system in which outdoor air is drawn into the recirculating air stream, and exhausted at an approximate rate for balance.

For cooling and heating purposes, the ventilation system must accommodate increased circulation needs. A high velocity air flow – rather than the number of air changes – is an important factor in the thermal comfort ventilation of a building. Since ventilation requirements differ according to regional climates and seasonal variations, a building must be designed and built to utilize any heat loss and heat gain techniques for the indigenous area. Air systems should have continuous cleaning treatments for outdoor and recirculating air.

Whatever benefits are perceived with efficient ventilation, thus

Fresh air...can do wonders in keeping Deacon Brown awake through the whole sermon!

temperature control, could be rendered woefully ineffective by:

- Ill-placed air openings
- Inadequate space and routing for ducts
- Excessive sound from mechanical equipment and circulating air

External surface colors – or the skin of a building – also will effect ventilation as it relates to controlling indoor air temperatures. Light-colored finishes will reflect radiation, thus reducing the amount of heat transfer to the interior. This is something to consider if your area enjoys long, hot summers and/or mild winters. Long, cold winters and mild summers call for medium-to-dark finish colors for radiation absorption.

If you are considering natural ventilation, there are two factors that move air through and within the interior space of a building: wind and temperature difference between indoor and outdoor air, or the "stack effect." To use natural wind forces for mild weather ventilation effectively, familiarize yourself with the prevailing breezes and their variations, along with any building structures, hills or vegetation that would interfere with the flow.

For optimum results of natural ventilation, any inlets (vents or windows) should be located on the side of the building directly facing the wind. The outlets, then, must be placed on the side or roof opposite the prevailing wind. In the stack effect, warm air rises and moves through the outlets which should be high in the space. The cooler air will be draw through the lower-placed inlets. An increased difference of indoor and outdoor temperatures requires the need for increased height between inlets and outlets. All openings should be equal in size to obtain the maximum air flow.

> *For optimum results of natural ventilation, any inlets (vents or windows) should be located on the side of the building directly facing the wind.*

Infiltration

In simple terms, infiltration is the flow of unwanted air that barges in each time a door is opened, or sneaks through cracks around doors and windows, or even in walls, roofs and floors. Exfiltration, as you may guess, is the quick and uncontrolled escape. While you're doing your best to heat or cool the church for every-one's thermal comfort, these two poachers can skew your entire space conditioning perspective and rob you blind at the same time.

An air lock or double entry at main entrances – or all entrances – will help decrease the problem by as much as 80 percent, since only the still-air space between interior and exterior doors will be effected. We also recommend that the main entrance is oriented away from the prevailing winds to reduce chill factor and velocity.

It's sad, but true: all edges around openings have the potential of leaking air. Properly applied weatherstripping and caulking around doors and windows can arrest infiltration/exfiltration by as much as 50 percent.

Fenestration

The design, proportioning and arrangement of all doors and windows in a building is referred to by the unwieldy word, "fenestration."

Windows are one of the largest factors in building energy consumption. And large expanses of glass will affect energy use for heating and cooling by as much as 20 to 30 percent. While they have tremendous potential for energy conservation, improper placement can be an energy drain in a facility's indoor space conditioning. Heat loss through a window during winter months is quite large compared to what is lost through a well-insulated wall.

Placement

The best placement, or orientation, for major glass areas in colder climates is one which results in the maximum heat gain through radiation in the winter and a minimum of loss. We suggest locating the largest window opening on the southeast, south and southwest. On the north, east and west side of the building, window areas should be smaller with shaded, heat-absorbing double glass utilized. Each situation has a singular consideration, of course, due to a church's geographical location, the desired aesthetics, its lighting, heating and cooling requirements, and time of occupancy during the day.

Glazing

Widows, doors, skylights and any other light-admitting areas are examples of glazing, which is actually a transparent or translucent covering of material such as glass or plastic. The application of a reflective metallic coating is an effective method of blocking the sun's rays. Obviously, two or three panes of glazing will reduce heat loss and heat gain more than just one pane.

Shading

The sun's energy is intensified as it penetrates glazed surfaces. So, during hot summer months or any other periods of over-heating the entire church building – and especially all glass areas – should be shaded. We recommend that south, southwest and southeast fenestration is shaded against the hot, persistent sun during summer months, with allowance for penetration during the winter.

Large expanses of glass will affect energy use for heating and cooling by as much as 20 to 30 percent.

Planting Concept for Cool Regions

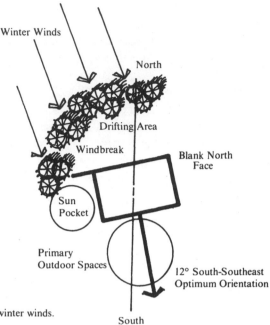

Cool Regions Objectives:

Maximize the warming effects of solar radiation; add protection from winter winds.

- Utilize south to south-west facing slopes as much as possible
- Utilize exterior walls and fences to capture the winter sun and reflect warmth into living zones
- Create protected sun pockets
- Utilize darker colors which absorb radiation
- Locate buildings on the lee side of hills in the "wind shadow"
- Utilize evergreens, earth mounds, and exterior walls to protect the northern exposures
- Flat or shallow pitched roofs collect and hold snow for added insulation
- Structures can be built into hillsides for natural insulation.

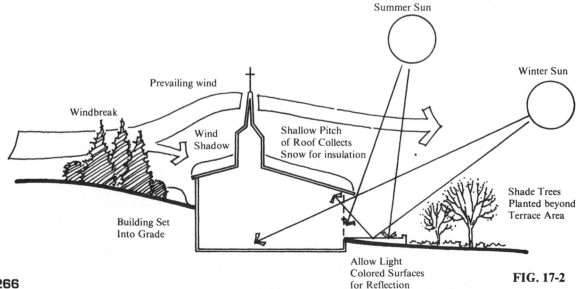

FIG. 17-2

Planting Concept for Temperate Regions

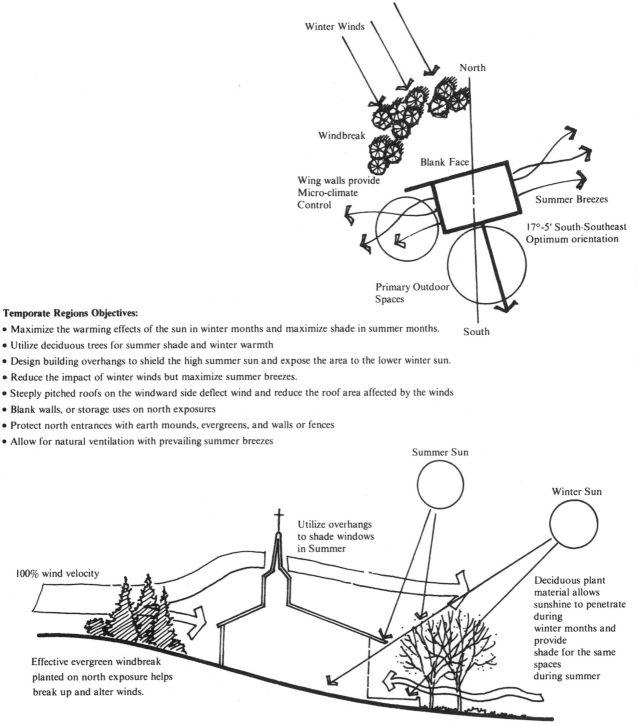

Temporate Regions Objectives:

- Maximize the warming effects of the sun in winter months and maximize shade in summer months.
- Utilize deciduous trees for summer shade and winter warmth
- Design building overhangs to shield the high summer sun and expose the area to the lower winter sun.
- Reduce the impact of winter winds but maximize summer breezes.
- Steeply pitched roofs on the windward side deflect wind and reduce the roof area affected by the winds
- Blank walls, or storage uses on north exposures
- Protect north entrances with earth mounds, evergreens, and walls or fences
- Allow for natural ventilation with prevailing summer breezes

FIG. 17-3

267

Planting Concept for Hot-Arid Regions

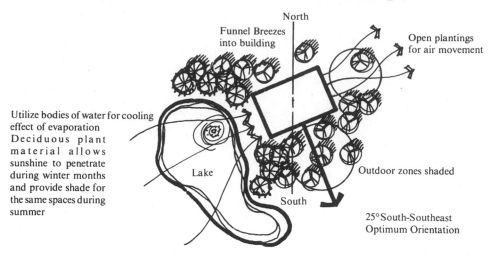

North

Funnel Breezes into building

Open plantings for air movement

Utilize bodies of water for cooling effect of evaporation Deciduous plant material allows sunshine to penetrate during winter months and provide shade for the same spaces during summer

Lake

Outdoor zones shaded

South

25° South-Southeast Optimum Orientation

Hot-Arid Regions
Objectives

- Maximize shade for late morning and afternoon.
  Glass areas should face north or south with adequate overhangs. Plant tall shade trees to shade windows from low east-west sun angles. Roof surfaces should be insulated and reflective.

- Maximize the humidity and cooling effects of evaporation across water bodies.

- Utilize the lower hillsides to benefit from cool natural air movements in early evening and warm air movements in early morning.

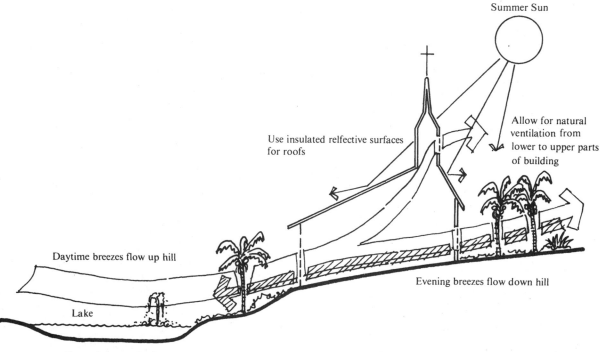

Summer Sun

Use insulated relfective surfaces for roofs

Allow for natural ventilation from lower to upper parts of building

Daytime breezes flow up hill

Evening breezes flow down hill

Lake

Evaporation cools air over water

FIG. 17-4

Planting Concept for Hot-Humid Regions

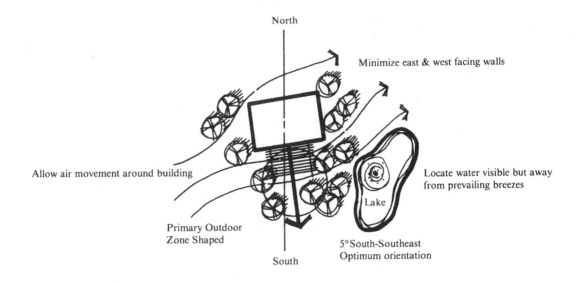

North

Minimize east & west facing walls

Allow air movement around building

Locate water visible but away
from prevailing breezes

Lake

Primary Outdoor
Zone Shaped

5° South-Southeast
Optimum orientation

South

Hot-Humid Regions Objectives

- Maximize shade throughout the day. Reduce the effects of high humidity by maximum exposure to air movements.
- Orient main open areas to the south with properly designed overhangs, trellis, or other sun control
- East or west windows should be avoided to minimize radiation with low sun angles
- Minimize energy intensive paving and building materials
- Orient streets and structures to maximize cool breezes. Prevailing winds vary with regions and micro climates
- Utilize the psychological effects of falling water or large water bodies but minimize the humidity of small water ponds and low areas

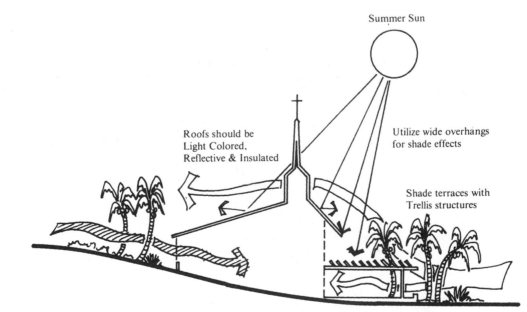

Summer Sun

Roofs should be
Light Colored,
Reflective & Insulated

Utilize wide overhangs
for shade effects

Shade terraces with
Trellis structures

Plantings should shade structure
as well as outdoor spaces but
allow air movement

FIG. 17-5

Summer and Winter Heat Gain and Loss

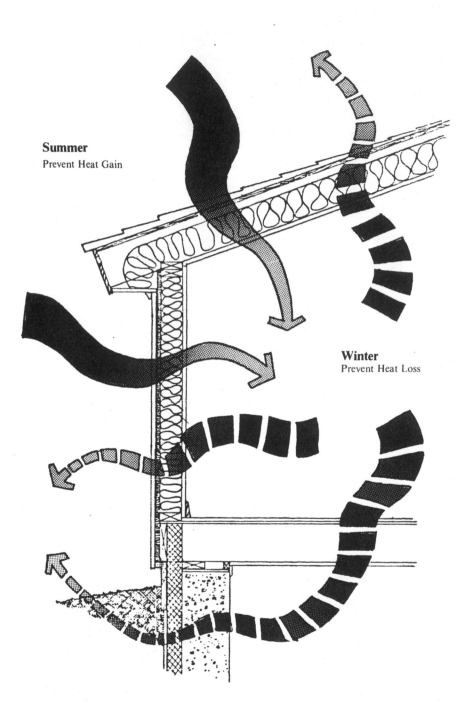

Summer
Prevent Heat Gain

Winter
Prevent Heat Loss

FIG. 17-6

Deciduous Trees A

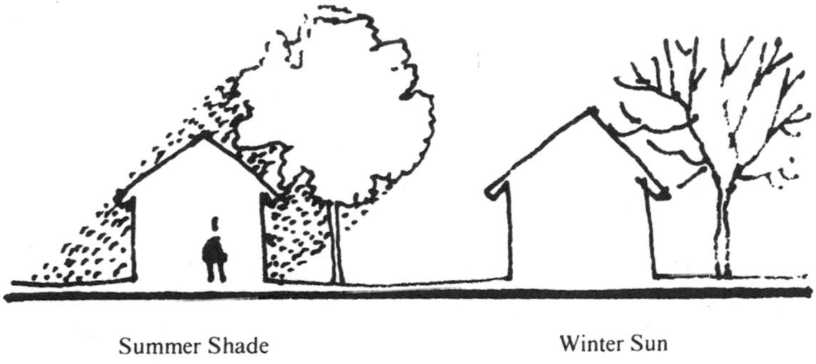

Summer Shade   Winter Sun

FIG. 17-7

Deciduous Trees B

Use tree or building shade

FIG. 17-8

Fixed or movable shading devices – indoor and outdoor should be designed to aid in the desired thermal control of your building. Fixed shading is usually not as expensive and gives less maintenance problems; however, movable devices can be more effective during seasons when solar radiation is needed for heating.

Some examples of exterior shading devices are building form design, sun screens, overhangs, vertical projections, awnings, shutters, trellises, trees and vegetation. In some cases, the necessary width of overhangs can be an eyesore for architectural aesthetics, so baffles or outdoor louvers might be the answer when full shade is the goal. Interior shading examples include drapes, roller shades and movable panels.

Landscaping

Deciduous trees that provide shade in the summer but allow light in the winter can be located around the south walls.

Insulation, ventilation, fenestration and shading devices are all important components in controlling heat loss and heat gain in your church facility. But we mustn't overlook the effect of landform and site vegetation on the total thermal control mechanism.

First of all, let's recognize the fact that the north side of a building is usually in the shade. It's cold. It's dark. It gets no direct sunlight in the winter, so ice and snow hang on like uninvited guests.

In designing a landscape for the ultimate in thermal control and energy conservation, the goals are to divert blustery winds, channel and capture the nice breezes, and utilize the sun's radiation depending on regional needs. Here are some suggestions for building in areas where extreme seasonal changes occur:

- Utilize warm, southern slopes to get the most of the sun's exposure. Avoid dense plantings or screening on south and southwest exposures that may block prevailing breezes.
- Incorporate earth berms on the north side to reduce exposure of the north wall and shadows cast by the building. This also will prevent heat gain in the summer.
- Evergreens planted around the north and northwest exposure provide a good wind screening during cold weather.
- Shade trees on the east and west sides of the church building give protection from the sun.
- Deciduous trees that provide shade in the summer but allow light in the winter can be located around the south walls.
- Walkways and paths should be shielded from cold winds and the summer sun by appropriate plantings.

The Solar Energy Concept

In the discussion of solar energy, there are two approaches to the subject: active and passive.

Active systems need mechanical equipment and hardware to collect and transport heat and provide cooling. Generally, the main elements needed are flat plate or focusing collectors, and a heat storage unit. Water or air goes through the collector, where heat is absorbed then transferred into the storage unit. A mechanical distribution system sends the heat from there into the building.

Passive systems utilize nonmechanical means to collect and transport heat. With passive solar heating and cooling, the building or some of its components actually is the system. Thermal energy comes from natural means such as radiation, conduction and convection. The two basic elements necessary for passive solar design are: glass or other glazing materials that will transmit radiation, or light, but are impenetrable to heat and serve as solar collectors; and certain materials, or thermal mass, that will absorb, store and distribute heat slowly to interior spaces.

Because equipment for active solar systems are still being developed, and can be expensive, we recommend that churches rely on their architect to design feasible and affordable elements that utilize all or parts of passive systems. Many suggestions throughout this chapter have incorporated design techniques for effective use of solar energy.

But to help establish a clearer understanding of passive systems, three concepts must be defined: direct gain, indirect gain and isolated gain. These, in turn, have five mutually dependent components:

- The collector draws the sun's radiation to the absorber.
- The absorber, then, makes heat from the radiation.
- The storage unit keeps any heat that is not used immediately.
- The distribution involves moving heat among the absorber, storage and interior spaces.
- Controls regulate heat loss and heat gain during cold winter months, while shading the collector and minimizing heat gain during the summer.

The workable formula for each of these components depend on which type of system is selected.

Direct gain

In this system – used primarily in milder climates – solar energy is collected and stored through windows, glass surfaces, walls and roofs. Through an expanse of south-facing windows, skylights, clerestories and glass doors, sunlight enters and is collected. Storage components are walls and floors which must be built of the proper material such as a stone, brick, adobe, concrete or concrete

We recommend that churches rely on their architect to design feasible and affordable elements that utilize all or parts of passive (solar) systems.

block. These materials can be used singularly or in combination. Another option for storing heat in this system is a water wall that is located where direct sunlight hits it throughout a major portion of the day. Materials used in constructing a water wall are generally metal and/or plastic.

Indirect gain

Thermal storage walls and roof ponds are two kinds of indirect gain systems of passive solar heating. In both cases, the concept relies on direct sunlight to strike a thermal mass located between the sun and interior space. Using a thermal storage wall, the sun's energy is absorbed, stored and/or transported to the space requiring heat. Again, south-facing fenestration is required for maximum gain and must be about 5 inches in front of the wall. In a roof pond system, the thermal mass is located on the roof. A metal deck, which can serve as a ceiling, supports water-filled plastic bags which act as a solar collector. A roof pond system is effective in heating and cooling.

Isolated gain

Simply stated, this approach to passive solar heating calls for a system that is built away from the facility and supplies heat and cooling only when needed. One application of this system is the natural convective loop which includes a flat plate collector and heat storage tank. Water and air, with rock storage, are two kinds of heat transfer. The design and construction of the convective loop is not unlike the procedures necessary for active solar systems.

Most space conditioning systems have their pros and cons; and it's no different with passive solar.

One of the biggest advantages of a passive (solar) system for a church is that in can be included with relative simplicity in the overall design.

One of the biggest advantages of a passive system for a church is that it can be included with relative simplicity in the overall design, operated and maintained with very little additional cost. There is no unsightly mechanical equipment to deal with and little noise pollution.

On the other hand, controlling the system for even temperatures is a major problem. Slow response to temperature changes is a built-in negative because of a system's large heat storage capacity. Another problem for a church building project is the site. The shape of the property must allow the building to be situated for a good southern exposure for maximum passive solar application.

Techniques for including passive solar systems in your church building should be considered, however. The interrelationship of architecture, construction, natural processes and the environment will be a positive step toward conserving energy and reducing maintenance costs in a time when the supply of fossil fuels is at risk.

18

ENJOY AND MAINTAIN YOUR NEW FACILITY

Getting the most out of what He has given

With the information we have provided in this book, you and your church building program should reach a happy conclusion! But as we all know, the end of one chapter usually means the beginning of another. Your new facility is a gift. And "every good gift and every perfect gift is from above" (James 1:17, KJV). We believe that it is God's intention for a church congregation to enjoy, thrive and grow in the "goodness" of a well-designed and well-constructed church building. Only by His generous outpouring of financial blessings – and the prudent management of those offerings – is this possible. So here is the next chapter: Good stewardship requires that His people continue the task by taking care of and overseeing the church site and facility. With proper maintenance, your new church can continue to be an effective instrument in His service for many years to come!*

> *The community, as a whole, will look critically at how well-kept a church is.*

As we have traveled throughout the United States – and built churches in most of them – we've had the tremendous opportunity to see thousands of churches and church programs. We have been equally impressed by one of the most important components of each church program: facility maintenance.

The first impression given by your church facility has impact. The community, as a whole, will look critically at how well-kept a church is – whether its members actually visit the church, or make a quick observance driving by. Efficient management in a church organization will be just as clearly interpreted by the general public as will be the private business down the street. The effects of good grooming, good people and a good budget will not fail to sell any product!

As you go through, then look beyond, your building program, please consider these three aspects of church maintenance: designing for maintenance, preventative maintenance, and ground maintenance. The following checklist hopefully will assist you in anticipating, thus avoiding, future maintenance problems. Some items may be repetitive statements from previous chapters, but it is our desire that you double-check all bases.

I. Designing for maintenance
   A. Assign a church committee or trustees to be responsible and make decisions.
      1. Meet at least bi-monthly.
      2. Identify specific areas, such as interior, exterior, grounds, and mechanical.
      3. Identify (a)projects completed, (b)projects pending, and (c) new items.
      4. Assign proper follow-up.
   B. Develop a job description for personnel involved in maintenance.
      1. Describe duties and qualifications.
      2. Remember the "who," "what," "where," "when," and "how." This will help both the employer and the employee.
      3. Determine the man-power to perform the tasks.
      4. Employ one person – a chief facilities' engineer, head custodian, housekeeping department director, or whatever title you assign the position – who is in charge, and who takes directions from the board. When the buck stops, it should be at this person's desk.
   C. Choosing building components and finish selections.
      1. Choose materials and methods of construction that are practical.
         a. Initial economical choices are usually more expensive in the long run.
         b. Provide protection against exposure wherever possible.
         c. Select finishes such as concrete, stone, brick, block, aluminum, stucco or synthetic cementitious surfaces.
         d. Minimize wood which rots, and steel which rusts.
      2. Windows and doors.
         a. Do choose aluminum, vinyl-clad, or anodized windows and frames. Don't choose wood or steel.
         b. Factory prefinished ready-to-set is preferred.

Minimize wood which rots, and steel which rusts.

   c. Use double-glazing glass and tempered glass when required.

   d. Require quality weather-stripping on all operable windows and doors.

3. Steeples, crosses and other elements.

   a. Purchase prefinished products, whenever possible, with aluminum, fiberglass or porcelain.

   b. Flashing all trim, attached elements and intersecting surfaces with copper trimming, where possible, is very important. Remember, building materials are only as good as the quality of the installer.

4. Walls and floors.

   a. Pre-cast – or cast in place – brick, stone, and concrete all come in a variety of textures and colors. Properly laid, tooled and sealed, these products are practically maintenance-free.

   b. Walls of prefinished metal panels are recommended.

   c. Floor materials can be sealed concrete, vinyl composition tile, quarry tile, ceramic tile or sheet vinyl.

   d. When utilizing carpet, evaluate the kind of fiber – nylon or olefin – and the weight of the material. We recommend direct glue-down throughout.

   e. Conventional wood floors require high maintenance. Current prefinished parquet flooring systems also are high-maintenance, but seem to hold the finishes longer.

   f. Several good synthetic sport floors are on the market. High-technology composition-backed carpets also are being used effectively on sport floors which double as fellowship areas for dining and worship spaces.

5. Mechanical systems.

   a. "You get what you pay for" is the tune for manufactured HVAC equipment.

   b. Require units of nationally-known brands. Specify medium-to-heavy commercial equipment. Require guarantees and warranties.

   c. Purchase only commercial plumbing fixtures.

   d. Conventional plumbing materials are copper water piping, and bronze or cast iron waste piping. Most codes are accepting some varieties of plastic pipes or venting waste pipes above grade.

6. Roofs. We saved the best for last! Faulty roofs are the Number One problem in building construction. Many

Walls of prefinished metal panels are recommended.

years, major studies, experiments, research – along with billions of dollars – have been expended by manufacturers, builders and owners to come up with the best products and techniques available. Yet, roofs – according to how they are attached to the walls – still leak.

KEEP IT SIMPLE.
a. Pitched roofs are the most desirable. They have the least amount of leakage problems.
b. Pitched roofs can be appealing in metal standing seam (prefinished), slate tile and fiberglass finishes.
c. Asphaltic shingles and wood shakes are very common, but have much shorter life spans. Specify national brands and as heavy a weight as the budget allows.
d. When using a pitched roof, realize that it means that mechanical equipment probably is on the ground or within the floor space.
e. As the worship space size gets larger, the exterior design and interior structure lends itself to what we call flat or semi-flat roof design. Seek your architect's guidance in selecting one of the many roof finish systems. It may be built-up bituminous with gravel ballast, or a single-ply monolithic sheet. This may seem over-simplified. But a whole book on leaks may be another book, another time!
f. Require and maintain a "positive" roof pitch. Have as few roof penetrations as possible.
g. Contract with licensed roofers who are established in the local area.
h. Utilize prefinished downspouts and gutters where possible. And be sure the water gets away from the building instead of running down the basement or foundation wall.
i. Keep your building insurance paid up and current!

II. Preventative maintenance
   A. Keep the building and its components clean and lubricated.
      1. Stop-gap measures are sometimes necessary. But we recommend that you permanently fix problems before they become larger and do further damage that will cost more in the long run.
      2. Cracked foundation walls and leaky pipes should not be

Asphaltic shingles and wood shakes are very common, but have much shorter life spans.

fixed with band-aids, unless you want to raise roofs, have stuck doors, or replace moldy wall and carpet on down the line.

3. The maintenance committee and/or administrative personnel should inspect the facility weekly and monthly. Good record-keeping and reports must be kept on the building. Work orders should be initiated, signed and filed when completed.
4. Roofing should be inspected regularly. Belts, pumps, fans. and other equipment should be checked, adjusted and greased.
5. Cooling and heating systems should be checked before each change-of-the-season.
6. Apply primers and paints to all wood and metal surfaces.
7. Keep doors and windows working free and easy. Any broken glass should be replaced immediately.
8. Paint and fill masonry walls.
9. Economical vinyl wall covering is a better investment than paint. Tape and pins abuse painted walls.
10. Use carpet base instead of vinyl rubber base on walls where possible.
11. Using carpet as a wainscoating on walls is a suggestion.

B. A schedule of repairs and cost estimates must be initiated so that decisions can be made. Have a plan. Know the bottom line cost.
1. Handle emergencies immediately.
2. Avoid large, sporadic installments to the maintenance budget, but provide funds on a regular, constant schedule.
3. Run the system like a business.

C. Operational maintenance.
1. Basically; labor and cleaning
2. The supervisor must be knowledgeable in cleaning products and procedures, and a good administrator of work and people.
3. Dry-brush masonry when needed.
4. Remove mold and mildew.
5. Refer to manufacturers' recommendations on priming and painting the many surfaces, such as wood and metal.

D. Safety. (The church facility is a public building and, as such, is bound to all the legal and ethical responsibilities associated with the keeping the public safe from hazards.)

Avoid large, sporadic installments to the maintenance budget, but provide funds on a regular, constant schedule.

1. The physical plant and its structures should be sound, and designed to withstand the elements that nature can hand out.
2. Fire resistance and electrical safety must be a top priority.
3. All exits, corridors, stairs and exits must be clear, and marked clearly.
4. Maintain clean and sanitary restrooms.
5. Locate janitors' closets close to major restrooms.

III. Maintenance of the grounds.
   A. Remember, keep it simple, keep it clean, and it will be attractive.
      1. Landscape can do more for the perceived value and aesthetics of a facility than anything else.
      2. The signage and the condition of the parking lot must be carefully maintained.
      3. Schedule mowing, pruning, fertilization, spraying, mulching, and controlling drainage.
      4. Snow and ice removal is very important, and takes proper equipment. Be prepared.
      5. Employ personnel who are experienced in care and maintenance of equipment.
   B. Driveways and parking areas.
      1. These areas must be paved if at all possible. Gravel lots are dusty, muddy and bumpy.
      2. Asphalt tends to be more economical than concrete, but has a shorter life. Asphalt can be repaired when necessary and recoated. It is also good for sports courts.
      3. Concrete is smoother and finished more exactly at areas such as walkways and entries. It tends to hold up better under heavy equipment use. Concrete cracks and joints can be repaired with bitumen or concrete patch.
      4. Concrete walkways are preferred. Ramps and steps should conform to all code requirements. Keep thresholds to a minimum for the physically challenged and the elderly.
      5. Select fence and wall materials that require little or no maintenance. These provide both security and privacy.
      6. Retaining walls can be expensive, but also are necessary devices to make the most out of site grading situations. Design and construction should be left to qualified professionals.
   C. Busing programs.
      1. Many busing programs are the strength and heartbeat of a ministry. Consider the outreach first.

In driveways and parking areas, asphalt tends to be more economical than concrete, but has a shorter life.

2. Provide parking, circulation and garages accordingly.
3. Bus maintenance should be funded and operated by a special budget, depending on the scope of the ministry.
4. Provide clean, safe and mechanically-sound buses.
5. Employ qualified bus drivers, and provide adequate insurance.

Anticipating future needs is a perfect way to live in the present. We trust that we have helped in some small way toward implementing God's plan in building your church of tomorrow. It's your ministry. And it's ours.

Anticipating future needs is a perfect way to live in the present.

Dr. Andrian Rogers, Pastor, Belleview Baptist Church, Memphis, TN, with Roe Messner

Belleview Baptist Church
Memphis, Tennessee

Illustrations

GLOSSARY

acoustics – the science relating to production, transmission, control, reception and effects of sound.

air lock – an intermediate space between the outer and inner air of a building structure; or between places of different atmospheric pressure and/or temperature.

ALcons – the articulate loss of consonants.

berm – a mound or hill of earth, man-made, and utilized for decorative and shelter purposes.

bituminous – having the qualities of bitumen, or asphalt.

cantilever – a bracket-shaped beam or other building component that is supported only at one end, and may, itself, support a building component.

change order – description of construction, or other work, to be done which is a change from the original contract documents. A change order could denote additional work, or the omission of work, and will specify the cost of change.

clerestories – vertically, or near-vertically-placed windows which are elevated in a structure to give natural lighting.

chroma – the combination of hue and saturation in a color quality.

coefficient – a constant factor as distinguished from a variable, and serving as a measure of a property.

dead air space – a still and confined space of air that reduces the heat gain and loss in a building.

decibel – a degree of loudness, or a unit that expresses relative intensities of sound on a scale from zero to approximately 130.

decidious – trees, or any other type of vegetation, which sheds leaves during the fall and winter months.

demographics – statistics that characterize a population, such as age, income and other information that may identify a certain market.

direct gain – energy from the sun that is collected through windows, walls or roofs - without special solar collection devices.

foyer – an anteroom, entrance hallway, or vestibule of a building.

fenestration – a description of openings in a building, such as windows, doors or clerestories, that admit light or air.

flashing – a sheet metal used for waterproofing.

gallery – refers normally to a projecting structure within the walls of an auditorium to accommodate additional people, above the ground level in the form of a balcony. However, the application may also refer to a portion of the balcony that extends from the upper level of the interior structure directly to the floor, or main auditorium, level.

glazing – glass, or any other transparent material utilized in window openings for the admission of light.

greenbelt – a "belt" of vegetation, such as parkways, that surrounds a building or community.

heat gain – the influx of heat within a space caused by solar radiation and the heat projected by other sources, such as machinery, lights, equipment or people.

heat loss – the decrease of heat in a contained space, as a result of heat flowing through windows, walls and other building components.

Hz – an abbreviation of "hertz" which is a unit of frequency that equals one cycle per second.

indirect gain – a term used for these purposes to describe a solar heating system that captures sunlight through a thermal mass, is then converted to heat and is transferred to the interior of a building.

infiltration – the movement of air into a building through cracks around walls, roofs and windows.

insulation – any building material that is effective in controlling heat gain and loss.

luminaries – a complete unit of lighting.

master plan – the visual creation of a complete and long-range site development, and the result of intense studies and surveys relating to realistic goals, "needs," "wants," and budget.

narthex – a foyer, or vestibule, that leads into the nave, or the sanctuary, of a church.

nave – the main part of a church, or the elevated hall leading into a church's primary worship center.

sacristy – a small room in the church where vessels and vestments are stored, and where the minister may robe for the service.

specular – having a mirror-like quality.

thermal mass – the quantity of possible heat storage in a structure's system, such as wall and floor materials and design.

topographical survey – the graphic delineation of a property's surface, including any natural or man-made features.

weatherstripping – the application of thin sections of material to stop infiltration, and exfiltration, of moisture and air around windows and doors.

written program – the accumulated information about the past, present and potential status of a church; community surveys; growth patterns and goals; and a detailed "wish list" that matches the budget. An architect/builder cannot proceed until a church program has been carefully researched and written.

INDEX

For those who are considering
building a new church facility,
contact.

Roe Messner
P.O. Box 1281
Matthews, NC 28105
704-841-8994